AWARENESS
OF DYING

BARNEY G. GLASER &
ANSELM L. STRAUSS

AWARENESS
OF DYING
BARNEY G. GLASER &
ANSELM L. STRAUSS

ALDINETRANSACTION
A DIVISION OF TRANSACTION PUBLISHERS
NEW BRUNSWICK (U.S.A.) AND LONDON (U.K.)

Paperback edition published 2005 by AldineTransaction, New Brunswick, New Jersey. Copyright © 1965 by Barney G. Glaser and Anselm L. Strauss. www.transactionpub.com

This book is printed on acid-free paper that meets the American National Standard for Permanence of Paper for Printed Library Materials.

Library of Congress Catalog Number: 2004058804
ISBN: 0-202-30763-8
Printed in the United States of America

Library of Congress Cataloging-in-Publication Data

Glaser, Barney G.
    Awareness of dying / Barney G. Glaser and Anselm L. Strauss.
      p. cm.
    Originally published: Chicago : Aldine Pub. Co., 1965.
    Includes bibliographical references and index.
    ISBN 0-202-30763-8 (pbk. : alk. paper)
    1. Death—Psychological aspects. 2. Physician and patient. 3. Sick—Psychology. I. Strauss, Anselm L. II. Title.

BF789.D4G5 2005
155.9'37—dc22
                                          2004058804

To

WALTER A. GLASER

and

MINNIE ROTHSCHILD STRAUSS

Preface

Once upon a time a patient died and went to heaven,
but was not certain where he was. Puzzled, he asked
a nurse who was standing nearby: "Nurse, am I dead?"
The answer she gave him was: "Have you asked your
doctor?"

—ANONYMOUS, circa 1964

Recently *The New York Times* reported: "VERY ILL CHILDREN
TOLD OF DISEASE; Leukcmia Patients at N.I.H. Not Shielded
From Truth. . . . A child should always be told the truth, even
when he has an incurable disease such as leukemia, according
to two researchers who interviewed 51 children hospitalized at
the National Cancer Institute, Bethesda, Maryland, for treatment of leukemia." This kind of news item reflects the growing
concern among researchers and public about matters which
touch on morality as much as on the technical aspects of medicine. The rapidly increasing proportion of elderly people in the
American population presents a range of personal and social
questions; not the least is how they view their newly won lon-
gevity (often including anticipated years of chronic disease) as
well as their attitudes toward death. In consequence, many geriatric specialists are beginning to study American attitudes
toward death, while others, spurred on by what seems a senseless prolonging of life within hospital walls by medical technology run wild, are raising questions about death and dying in
American life.

Our book is no exception to this trend; indeed, we would
further it. We wish to contribute toward making the management of dying—by patients, families and health professionals—

more rational and compassionate (and the two are far from incompatible). The chief differences between our approach and others' can be quickly summarized. Recognizing that most Americans are now dying inside hospitals, we have focused upon what happens when people die there. We have focused on the interaction between hospital staffs and patients, rather than on the patients themselves. We have reported on contexts of action rather than merely on "attitudes toward death." And we have been less concerned with death itself than the process of dying—a process often of considerable duration.

This approach reflects our sociological perspective, for we have attempted to channel our reforming impulses into an inquiry not at all medical in character. If increasingly Americans are dying within medical establishments, surrounded more by nurses and physicians than by kinsmen, then how do these representatives of the wider society manage themselves and their patients while the latter are dying? How is the hospital's organization capitalized upon in this process? What forms of social action, transitory or more permanent, arise while handling the dying of people? What are the social consequences for the hospital and its staff, as well as for the patients and their families?

To answer these kinds of questions, we did intensive fieldwork (involving a combination of observation and interviewing) at six hospitals located in the Bay area of San Francisco. We chose a number of medical services at each hospital, selected, as we shall explain later, to give us maximum exposure to different aspects of dying—locales where death was sometimes speedy, sometimes slow; sometimes expected, sometimes unexpected! sometimes unanticipated by the patient, sometimes anticipated; and so on. The reader who is unacquainted with this style of field research need only imagine the sociologist moving rather freely within each medical service, having announced his intention of "studying terminal patients and what happens around them" to the personnel. The sociologist trails personnel around the service, watching them at work, sometimes questioning them about its details. He sits at the nursing station. He listens to conversations himself. Occasionally he queries the staff members, either about events he has seen or events someone has told him about. Sometimes he interviews personnel at considerable length, announcing "an interview," perhaps even using a tape recorder. He sits in on staff meetings. He follows, day by day, the progress of certain patients, observing staff interaction with those patients and conversation about the patients among the personnel. He talks with patients, telling them only that he is "studying the hospital." His fieldwork takes place during day, evening and night, and may last from ten minutes to many hours.

In presenting what we observed by such methods, we might have organized our analysis in this book to highlight differences and similarities among the various medical services. Instead, we chose to offer our readers a more abstract—and so more powerful—explanatory theoretical scheme. This scheme arose from scrutiny of the data and should illuminate the data far more than a comparative analysis of the medical services. Our analysis is based upon what we term "awareness context," which is discussed in Chapter I; here we need only note that this term refers to who, in the dying situation, knows what about the probabilities of death for the dying patient. It makes a great deal of difference who knows what, and the use of this scheme allows the organization of many events that otherwise might seem disconnected or paradoxical.

The efficiency of the scheme allows us to claim—we believe with some persuasiveness—that discernible patterns of interaction occur predictably, or at least non-fortuitously, during the process of hospitalized dying, and that explicit knowledge of these patterns would help the medical staff in its care of dying patients. Physicians and nurses tend to regard such events either in mythological terms (some mythologies are touched upon later) or to discount patterned events in favor of the uniqueness of events (everyone is "a different personality," so dies differently and must be handled differently). A group of eminent physicians hearing of our analysis before its actual publication, we were told, remarked flatly that sociologists have nothing useful to offer physicians. Theirs was a natural reaction to the invasion by outsiders of a delicate and somewhat mysterious realm. We have not meant to scientize this realm, nor to offer commentary that would freeze and prematurely professionalize care for the dying by hospital staffs. Our intent was, above all, to ask whether people can die socially before they die biologically, and what this means for human relationships. If our report makes matters easier for people who must live around the dying (and vice versa), it will only be because critical intelligence is brought to bear on our findings and on common practices in American hospitals. Perhaps, then, hospital personnel will not laugh quite so wryly at the anonymous lines, quoted above, about the patient's puzzled query of a nurse.

Awareness of Dying was planned as the first of a series of four monographs resulting from a six-year research financed by the National Institutes of Health (grant number NU 00047). The second monograph will discuss the course, or trajectory, of dying; and the third, by Jeanne Quint, will be titled *The Nurse Student and the Dying Patient*. A fourth volume will deal with staff-family interaction in dying situations.

The authors of *Awareness of Dying* are indebted to a great many people. They wish especially to thank the third member of the project team, Miss Jeanne Quint, for her almost daily invaluable support; also Mrs. Elaine MacDonald and Miss Ruth Fleshman, who assisted in data collection during an early phase of the project. Howard Becker, editor of the "Observations" series in which this book appears, read our original manuscript with an appreciative but unusually critical eye, and we wish to thank him here. From a number of colleagues, we received general support and specific commentary: among them, Herbert Blumer, Fred Davis, and Louis Schaw. Strauss appreciates his conversations with Leonard Schatzman. We had a very useful early exchange with Dr. Melvin Sabshin and equally useful later conversations with several nurse educators, especially Miss Helen Nahm, Miss Jeanne Hallburg and Mrs. Mildred McIntyre.

Like all field researchers, we are especially indebted to many persons who worked at the field-work locales. They are far too many to cite by name, but we wish at least to express our gratitude to them and their institutions: especially Moffitt Hospital (University of California Medical Center, San Francisco); Providence Hospital, Oakland; the Veterans Administration Hospital at Oakland; the Napa State Mental Hospital; the San Francisco General Hospital; and Highland Hospital in Oakland.

Miss Karen Many edited and Mrs. Kathleen Williams helped to type first draft manuscript. Miss Bess Sonoda, our project secretary, is the hitherto "without whom" unsung heroine of our manuscript; we thank her, too.

Barney G. Glaser and Anselm L. Strauss
San Francisco

Contents

Part One

Introduction

1

The Problem
of Awareness of Dying

American perspectives on death seem strangely paradoxical. Our newspapers confront the brutal fact of death directly, from the front page headlines to the back page funeral announcements. Americans *seem* capable of accepting death as an everyday affair—someone is always dying somewhere, frequently under most unhappy circumstances. To account for this absorbing interest in death (even death by violence), one need not attribute to the reading public an especially vigorous appetite for gruesome details. Death is, after all, one of the characteristic features of human existence, and the people of any society must find the means to deal with this recurring crisis. Presumably one way to deal with it is to talk and read about it.

Curiously, however, Americans generally seem to prefer to talk about particular deaths rather than about death in the abstract. Death as such has been described as a taboo topic for us, and we engage in very little abstract or philosophical discussion of death.[1] Public discussion is generally limited to the social consequences of capital punishment or euthanasia.

Americans are characteristically unwilling to talk openly about the *process* of dying itself; and they are prone to avoid telling a dying person that he is dying. This is, in part, a moral attitude: life is preferable to whatever may follow it, and one should not look forward to death unless he is in great pain.

This moral attitude appears to be shared by the professional people who work with or near the patients who die in our

[1] Herman Feifel, "Death," in Norman L. Farberow, *Taboo Topics* (New York: Atherton Press, 1963), pp. 8-21.

3

hospitals. Although trained to give specialized medical or nursing care to terminal patients, much of their behavior towards death resembles the layman's. The training that physicians and nurses receive in schools of medicine or nursing equips them principally for the technical aspects of dealing with patients. Medical students learn not to kill patients through error, and to save patients' lives through diagnosis and treatment, but their teachers emphasize very little, or not at all, how to talk with dying patients, how—or whether—to disclose an impending death, or even how to approach the subject with the wives, children and parents of dying patients.[2]

Similarly, students at schools of nursing are taught how to give nursing care to terminal patients, as well as how to give "post-mortem care," but only recently have the "psychological aspects" of nursing care been included in their training. Few teachers talk about such matters, and they generally confine themselves to a lecture or two near the end of the course, sometimes calling in a psychiatrist to give a kind of "expert testimony."[3] Although doctors and nurses in training do have some experience with dying patients, the emphasis is on the necessary techniques of medicine or nursing, not on the fact of dying itself. As a result, sometimes they do not even know they are treating or caring for a dying patient.

Although physicians and nurses may thus exhibit considerable technical skill in handling the bodies of terminal patients, their behavior to them otherwise is actually outside the province of professional standards. In hospitals, as in medical and nursing schools, discussion of the proper ways to manage dying patients tends to be only in strictly technical medical and nursing terms. Also, staff members are not required to report to

[2] These statements are the result of a secondary analysis of field-notes from a study of the University of Kansas Medical School; see Howard S. Becker, Blanche Geer, Everett C. Hughes, and Anselm L. Strauss, *Boys in White* (Chicago: University of Chicago Press, 1961).

[3] Jeanne C. Quint and Anselm L. Strauss, "Nursing Students, Assignments, and Dying Patients." *Nursing Outlook,* Vol. 12 (January 1964); also Jeanne C. Quint, *The Nurse Student and the Dying Patient* (New York: The Macmillan Company, in press, 1966).

each other, or to their superiors, what they have talked about with dying patients. As we will discuss later, they are "accountable" only for the technical aspects of their work with the dying.[4]

Medical and nursing personnel commonly recognize that working with and around dying patients is upsetting and sometimes traumatic. Consequently some physicians purposely specialize in branches of medicine that will minimize their chances of encountering dying patients; many nurses frankly admit a preference for wards or fields of nursing where there is little confrontation with death. Those who bear the brunt of caring for terminal patients tend to regard its hazards as inevitable— either one "can take" working with these patients or he cannot. Physicians and nurses understandably develop both standardized and idiosyncratic modes of coping with the worst hazards. The most standard mode—recognized by physicians and nurses themselves—is a tendency to avoid contact with those patients who, as yet unaware of impending death, are inclined to question staff members, with those who have not "accepted" their approaching deaths, and with those whose terminality is accompanied by great pain. As our book will attest, staff members' efforts to cope with terminality often have undesirable effects on both the social and psychological aspects of patient care and their own comfort. Personnel in contact with terminal patients are always somewhat disturbed by their own ineptness in handling the dying.

The social and psychological problems involved in terminality are perhaps most acute when the dying person knows that he is dying. For this reason, among others, American physicians are quite reluctant to disclose impending death to their patients,[5] and nurses are expected not to disclose it without the consent of the responsible physicians. Yet there is a prevailing belief among them that a patient who really wants to know will

[4] Anselm L. Strauss, Barney G. Glaser, and Jeanne C. Quint, "The Nonaccountability of Terminal Care," *Hospitals,* 38 (January 16, 1964), pp. 73-87.
[5] Feifel, *op. cit.,* p. 17.

somehow discover the truth without being told explicitly. Some physicians, too, maneuver conversations with patients so that disclosure is made indirectly. In any event, the demeanor and actions of a patient who knows or suspects that he is dying differ from those of a patient who is not aware of his terminality. The problem of "awareness" is crucial to what happens both to the dying patient and to the people who give him medical and nursing care.

From one point of view the problem of awareness is a technical one: should the patient be told he is dying—and what is to be done if he knows, does not know, or only suspects? But the problem is also a moral one, involving professional ethics, social issues, and personal values. Is it really proper, some people have asked, to deny a dying person the opportunity to make his peace with his conscience and with his God, to settle his affairs and provide for the future of his family, and to control his style of dying, much as he controlled his style of living? Does anyone, the physician included, have the right to withhold such information? Someone must decide whether to disclose, and when to disclose, but on whose shoulders should this responsibility fall—the physician, the family, or the patient? The rationale for making such decisions, as well as for designating who will make them, is not based on technical reasoning alone but also on various ethical, moral and human considerations.

Both the human and the technical aspects of the awareness problem are becoming increasingly momentous, for at least two reasons. One is that most Americans no longer die at home. Last year in the United States, 53 per cent of all deaths occurred in hospitals, and many more in nursing homes.[6] The family may be present much of the time while a person is dying, but he is also surrounded by many strangers, however compassionate and technically skilled they may be. Dying away from home is compounded by a noticeable and important medical

[6] Robert Fulton, "Death and Self," *Journal of Religion and Health,* 3 (July 1964), p. 364.

trend: because medical technology has vastly improved, fewer people are dying from acute diseases and more from chronic diseases. Moreover, the usual duration of most chronic diseases has increased, so that terminal patients, in the aggregate, take longer to die than they used to. They may spend this time in the hospital, or return several times to the hospital while they are dying.

Dying away from home, and from a chronic disease, will become more common during the next decades, making the problem of "awareness" even more salient to everyone concerned. Hospitals are scientific establishments and staff members are expected to make competent judgments about what is wrong with patients and to assess their prospects for recovering —or not recovering. For this very reason more and more terminal patients will persist in asking questions, and in expecting explicit, detailed answers, about the nature of their illness, how long the hospitalization will last, and why, and in what shape they will leave for home. Inevitably, more of them will discover, or be told, the truth. (The widespread improvement in educational level will strengthen these trends.) And so it is predictable that the problem of awareness will become more and more central to what happens as people pass from life to death in American hospitals. That problem is the principal subject of our book.

AWARENESS AND THE STUDY OF INTERACTION

This book will be directed to two audiences: those who are concerned with dying in our hospitals (especially those who must deal with it), and sociologists (especially those who study social interaction). Our book, then, can be read for its practical details as well as for its theoretical aspects. Writing to such a double audience is only slightly hazardous, we believe, because we are convinced that sociologists cannot say anything profoundly useful unless it is of theoretical interest to sociologists themselves.

As noted, our book is based upon extensive field observation and interviewing done at hospitals in the San Francisco metropolitan area. The research was part of a larger study
of how nursing and medical personnel give care to terminal
patients. In Appendix A, both the larger project and the fieldwork methods which underlie our conclusions in this book are
described briefly. In general, our project was focused on what
kinds of thing happen around patients as they lie dying in
American hospitals. In this book, we began by narrowing that
focus to the following questions. What are the recurrent kinds
of *interaction* between dying patient and hospital personnel?
What kinds of *tactics* are used by the personnel who deal with
the patient? Under what conditions of hospital organization do
these kinds of interaction and these tactics occur, and how do
they affect the patient, his family, the staff, and the hospital
itself, all of whom are involved in the situations surrounding
dying? In finding answers to these questions, we discovered
that most variations could be accounted for by what each party
to the dying situation was aware of about the patient's fate.
Thus we further narrowed our focus to dealing with these
questions as they related to awareness: a powerful explanatory
variable.

These questions are of immense practical relevance to hospital personnel, who are confronted daily with the exceedingly
delicate and difficult task of caring for terminal patients. But
outsiders like ourselves, however observant, can contribute
little by merely narrating the difficulties experienced by hospital "insiders," and even less by offering a few suggestions for
coping better with those difficulties. (We are chary of prescriptions and evaluations, though in Chapter 14 we shall address
ourselves to how our theory of awareness bears upon issues of
practical understanding and control.) A sociologist contributes
most when he reports what he has observed in such a fashion
that his account rings true to insiders, but also in such a
fashion that they themselves would not have written it. That

is, most useful sociological accounts are precisely those which insiders recognize as sufficiently inside to be true but not so "inside" that they reveal only what is already known. And since insiders, especially those in stressful circumstances, do not always agree with each other on all matters, a sociological narrative must also take this disagreement into account. The sociologist's obligation is to report honestly but according to his own lights.

These two factors—how the report is written and what it adds to what is already known by insiders—also permit the sociologist to contribute to the factual knowledge of his own craft. To the degree that the sociologist treats his data abstractly, he also has an opportunity to say something important to his own colleagues. So, in this book, we address ourselves to the problem of how to conceptualize and *account* for "social interaction." This problem is a central sociological issue: virtually all the influential theorists in sociology—Max Weber, Durkheim, Thomas, Mead, Parsons and Goffman, to name but a few—have grappled with the issue. Researchers, too, must often decide how to characterize and explain the interaction that takes place within groups, organizations and institutions.

AWARENESS CONTEXTS

Our own approach to social interaction and awareness has been much influenced by our study of the situation of dying people. When a patient is brought to the hospital irrevocably comatose, and diagnosed as dying, then there is no question that he will ever become aware of that diagnosis. It is possible that nurses and physicians may define this patient's status differently, but such disagreement is unlikely. On the other hand, when a patient arrives sentient, and there is some question about whether or not he is dying, then of course his definition may diverge sharply from theirs, and theirs vary among themselves. What *each* interacting person knows of the patient's defined status,[7] along with his recognition of the others' awarenesses of his own definition—the total picture as a sociologist might construct it—we shall call an *awareness context*. It is the context within which these people interact while taking cognizance of it. Plainly, that context is complex, and it may change over time, especially as the patient's condition worsens and as explicit or implicit messages on his condition get through to him.

If we assume that a number of persons are party to the interaction, then the logical combinations of who knows what yield a great many different types of awareness context.[8] For Part II of this book, we have selected several that recur empirically—and are immensely important for "what goes on around the patient"—when only *two* interactants are assumed. Those two are the patient and the hospital staff. To simplify matters, we assume that the staff acts mainly as though all its members share the same awareness. For Part III, we do not make the assumption of staff consensus, but discuss what happens under various conditions of agreement and disagreement. When discussing the patient's family in Part III, we shall not assume consensus either.

Each chapter in Part II is organized around specific awareness contexts, each turning around the confrontation of patient and hospital personnel and the characteristic modes of interaction that appear within the context.[9] For instance, there is

[7] In Chapter 2 we analyze the elements of this definition of the dying status.

[8] Barney G. Glaser and Anselm L. Strauss, "Awareness Contexts and Social Interaction," *American Sociological Review*, 29 (1964), pp. 669-79. In this paper we consider the various dimensions that make up the types considered in this book and that could make up thirty-six possible types. These dimensions are (1) number of people involved; (2) acknowledgment of awareness (pretense or not); (3) degree of awareness (aware, suspicion, unaware); (4) object of awareness (in our case a death expectation); and (5) awareness of other person's awareness of object.

[9] These interactional modes may occur also in other types of awareness context, but in less empirically significant form or magnitude.

the situation where the patient does not recognize his impending death even though everyone else does. There is the situation where the patient suspects what the others know and therefore attempts to confirm or invalidate his suspicion. There is the situation where each party defines the patient as dying, but each pretends that the other has not done so. And, of course, there is also the situation where personnel and patient both are aware that he is dying, and where they act on this awareness relatively openly. We shall refer to these situations as, respectively, the following types of awareness context: *closed awareness, suspected awareness, mutual pretense awareness,* and *open awareness.*

The impact of each type of awareness context upon the interplay between patients and personnel is profound, for people guide their talk and actions according to who knows what and with what certainty. As talk, action, and the accompanying cues unfold, certain awareness contexts tend to evolve into other contexts. Said another way, interaction evolves or develops; it does not remain static. Our task will be to trace typical patterns of interactional development, and to link them with awareness contexts, according to the following paradigm for the study of awareness contexts and interaction: (1) a description of each awareness context, (2) the social structural conditions that enter into the context, (3) the consequent interaction, including various tactics and countertactics, (4) the change of interaction from one type of awareness to another, (5) the ways in which various interactants engineer changes of awareness context, and (6) various consequences of the interaction—for the interactants, for the hospital, and for further interaction. Each chapter in Part II is organized according to the above design. The purpose of these chapters is to show how our theory discriminates various interactional modes and processes. Thus, they show that the theory works.

Part III, which then follows, is focused on various general problems associated with awareness contexts: notably as they bear upon the patient, his family and the hospital staff. These chapters develop models for understanding and explaining problems of awareness of dying which will be useful to both medical practitioners and sociologists. The analysis in each chapter is carried on according to the prescriptions of the awareness context paradigm, but not with the same organization. They are organized, rather, by the substantive issues of the problem under consideration. Thus these chapters show our theory applied to substantive issues. In Part IV we consider some implications of our general analysis for nursing and medical care and for awareness and interactional theory.

In so arranging our book, we hope to link together our dual commitment to practical and theoretical affairs. Surely we shall not have said all there is to say—indeed not all we ourselves have to say—about dying in American hospitals. But we hope that our account will help establish surer ground than now exists for understanding the social-psychological dimensions of terminal care, as well as contribute to sociological theory.

It will prove useful to note a few general features of awareness contexts in the dying situation as they contrast with other situations involving the problem of awareness. Other features will be noted in succeeding chapters. First, unlike some secrets that may be kept or disclosed, a man's approaching death is almost certain to be bad news to him when and if he learns of it (unless he is very old or in tremendous pain). Consequently, the stakes involved in this particular awareness are very high. For the staff, the stakes are also frequently high, because of various reasons soon to be detailed. Second, the dying situation involves a single individual (the patient) who is pitted against a group of others (the staff). Each staff member usually acts as a group representative when interacting with the patient. This situation can be contrasted with spy dramas, where spies and counterspies, on both (or even more than two) sides, all belong to teams. Third, the signs of the patient's terminality are not always visible to him, and, if visible, may not usually be very meaningful to him. Their meaning is not always apparent, either, to all other interactants. Again this situation contrasts with some other awareness situations where a single sign (say, dark skin) is likely to be interpreted specifically by most interactants ("race"). These different features of different awareness situations suggest the generality of "awareness context" as a concept. We shall develop this theme of generality in the closing chapter of this book. Initially, it is enough to say that the human condition is such that men often act without full surety of knowing one another's true identity. Action proceeds on faith, and on the basis of canniness and tactics, as well as on mutual understanding of motives and statuses.

SOCIAL ORDER AND THE ANALYSIS OF INTERACTION

Other sociologists have duly taken into account this phenomenon of problematic identity, or assumed its existence, but few of them have analyzed awareness of identity and interaction in detail. Some theorists (Simmel, Cooley, Mead, Icheiser, Goffman and Davis) have written in detail about awareness and consequent interaction, but generally there has been little theoretical cognizance of either the structural context within which types of awareness occur, or the structure of the awareness context itself. As a result, they have tended to restrict their range in considering the problem of awareness. Their characteristic theoretical perspectives and concerns may have led them to focus on one or two types of awareness: George Mead's concern with the implications of mutual understanding is a good example. Or a writer's ideas may be directly affected by the particular kinds of data with which he has worked.[10]

Our own approach to the problem of interaction is much affected by a set of convictions about the maintenance of social order. Concerning social order, Norton Long, a political scien-

[10] See "Awareness Contexts and Social Interaction," *op. cit.*, for full discussion.

tist, recently wrote that there is a sociology of John Locke
and a sociology of Thomas Hobbes: the one emphasizes a
realm of stable unquestioned values underlying the social order,
and the other, the highly problematic character of social order.[11]
George Mead earlier rephrased the Hobbesian view by noting
that social changes occur constantly; he argued that the human
task is "to bring those changes about in an orderly fashion,"
to direct change so that it is not chaotic, or in Hobbes' language,
anarchistic.[12] Our version, which combines both views of this
overdrawn dichotomy, is that the bases of social order must
be reconstituted continually, must be "worked at," both according to established values and with the purpose of establish-
ing values to preserve order.[13] The maintenance of social order,
whether in society, organizations, groups or interaction, we
believe, turns about handling relatively unforeseen consequences
in this twofold manner.

Our assumptions about social order have naturally lead
us to explore the developmental possibilities of interaction,
though our assumptions need not be accepted to legitimate this
aim as of immense sociological importance. In his recent *Behavior in Public Places*, Erving Goffman analyzed interaction
in terms of the social regulations that subtly govern it and
make it the genuine embodiment of social order; [14] in contrast,

[11] "The Political Act as an Act of Will," *American Journal of Sociology*, 69 (July 1963), pp. 1-6.
[12] "The Problem of Society—How We Become Selves," *Movements
of Thought in the Nineteenth Century* (Chicago: University of Chicago
Press, 1936), pp. 360-61. See also Herbert Blumer, "Society as Symbolic Interaction," in Arnold Rose (ed.), *Human Behavior and Social
Processes* (Boston: Houghton Mifflin, 1962), pp. 179-192.
[13] For an analysis of "working at" social order, see Anselm Strauss,
Leonard Schatzman, Rue Bucher, Danuta Ehrlich, and Melvin Sabshin,
"The Hospital and Its Negotiated Order," in Eliot Freidson (ed.), *The
Hospital in Modern Society* (New York: Free Press of Glencoe, 1964),
pp. 147-169; also by Strauss *et al.*, *Psychiatric Ideologies and Institutions* (New York: Free Press of Glencoe, 1964), pp. 292-315.
[14] Erving Goffman, *Behavior in Public Places* (New York: Free
Press of Glencoe, 1963). For our contrasting view, see Anselm Strauss,
Mirrors and Masks (Chicago: Free Press of Glencoe, 1959), especially
the section on "Self-appraisals and the Course of Action," and "Interaction," pp. 31-88.

we are cognizant of rules but are principally interested in analyzing interaction in terms of its open-ended and problematic character. Rather than focusing on interactional *stability*, we shall be preoccupied in this book with *changes* that may occur during the course of interaction. However, relatively stable or purely repetitive interaction also demands analysis beyond detailing the governing regulations: that is, one must also consider the tactics sustaining that stasis which constantly is subjected to change and unforeseen consequences; one must combine both the rule and the "working at" basis of social order. Thus, in our account of the interaction that centers around dying patients, we shall be interested not only in the social regulations and other structural conditions entering into the interaction, but also in the tendency for interaction to move out of regulated social bounds and into new interactional modes.

2
Expectations of Death: A Problem in Social Definition

The issue discussed in this chapter is basic to all discussions of interaction: How do the interacting persons come to define both themselves and others *as* interactants—and how do they make redefinitions, if necessary, as the interaction continues? As it pertains to the dying patient, the question is how hospital personnel come to see the patient as due to die within some approximate time period, and how they define their status and sometimes their "selves" in their relations with this patient. The patient must do the same with them, in reverse, even if he never discovers their true definitions of him.

Some years ago the Swedish social scientist Gunnar Myrdal, in his book about race relations in the United States, remarked upon the importance of criteria, in this instance especially a single criterion, skin color, for defining statuses. He writes:

> I had once another experience which throws light on the same problem. . . . The N.A.A.C.P. had, in 1939, their annual convention in Richmond, Virginia. I visited the meetings and took part in a boat excursion which ended the convention. On board I approached a group of officers and crew (whites) who held themselves strictly apart, looking on the Association members who had crowded their ship for the day with an unmistakable mixture of superiority, dislike, embarrassment, interest and friendly humor. . . . I told them that I was a stranger who by chance had come on the boat, just for

16

the excursion. . . . [They] entertained me for more than an hour by telling me everything about the Negro and the Negro problem in America. During the course of our conversation I remarked that there were apparently a lot of white people, too, on the boat. At first they just laughed at my remark and insisted that all persons present were Negroes. Some Negroes are so fair, they told me, that only Southerners, who know them by life-long intimate association can distinguish them from whites. I insisted and pointed to Mr. Walter White, the secretary of the N.A.A.C.P. and some other "white" Negroes, and actually succeeded in drawing an acknowl-edgment that he and some other men (who I knew were all Negroes) were, indeed, white upon closer observa-tion. One of my interlocutors went to have a closer look at the persons I had pointed out, and came back and confirmed authoritatively that they were indeed white. "There are some 'nigger lovers' in the North and we have a few down here, too," he commented.[1]

The whites first saw the passengers as Negroes primarily be-cause of skin color, and then misperceived some as "whites" for the same reason. This imperious role of skin color in American race relations was brought home recently when a white journalist, John Griffin, ingeniously changed his skin color and passed as Negro without once being challenged by either southern whites or Negroes.[2] Griffin's passing seems even more ironic in light of a remark by a young sociologist, unaware of the book, that a white sociologist could not study Negro social relations in depth because he could not pass as a Negro—both Negroes and whites would discover who he really was.

But in most cases a single criterion rarely is the basis for interactional definition. The complexity of the process of making definitions in interaction will become clear in our discus-sion of the specifics of defining dying patients.

[1] Gunnar Myrdal, *An American Dilemma* (New York: Harper and Bros., 1944), Vol. 1, p. 68.
[2] John Griffin, *Black Like Me* (Boston: Houghton Mifflin Co., 1960).

DIAGNOSIS AND PROGNOSIS AS
DEFINITIONAL QUESTIONS

When a patient enters a hospital, one of the most important initial questions is "what's the diagnosis?" This question is no less important when the patient is fated soon to die, unless death is so imminent that diagnosis is meaningless. What is done to and for most patients depends mainly on the answer to the diagnostic (and its allied prognostic) question. Modern hospitals are organized to insure a relatively speedy answer. If diagnosis is uncertain, then additional diagnostic soundings are typically made, and the course of the illness itself, during the next few days, may prompt more accurate answers.

From a sociological perspective, the important thing about any diagnosis, whether correctly established or not, is that it involves questions of definition. Even with a known terminal patient, another important question—how fast he will die— must still be determined. Many a hospital patient poses for the staff both questions simultaneously: Is this patient going to die here, and when? The first of these questions refers to "uncertainty of death" while the second refers to "time of death." Even more specifically, let us say that *certainty* of death means the degree to which the defining person (physician, nurse, or even the patient himself) is convinced that the patient will die. Let us say that *time* of death means the expectation of either (a) when the certain death will occur, or (b) when the uncertainty about death will be resolved. Time units can be from minutes to months, varying with the nature of the illness and the patient's location in the hospital. For example, on emergency wards only a few minutes may pass before it is known for certain whether a patient will live. About premature babies, nurses usually think of death in terms of hours or a few days at most; while for cancer patients, the time unit may be months.

In combination, certainty and time yield four types of "death expectations:" (1) certain death at a known time,

(2) certain death at an unknown time, (3) uncertain death but a known time when the question will be resolved, and (4) uncertain death and unknown time when the question will be resolved. As we shall show later, these types of expectations have varying effects on the interaction of participants in the dying situations.

ESTABLISHING EXPECTATIONS OF DEATH

Anyone may read the medical signs and draw his own conclusions, the terminal patient included. But in American hospitals, the attending physician is the only one who can legitimately define the patient's condition, because of his professional expertise and the professional mandate that he be medically responsible for the patient. Ordinarily, only he may tell patients that they are dying. Under extraordinary conditions, nurses tell patients or relatives directly, but this is not the usual practice. (The physician's problems in reading the medical signs correctly will not concern us here, though it is worth noting that uncertainty in medical diagnosis and prognosis, and the need to train young physicians to manage it, has produced a special literature.[3])

Nurses must *also* correctly assess whether the patient is dying and when he will die. To make those assessments is often no easy matter. In forming their expectations, the nurses may rely on their own reading of cues—how the patient looks and acts, what his charts report about him—as well as on cues

[3] Talcott Parsons, *The Social System* (New York: Free Press of Glencoe, 1951), pp. 447-466; Renée Fox, "Training for Uncertainty," in Robert K. Merton, *et al.* (eds.), *The Student Physician* (Cambridge: Harvard University Press, 1957), pp. 207-241; Renée Fox, *Experiment Perilous* (New York: Free Press of Glencoe, 1959), see index on page 262 for diverse sources; Fred Davis, "Uncertainty in Medical Prognosis," *American Journal of Sociology*, 66 (July, 1960), pp. 41-47; Fred Davis, "Definitions of Time and Recovery in Paralytic Polio Convalescence," *American Journal of Sociology*, 61 (May 1956), pp. 582-587; Julius A. Roth, *Timetables* (Indianapolis: Bobbs-Merrill, 1963); and Howard S. Becker, Blanche Geer, E. C. Hughes, and Anselm L. Strauss, *Boys in White* (Chicago: University of Chicago Press, 1961).

flashed, perhaps unwittingly or obliquely, by the doctor. Sometimes they also receive direct information from the doctor; typically, they trust this source more than their own individual or collective reading of cues, though of course the reverse may be true if they are experienced nurses and the doctor seems inexperienced, incompetent, or not well acquainted with the case. Sometimes the cues are so obvious that the physician needs to say little or nothing. So, although the most legitimate source for forming death expectations is the physician, the nurses also observe cues constantly.

Doctors vary considerably as to whether they give nurses a legitimate basis for death expectations. ("The doctor may or may not tell us a patient is critical. We decide. They expect us to use our beans.") It is unusual for a nurse to ask the doctor directly, but there may be an implicit understanding that he will tell her, or she can hint that he should tell her or give her cues. He may tell her obliquely at first, but more directly later when the patient nears death. In one Catholic hospital a nurse told us, "There is no formal declaration that a patient is terminal. Sometimes a doctor will tell the nurse, but usually you just pick it up." She added: "If the doctor knows that a patient is going to die, I prefer to know it." This nurse wants legitimate expectations, but she is forced to rely mainly on cues. Sometimes nothing much needs to be said, as when a cancer patient who has returned often to the service returns now in obviously critical condition, and everyone, residents and nurses alike, agree that "this is the last time." Sometimes the cues are as explicit as words might be, as when a feeble patient who still seems to have a chance to live is taken off intravenous blood injections.

In some hospitals, the doctor is required to deal with the uncertainty dimension by putting the patient on a critically, dangerously or seriously ill list, or by including that information on an admission card. A patient's appearance on such a critical list initiates many activities. In one veterans' hospital, for example, families are allowed to stay around the clock with the patient; if relatives are not on hand they are sent a wire stating that "Your (kin) has been put on the seriously ill list, please come at once." The physician then has a talk with the family, while social workers and the chaplain drop in to help. To be sure, medical personnel at this hospital are reluctant to initiate all this activity by formally indicating the patient's impending death, and they wait until the last moment to put patients on the critical list. Paradoxically, the nurses therefore must work longer with cues unless given explicit information by the doctor.

Two principal types of cues that can be read by the nurses are the patient's physical condition and the temporal references made either by themselves or the medical staff. Physical cues, ranging from those that spell hope to those that indicate immediate death, generally establish the certainty aspect of death expectations. Temporal cues, however, have many reference points. A major one is the typical progression of the disease, against which the patient's actual movement is measured (he is "going fast" or "lingering"). Another is the doctor's expectation about how long the patient will remain in the hospital. For instance, one patient's hospitalization was "lasting longer" than the short while anticipated by the physician. Work schedules also provide a temporal reference: nurses adjust their expectations according to whether the patient can continue being bathed, turned, fed, and given sedation regularly. All such references pertain to the temporal aspect of dying; that is, to how long the patient is expected to live.

Because physical cues are generally easier to read, and their presence helps to establish some degree of certainty about dying, temporal cues are rather indeterminate when the physical ones are absent. The patient may die "sometime" or "at any time." As both types of cues accumulate, they may support each other; for example, as a patient's condition becomes more grave his hospitalization grows longer. But physical and temporal cues can also cancel each other: thus, an unduly long hospitalization can be balanced or even negated by increasingly hopeful physical cues. When cues cancel each other, nurses can use the more hopeful one (he is going home sooner than expected) to balance or deny the less hopeful (he looks bad). As physical and temporal cues accumulate faster and become more severe, they become harder to deny, and the expectation of death is gradually more firmly established.

About the patient's own expectation of death we shall have much to say in succeeding chapters. Here we need note only the most general sources of his expectations. The most impeccable source is the physician himself, who may choose to announce directly "you have little chance to live" or "your disease is fatal." However, as noted in Chapter 1, American physicians very infrequently make such announcements. Much more frequently they drop gentle, oblique references, relying on the patient's willingness to read those references correctly— but if he chooses to ignore their sombre meaning, then physicians assume that the patient really does not wish to confront the fact of his own death.[4]

Besides the physician's word, what else can the patient depend on if he does want to know his fate? If one were to write a set of directives for such a patient it would go as follows: Apart from making your physician tell you, listen carefully to what the staff says about you. Listen carefully also to anything the medical or nursing personnel may tell you, obliquely, about your condition; for sometimes they flash cues, perhaps knowingly or perhaps unwittingly, about you. And do not forget that you can sometimes force more cues out of the staff members; by being canny and clever, you can catch them unawares. Many patients, of course, figure out for themselves such methods for discovering what the staff knows. In addition, they can attempt to read the physical cues in their own bodies. These are sometimes unambiguous enough to be read correctly by very aged patients or patients with chronic retrogressive diseases. Again, as with the nurses themselves, temporal cues

---

[4] This topic of disclosure to patients by doctors is taken up in detail in Chapter 8.

are less dependable but operate in conjunction with the other cues just mentioned.[5]

CHANGING EXPECTATIONS

We shall leave for later pages further references to the patient's definitions of his condition and turn now to ways in which expectations of a patient's death may change.

Nurses' definitions of the patient's illness status—that is, their expectations—affect their behavior toward him. Therefore, the moment when their expectations change is significant. For example, even when the physician's cues imply that the patient is doomed, as when he stops blood transfusions, the nurses may still not be absolutely sure that the implied prediction is accurate. They may not lower their levels of alertness or reduce their effort to save the patient. They may say of the patient, as one nurse did, "If he comes out of it, we'll work on him. He only has to give us the slightest cue." Since the doctor has said nothing official, even nurses who believe the patient is dying can still give him an outside chance and stand ready to save him. They remain constantly alert to countercues. "Everybody is simply waiting," said one nurse. If the doctor had indicated that the patient would die within the day, nurses would have ceased their constant watch for countercues and reduced their efforts to save him, concentrating instead on giving comfort to the last, with no undue prolonging of life. Thus, the nurses' changing expectations can have considerable impact on their care of dying patients.[6]

[5] For a book length discussion of how one type of patient may survive in a hospital with the aid of sociological knowledge see Julius A. Roth, *Handbook for Tuberculosis Hospital Patients or How to Survive the Treatment* (Mimeo: April, 1963). Much of the discussion in our book on awareness could also be written as a hand book of prescriptions to patients on how to cope with the hospital organization, the staff and the medical rigors of dying, in order to bring one's life to a close in a more satisfying way than often allowed by medical treatment, staff and hospital organization.

[6] Chapters 11, 12 and 13 examine in detail the effects of changing expectations on medical care, nursing care, and on the nurse, respectively.

The changing expectations of nurses and physicians actually map out the patient's changes of status. Many patterns of "status passage," [7] with typical rates of movement, are well known. A classical pattern is the lingering patient: he is certain to die, but when he will do so is unknown and he does not die for some while. On one cancer ward we studied, an all-too-typical sequence of expectations for the lingering patient ran the gamut of various stages of determinancy: from original prognosis of certain death but uncertain time, through the weeks when the patient began obviously to decline, to the time that his precise time of death finally became relatively certain. Of course, before the final decline takes place, such patients may alternate between hospital visits and periods at home. Often the nurses feel that a lingering patient is taking more time than is proper, because there is really no hope for him. (In this sense, even an unknown time period has limits.)

A patient expected to die on time, but who suddenly begins to recover slightly or to linger—the short-term reprieve pattern —can cause problems for nurses, family, physicians, and hospital administrators. Here is an example: one patient who was expected to die within four hours had no money, but needed a special machine during his last days. A private hospital, at which he had been a frequent paying patient for thirty years, agreed to receive him as a charity patient. He did not die immediately but started to linger indefinitely, even to the point where there was some hope that he might live. The money problem, however, created much concern among both his family members and the hospital administrators. Paradoxically, the doctor had continually to reassure both parties that this patient, who actually lasted six weeks, would soon die; that is, to try to change their expectations back to "certain to die on time."

Another pattern, which may be called the vacillating pattern, is a variation on the short-term reprieve. The patient alternates from "certain to die on time" to "lingering." The

[7] Barney G. Glaser and Anselm L. Strauss, "Temporal Aspects of Dying as a Non-scheduled Status Passage," *American Journal of Sociology* (June, 1965).

alternation may occur sufficiently often to cause stress among family members and hospital personnel. Whenever the patient genuinely starts to fade, the nurses may call the family, for as one nurse said, "If you do not call the family and the patients die, that's wrong." The family members arrive for their last look at the dying man, but he begins to linger. They finally leave saying, "please call us again" when he begins to die. Family and nurses may go repeatedly through this stressful cycle.[8] The physician and chaplain may also be affected. Changes in the activities and moods of the various participants are thus linked with this vacillating pattern, and the nurses' typical mood is relief when at last they can forecast the end of the unusual lingering.

In contrast, some patients are the focus of what is commonly known in the hospital as "heroics"; that is, speedy and all-out attempts to stave off death. Patients on emergency, premature baby, and intensive-care units sometimes are the recipients of such heroic measures. (So are patients who are deemed especially valuable: extreme cases being Dr. Ward of the recent British political scandal and a famous Soviet scientist who has been saved repeatedly through heroic hospital measures.) Heroic measures signify uncertain prognosis, which will be quickly resolved, with an appropriate change in staff expectations.

The two extremes toward which patients may progress are either getting well or being certain to die at a specific time, but the nurses and physicians may have other intermediate expectations for a given patient who leaves the hospital. He may have arrived with uncertain prognosis, but been sent home diagnosed as cancerous: certain to die, but "when" is quite unknown. The prognoses of more puzzling cases may be uncertain on both counts.

The staff may be surprised by unexpected changes in the expected passage of patients toward death. Among the most

[8] Chapters 9 and 10 focus on the changing expectations of the family.

surprising changes are the sudden death, or onset of death, of a patient who previously had prognoses of doubtful certainty and time. Of course, the surprise is greatest when there has been no death expectation whatever, as when seemingly healthy patients die. When such patients die on the operating table, the resulting impact is tremendous. The patient's death is too sudden: there is no time to prepare oneself for it. (In one instance, a surgeon much admired by his nursing staff shocked them with an unexpected loss on the operating table. Rumors of negligence were rife, until autopsy showed that the man had died of unanticipated natural causes.) In less traumatic instances, when expectations are revised as the patient moves toward death, but his progress turns out to be unusual, personnel may experience a disquieting feeling of having missed certain steps.

The dying process can become exceedingly complex, for doctors, nurses, family and patient can have different death expectations based on different sources, or they may interpret the same cues differently. The total combinations of these differential expectations make up the "what" we referred to in the first chapter, in our definition of the "awareness context" around the patient.[9]

[9] We wish to underscore the theoretical step we have taken from two important papers by Fred Davis (see Note 3), each of which brought out the notion of differential perceptions. In his medical prognosis article, Davis discussed the differential perceptions of certainty of prognosis held by doctor, patient, and family, and in his "Definitions of Time . . ." he discussed differential perceptions of time of recovery. In our study each participant defines the dying patient situation in terms of both certainty and time. This yields more complex, but more determinant, sets of differential perceptions than Davis deals with explicitly, and these, in turn, have led us to the concept of "awareness context."

Part Two

Types of
Awareness
Contexts

3

Closed
Awareness

In American hospitals, frequently the patient does not recognize his impending death even though the hospital personnel have the information. This situation can be described as a "closed awareness" context. Providing the physician decides to keep the patient from realizing, or even seriously suspecting, what his true status is, the problem is to *maintain* the context as a closed one. With a genuinely comatose patient, the staff members naturally need not guard against disclosure of his terminal condition. As an interactant, the comatose person is what Goffman has called a "non-person." [1] Two nurses caring for him can speak in his presence without fear that, overhearing them, he will suspect or understand what they are saying about him. Neither they nor the physicians need to engage in tactics to protect him from any dread knowledge. And of course with terminal babies, no precautions against disclosure are needed either. But with conscious patients, care must be taken not to disclose the staff's secret.

CONTRIBUTING STRUCTURAL CONDITIONS

There are at least five important structural conditions which contribute to the existence and maintenance of the closed awareness context. [2] First, most patients are not especially

[1] Erving Goffman, *The Presentation of Self in Everyday Life* (Edinburgh, Scotland: University of Edinburgh, 1956), pp. 95-96.
[2] *Cf.* Barney Glaser and Anselm Strauss, "Awareness Contexts and Social Interaction," *American Sociological Review*, 29 (October, 1964), pp. 669-679.

experienced at recognizing the signs of impending death. Of course, a patient who has been in an auto accident and is injured terribly, although still conscious, may recognize how close death is. He may also recognize it if he is himself a physician or a nurse, or if as a chronic hospitalized patient he has encountered fatal signs in dying comrades.[3] But most Americans have not had such opportunities to witness rehearsals for their own deaths.

A second structural condition is that American physicians ordinarily do not tell patients outright that death is probable or inevitable. As a number of studies have shown, physicians find medical justifications for not disclosing dying status to their patients.[4] For instance, Dr. Donald Oken has recently demonstrated that a chief reason offered is "clinical experience." [5] The physician states from "clinical experience," that when one announces terminality to a patient, he is likely to "go to pieces"; one must therefore carefully judge whether or not to tell after sizing up the individual patient. In actual fact, Oken notes, the clinical experience is not genuinely grounded experience, but a species of personal mythology. Generally the experience consists of one or two unfortunate incidents—or even incidents recounted by colleagues—and this effectively cuts off further clinical experimentation to discover the possible range of consequences of disclosure.

Among several articles of faith in professional ideology which support not disclosing terminality, is the belief that patients really do not wish to know whether they are dying. If they did, then they would find out anyhow, so there is no

[3] Renée Fox, *Experiment Perilous* (New York: Free Press of Glencoe, 1959).

[4] Herman Feifel, "Death" in Norman L. Farberow, *Taboo Topics* (New York: Atherton Press, 1963), p. 17.

[5] Donald Oken, "What to Tell Cancer Patients: A Study of Medical Attitudes," *Journal of the American Medical Association,* 175 (April 1, 1961), pp. 1120-28. See the bibliography cited in his paper for further studies on physician's tendency not to announce terminality. See also our further discussion in Chapter 8 of physicians' announcements. ·

sense telling them directly. Presumably some patients do not wish to know their fates, but there is no really good evidence that *all* wish to remain in blissful ignorance or that these patients will find out while in the hospital. And there is some good evidence that they do wish to know.[6] Quite possibly also, physicians, like other Americans, shy away from the embarrassment and brutality of making direct reference to another person about his impending death. They also undoubtedly would rather avoid the scene that an announcement of impending death is likely to precipitate.

A third structural condition is that families also tend to guard the secret. Family members sometimes may reveal it, but in our own study we never witnessed deliberate disclosure by a family member. One psychiatrist told us, however, that he had disagreed with his father's physician about the wisdom of not telling his father, and so had made the disclosure himself. (Family members, of course, usually confirm what the physician has already announced.) An interesting contrast is the usual practice in Asian countries, where the extended kin gather around the hospital death bed, two or more days before death is expected, openly indicating to the patient that they are there to keep him company during his passage out of life.

A fourth structural condition is related both to the organization of hospitals and to the commitments of personnel who work within them. Our hospitals are admirably arranged, both by accident and by design, to hide medical information from patients. Records are kept out of reach. Staff is skilled at withholding information. Medical talk about patients generally occurs in far-removed places, and if it occurs nearby it is couched in medical jargon. Staff members are trained to discuss with patients only the surface aspects of their illnesses, and, as we shall see, they are accustomed to acting collusively around patients so as not to disclose medical secrets.

A fifth structural condition, perhaps somewhat less apparent,

[6] Eighty-two percent of Feifel's sample of sixty patients wanted to be informed about their condition.

is that ordinarily the patient has no allies who reveal or help him discover the staff's knowledge of his impending death. Not only his family but other patients withhold that information, if they know. When a patient wants less distressing information, he may readily find allies among the other patients; but when he lies dying, the other patients follow ordinary rules of tact, keeping their knowledge to themselves or at least away from the doomed person. There may be exceptional incidents: the parents of a dying teenager told neighbors about his condition, and these neighbors told their son who in turn spilled out this information to the patient himself. Among adults, such failures of secrecy ordinarily do not occur.

While together these structural conditions contribute to the occurrence and maintenance of the closed awareness context, a change in any one condition may precipitate a change to another type of context. For example, the physician may decide to tell the patient—which leads to an "open awareness" context; or a patient begins to suspect something amiss because he begins to learn some of the indicators relevant to increasingly grave illness—which leads to a "suspicion awareness" context. In a later section of this chapter we shall discuss how changing structural conditions may transform the closed awareness context.

THE PATIENT'S FICTIONAL BIOGRAPHY

A newly hospitalized patient has some basic questions about his condition. He wants to know, if he does not know already, just how ill he is, and whether he is going to get better or worse, *how* much better or worse, and how quickly he will progress or retrogress. In short, he ordinarily is passionately concerned with his own sick status—he wishes to know what may usefully be referred to as his "future biography."

The patient who is dying but who has not yet discovered or been told of his terminality faces a peculiar problem in getting an accurate assessment of his condition from the medical and nursing personnel. Can he trust the doctor, can he trust the nurses and aides, to yield him a true account of his story? [7] Or will their account be tinged by deceit and perhaps thoroughly false? A false account is a real possibility, although the patient may not recognize it as such. So trust is important in his transactions with the staff members.

Developing trust is also basic in the staff's transactions with the patient. To keep the patient unaware of his terminality, the staff members must construct a *fictional* future biography. for him, and they must sustain his belief in that biography by getting and keeping his trust.

What is involved in winning the patient's "trust?" First, consider a child who is old enough to know about death but still too young to doubt that his elders will properly care for him during his illness. The essence of his relations with adults is that he takes their actions at face value. What they are doing to him, and what they make him do is, as they explain, to make him get better. With children of this age, hospital personnel need not be so concerned about betraying their own behind-the-scenes knowledge. Such suspicions as the child may have will be more "I don't trust them to help me" rather than "I don't trust them because they are not telling me the truth about my condition." Consequently, personnel on pediatric wards report no great danger of unwarily letting their younger patients know they are dying. Indeed, they report that less control of one's face in a child's presence is needed, as he is not so apt to draw conclusions from an expression.

With adults the matter of trust in physicians and nurses is

---

[7] Research in hospitals where psychotherapy is practiced indicates the patients collectively develop a philosophy that one must have faith in one's doctor. *Cf.* William Caudill *et al.,* "Social Structure and the Interaction Process on a Psychiatric Ward," *American Journal of Psychiatry,* 22 (1952), pp. 314-334; also Anselm Strauss *et al., Psychiatric Ideologies and Institutions* (New York: Free Press of Glencoe, 1964), pp. 271-273. But compare with the frequent distrust of doctors found in TB hospitals: Julius Roth, *Timetables* (Indianapolis: Bobbs-Merrill, 1963).

rather more complicated. Trust does not arise automatically; it must either be part of the history of a particular relationship or it must be earned. Furthermore, once earned it must be maintained. The importance of keeping trust can be seen in the dilemma of an unaware patient who has long placed trust in a particular physician, but whose suspicions have now been aroused by some incident or remark. Can the man still be trusted in this new domain, trusted not only to "pull me through my illness" but "to tell me the worst?" In general, the physician and others must not arouse any suspicion by their words and actions that they are concealing knowledge about terminality. They must not even seem to fail in giving honest answers to any questions that might touch upon terminality. When staff members succeed in acting convincingly, the patient accepts their account of his future biography as accurate, or at least as accurate as they know how to make it.

ASSESSMENT MANAGEMENT

To sustain the unaware patient's belief in their version of his future biography, the staff members must control his assessments of those events and cues which might lead him to suspect or gain knowledge of his terminality. Their attempts at managing his assessments involve them in a silent game played to and around him; during which they project themselves to him as people who are trying to help him get better, or at least to keep him from getting worse. They must be sufficiently committed to this game, and sufficiently skilled at it, not to give it away. Their advantage is that they can collaborate as a team, sometimes a very experienced one, against an opponent who, as noted earlier, has ordinarily not much experience in discovering or correctly interpreting signs of impending death, and who is usually without allies.

Though the staff's explanations of his condition initially may seem convincing to the unaware patient, and though he may greatly trust the staff, he may begin to see and hear things that arouse his suspicions about his condition. Inevitably he wonders about, and requires explanation for, a host of events: Why is he given certain treatments or exposed to certain tests and procedures? Why is he moved from one room to another? Why has one more physician dropped into his room to examine him? Why is he not getting better more quickly? He wants answers to questions stimulated by various events even when he does not in the slightest suspect their true significance.

The staff members usually hasten to give him reasonable interpretations of those events. Frequently they even offer interpretations before he requests them, because they calculate he may otherwise secretly suspect the real meanings of those events. Their interpretations may be intentionally incorrect or only partly correct—if they feel that a correct one will potentially or actually reveal terminality to the patient. Thus, many of their interpretations are meant to mislead him. Of course a correct interpretation is offered when the staff member judges it will neither disclose nor arouse suspicions of terminality.

A patient near death, for instance, may be moved to a special space or room, but is informed that this move is only to permit more intensive care. A patient may even be sent home to die on request of his family, but his discharge from the hospital is explained in quite other terms. Occasionally the physician will give a patient an incorrect or incomplete diagnosis to explain his symptoms—as in one instance when a patient was discovered, through a diagnostic operation, to have incurable cancer of the pancreas but was sent home with a diagnosis of diabetes and given instructions in the use of insulin. If the patient believes that he has taken a turn for the worse, or at least is not improving, staff members are ready with reasonable answers that are meant to mislead him. At the very least, certain of his symptoms must be explained away, discounted, as signifying something much less alarming than they appear to him. Sometimes the physician warns him of anticipated symptoms, discounting them in advance. The physician and the nurses may also go out of their way continually to reassure him that things will turn out "all right," and indeed are "coming along fine." They will fabricate, hint at, or suggest favorable progress. Nurses especially compare the patient's condition, and his progress, with that of other patients they have known (including themselves), thus suggesting reasons for optimism. If the patient asks the nurses "Am I going to die?" as occasionally patients do without even real suspicion, they refer him to his physician for an answer ("Have you asked your physician?"), or change the subject without answering the question, or turn it aside with a stock answer (for instance, "We all have to go sometime"). When a patient asks the same question of the physician, the latter may simply lie.

The staff members also use tactics intended to encourage the patient to make his own interpretations inaccurately optimistic. They will comment favorably on his daily appearance, hoping he will interpret their comments optimistically. Some comments are downright misrepresentations and others are ambiguous enough to be misread easily. Staff members will attempt to establish a mood consonant less with terminality than with "things are not so bad even if not yet better." They also practice a sleight of hand, like magicians, drawing the patient's attention away from a dangerous cue by focusing his attention on an innocent one. They raise false scents, sometimes displaying elaborate interest in the symptoms he himself brings up for consideration. The physician may even put on diagnostic dramas for him, sending him for irrelevant tests. A certain amount of conversation with him about his imminent, or eventual, return home may occur; and his own reading of physical and temporal cues that represent progress to him may be supported. There is also what one might call a "sociability shield," or conversation that circumvents disclosure; during this conversation, personnel carry on as if the entire situation were quite normal. With such interactional devices, the staff simultaneously projects their own trustworthy medical identities, conveying to the patient that he is not expected to die.

In addition to all these devices, other techniques reduce cues that might arouse the patient's suspicion. Space is carefully managed, so that talk about him occurs away from his presence. If a nurse believes her involvement with, or sadness about, the patient might give the secret away, she may move quickly outside his visual range. She may even request an assignment away from him. Possibly revealing cues are also reduced by decreasing the time spent with the patient. Personnel who fear that they may unwittingly disclose something may remain with the patient very little, or choose to work on his body rather than talk much with him. They may keep tabs on his physical condition by popping in and out of his room, but thereby keep conversation at a minimum. Sometimes, when the patient is extremely close to death but there is nothing much to be done for him, staff members tend to go no farther than the doorway. If the patient becomes genuinely comatose, nurses or aides can again circulate freely in the patient's room.

The disclosing cues are minimized most subtly by reducing the range of expression and topic. The face can be managed so as to minimize the dangerous cues it conveys; hence the conventionally bland or cheerful faces of nurse and physician. A less obvious mode of minimizing such cues is to censor and select conversational topics. Staff members, for instance, steer conversation away from potentially revealing subjects and toward safer ones. They may talk, especially, about the relatively straightforward meanings of procedures being used on the patient's body, providing those meanings are not revealing.

One aspect of talk that personnel are cautious about is its present-future orientation. When a patient is defined as certain to die within a few days, nurses tend to focus their conversation with him on the immediate present, discussing such matters as current doses of medication for pain relief or other topics relevant to his comfort. But if they do not anticipate death for some time, then they will extend the temporal range implied in their talk. One nurse thus said, before leaving for a weekend, "See you next week." Another told a patient that he would need another X ray in two weeks. Similarly, they talk about blood tests to be done next week, or about the family's impending visit. One young nurse told us that she used to chat with a young patient about his future dates and parties, but that after discovering his certain and imminent death, she unwittingly cut out all references to the distant future. It is not easy to carry on a future-oriented conversation without revealing one's knowledge that the conversation is, in some sense, fraudulent, especially if the speaker is relatively inexperienced.

Staff members, again especially if they are inexperienced, must also guard against displaying those of their private reactions to him and to his impending death as might rouse the patient's suspicions of his terminality. For instance, young nurses are sometimes affected by terminal patients of their own age whose deaths become standing reminders of their own potential death. ("I found . . . that the patients who concerned me most when they died were women of my own age. . . .") Identification of this kind is quite common, and makes more difficult the staff members' control of their behavioral cues.

Their reactions to the patient's "social loss" [8] can also be revealing. In our society, certain values are highly esteemed— among them youth, beauty, integrity, talent, and parental and marital responsibility—and when a terminal patient strikingly embodies such values, staff members tend to react to the potential or actual loss to his family or to society. But such reactions must not be allowed to intrude into the fictionalized future biography that is directly and indirectly proffered to the patient. Since personnel tend to share a common attribution of social value, that intrusion is quite possible unless they keep

[8] Barney Glaser and Anselm Strauss, "The Social Loss of Dying Patients," *American Journal of Nursing* (June 1964), pp. 119-121.

tight control over their reactions. Although the staff's control is not always fully conscious, it is no less real.

Finally, because the patient is usually in contact with many staff members during each day, his suspicions of terminality may be aroused if they do not give consistent answers to his questions or if their behavior yields him inconsistent cues. So they must strive for consistency. But if he queries any inconsistency, then the staff members must offer him reasonable interpretations to explain away the "apparent" inconsistency.

FROM CLOSED TO OTHER AWARENESS CONTEXTS

Inherently, this closed awareness context tends toward instability, as the patient moves either to suspicion or full awareness of his terminality. The principal reasons for the instability of closed awareness require only brief notation, as they have already been adumbrated. First, any breakdown in the structural conditions that make for the closed awareness context may lead to its disappearance.[9] Those conditions include the physician's decision not to tell the patient, the family's supporting agreement, and the tactful silence of other patients. For example, such a break occurs repeatedly at one Veterans Administration hospital we studied, where patients who are eventually judged to be hopelessly terminal are sometimes asked whether they would care to become research subjects and receive medication that might prolong their lives.

Some unanticipated disclosures or tip offs, stemming from organizational conditions, can also occur. The staff members who work in emergency rooms in hospitals need to be especially careful in controlling their facial surprises or immediately

[9] The Catholic practice of giving the sacrament requires calling in a priest prior to possible death, and this may function as an announcement to the dying patient. But non-Catholics probably need to be told that this is done only to insure that the patient does not die without the sacrament. If he recovers, whether to live for many years or merely days, then he may receive the sacrament once or perhaps several times again.

compassionate distress when suddenly confronted by obviously dying patients, often the battered victims of accidents caused by others' carelessness. Staff members' control in these instances is not always successful. On other hospital services, rotation of nursing staff may bring the patient into contact with new persons who do not always know of his terminality or who have not been coached properly in the history of how the staff has conducted itself in the presence of this patient. Even the daily shift carries hidden dangers. For instance, the doctor may inform the day shift that his patient is dying, but unless specific measures are taken to transmit this information to the night shift, the patient may be cared for by personnel not sufficiently alert to the dangers of unwitting disclosure. This danger is especially grave when the patient is worried about certain new symptoms.

New symptoms understandably are likely to perplex and alarm the patient; and the longer his retrogressive course, the more difficult it becomes to give him plausible explanations, though a very complicated misrepresentational drama can be played for his benefit. Even so, it becomes somewhat more difficult to retain the patient's trust over a long time. When a patient's physical symptoms become compelling, sometimes he can force nurses into almost an open admission of the truth. Not to hint at, or tacitly admit to, the truth would be to risk losing his trust altogether. So it is not unknown for the staff to "snow a patient under" with drugs as he nears death, partly to reduce his suffering (and perhaps their own) and partly to reduce the likelihood that finally he will correctly read the fateful signs. Indeed, sometimes a race with time occurs, there being some question whether the patient will die, or at least become comatose, before he becomes suspicious or aware of his terminality.

Another threat to closed awareness, closely linked with retrogressive physical symptoms, is that some treatments make little sense to a patient who does not recognize that he is dying. Just as many polio patients will not take full advantage of rehabilitation programs because they do not anticipate being cured, so a terminal patient may refuse a medicine, a machine, an awkward position or an inconvenient diet.[10] To accomplish her task, the nurse may have to hint at the extreme seriousness of her patient's condition, hoping that he will get the point just long enough for her to complete the procedure. But if this tactic works, it may then also stimulate an attempt by the patient to discover what is really happening to him. The staff then must redouble its assessment management. For instance, the nurse who alarmed him must immediately assure him that he has interpreted her words incorrectly—but she may not be wholly or at all successful. The physician can also have problems when explaining to his patient why he must undergo certain additional treatments, tests and operations, or why he needs to return to the hospital "for a while."

At times, moreover, a patient may be unable to cope with his immensely deteriorating physical condition unless nurses interpret that condition and its symptoms to him. To do this, nurses may feel forced to talk of his dying. Not to disclose at this desperate point can torture and isolate the patient, which runs counter to a central value of nursing care, namely to make the patient as comfortable as possible. Similarly, the physician's inaccessibility may force nurses to disclose the truth in order to do something immediately for, or with the patient.

The danger that staff members will give the show away by relaxing their usual tight control also increases as the patient nears death, especially when the dying takes place slowly. For instance, concerned personnel will continually pause at the patient's door, popping their heads into his room to see how he is—or if he is still alive. Sometimes a patient very close to death will be given more privileges because of simple compassion for him (like permitting him to eat previously denied favorite foods or to take an automobile ride or even to return home

---

[10] *Cf.* Fred Davis, "Uncertainty in Medical Prognosis," *American Journal of Sociology*, 66 (July 1960), p. 45.

permanently); occasionally this can cue him into suspicion awareness. The staff will also sometimes relax their guard when they believe the patient is too far gone (physically dazed, comatose, or senile) to understand what would otherwise be revealing cues or downright disclosing conversations—but he may be sentient enough to understand.

This last set of conditions brings us to the question of whether, and how, personnel actually may engineer a change of the closed awareness context. For instance, a physician may drop hints to the patient that he is dying, giving the information gradually, and hoping that eventually the patient will comprehend the finality of his medical condition. Nurses have so often confided to us that they hoped certain patients were really aware of impending death that we can be sure they have signaled, however ambiguously, to such patients, especially when the latter are well beloved and the nurses can see no good reason why they should not be prepared for death even though the physicians choose not to tell. The true situation can be deliberately conveyed to a patient by facial expression, by carefully oblique phrasing of words, or merely by failure to reassure him about his symptoms and prognosis. And of course the family members may occasionally signal or hint at the dreadful truth. Indeed, when the family actually knows the truth, the hazards to maintaining closed awareness probably are much increased, if only because kin are more strongly tempted to signal the truth.

CONSEQUENCES OF CLOSED AWARENESS

So many discrete consequences seem to flow from this closed awareness context that we must restrict our attention to a few of its consequences for the patient, his family, the hospital personnel, and the hospital itself. We shall return to this discussion of interactional consequences in later chapters; here we shall merely initiate it.

We can approach the consequences of closed awareness by

touching on a contrasting situation. In her book *Experiment Perilous,* Renée Fox has described a small research hospital whose patients recognized their own inevitable terminality because that was why they were research patients.[11] Death was an open and everyday occurrence. Patients could talk familiarly to each other, about their respective fatal conditions, as well as to the staff members. Various consequences seemed to flow from this generally *open* situation, including the following: Patients could give each other support; and the staff could support patients. Patients could even raise the flagging spirits of the staff! From their deathbeds, they could thank the physicians for their unstinting efforts and wish them luck in solving their research problems in time to save other patients. They could close their lives with proper rituals, such as letter writing and praying. They could review their lives and plan realistically for their families' futures. All these various possibilities, available to aware patients in the open awareness situation, are of course not available to unaware patients in the closed awareness situation.

When patients are kept unaware of their terminality, then other consequences emerge. Since the unaware patient believes he will recover, he acts on that supposition. He may often be extremely cooperative with physicians and nurses because he believes faithful following of their orders will return him to good health. He talks and thinks as if his period of illness is only an interruption of normal life. Thus he may convert his sick room into a temporary workplace, writing his unfinished book, telephoning his business partners, and in other ways carrying on his work somewhat "as usual." He carries on his family life and friendship relations, also, with only the interruption necessitated by temporary illness. And of course, he can plan, if plans are called for, as if life stretched away before him. Since, in reality, it does not, other consequences may attend his acting as though it did. He may work less feverishly on his unfinished book than if he knew time was short, and

[11] Renée Fox, *op. cit.*

so fail to finish it. He may set plans into operation that make little sense because he will soon be dead, and the plans will have to be undone after his death. Also, the unaware patient may unwittingly shorten his life because he does not realize that special care is necessary to extend it. Thus he may not understand the necessity for certain treatments and refuse them. Unaware cardiac patients, as another instance, may even destroy themselves by insisting upon undue activity.

A word or two should be said about the next of kin. It is commonly recognized that it is in some ways easier for the family to face a patient who does not know of his terminality, especially if he is the kind of person who is likely to die "gracelessly." And if an unaware person is suddenly stricken and dies, sometimes his family is grateful that "he died without knowing." On the other hand, when the kin must participate in the non-disclosure drama, especially if it lasts very long, the experience can be very painful. What is more, family members suffer sometimes because they cannot express their grief openly to the dying person; this is especially true of husbands and wives who are accustomed to sharing their private lives. Other consequences for the family of a patient who dies without awareness are poignantly suggested in the following anecdote: The dying man's wife had been informed by the doctor, and had shared this information with friends, whose daughter told the patient's young son. The son developed a strong distrust for the doctor, and felt in a way disinherited by his father since they had not discussed the responsibilities that would fall to him in the future (nor could they). The father, of course, could do nothing to ameliorate this situation because he did not know that he was going to die; and so, this closed awareness situation was, perhaps unnecessarily, made more painful and difficult for the family members.

We have already indicated in detail what difficulties the closed awareness context creates for the hospital staff, especially for the nurses. Nurses may sometimes actually be relieved when the patient talks openly about his demise and they no longer have to guard against disclosure. By contrast, the closed context instituted by the physician permits him to avoid the potentially distressing scene that may follow an announcement to his patient, but subjects nurses to strain, for they must spend the most time with the unaware patient, guarding constantly against disclosure. The attending physician visits the patient briefly and intermittently, sometimes rarely.

On the other hand, under certain conditions, nurses prefer the closed context. Some do not care to talk about death with a patient, especially a patient who does not accept it with fortitude. An unaware person is sometimes easier to handle anyway, for precisely the reason that he has not "given up," or is not taking death "badly" or "hard." (At one county hospital where we observed both nurses and interns, it was remarkable how little strain they experienced in their frequent contact with extremely ill, but unaware, terminal patients.) Nonetheless, as we shall show later in more detail, the closed awareness situation prevents staff members from enjoying certain advantages that accompany a patient's resigned—or joyous—meeting with death.

As for the hospital itself, the important consequences of closed awareness derive mainly from the consequences for the staff. Unaware patients who die quickly tend to do so without fuss, so the hospital's routine work is delayed less. On the other hand, as one can readily imagine, a patient who moves explosively and resentfully from an unaware to a highly suspicious or fully aware state is relatively disruptive. But these are only transitory consequences; the long-run consequences are most important.

The most crucial institutional consequence has already been mentioned: because American physicians choose not to tell most patients about terminality, the burden of dealing with unaware patients falls squarely and persistently upon the nursing personnel. Quite literally, if subtly, this considerable burden is built into the organization of the hospital services that deal with terminal patients. Another social structural condition intrinsic to the functioning of American hospitals also increases the nurse's burden. We refer to the nursing staff's commitment to work relatively closely with and around patients. Again, this structural condition can be better appreciated if one thinks of the contrast in Asian hospitals, where the family clusters thickly and persistently around the dying patient. A corollary of this familial clustering is that the nursing personnel can remain at a relatively great emotional distance from, and spend relatively little time with, the patient. The enormously high patient-to-personnel ratio increases the probability of great distance and little contact. Although American nurses are sometimes criticized for a propensity to anchor themselves at the nurses' station, they do spend more time with fewer patients, including those who are dying unaware.

Finally, we must ask about the consequences of closed awareness for continued interaction with the patient. Perhaps little need be said about this aspect of the closed awareness context. It should be abundantly clear that closed awareness can change smoothly and easily, or explosively and brutally, into another type of awareness context, depending on how the closed awareness was managed, and on the conditions under which the terminal patient discovered what the staff members were doing to or for him. At the most painful extreme, he can feel betrayed; the happiest outcome is that he feels grateful for their protection and genuine sensibility.

4
Suspicion Awareness: The Contest for Control

How does a patient who suspects that he is dying try to verify his suspicions while others, who recognize that he suspects, simultaneously attempt to negate his suspicions? The hallmark of this awareness context is that the patient does not know, but only suspects with varying degrees of certainty, that the hospital personnel believe him to be dying. The consequential interaction—to run a bit ahead of the story—can be described metaphorically as a fencing match, wherein the patient is on the offensive and staff members are carefully and cannily on the defensive. Under conditions of closed awareness there was little contest for interactional control; now a contest between patient and staff is characteristic.

This particular awareness context should be distinguished from two others involving suspicion, neither of which we shall analyze but which require mention. These are both "closed suspicion" contexts. One type is closed because, though the patient is suspicious, the staff does *not* recognize his suspicion. A patient may choose not to reveal his suspicion, and manage that game for some while, but only rarely can he maintain this silent and difficult pose for any considerable time without either being discovered or confirming his suspicions about his true status. Perhaps a more important type of awareness context, for our purposes, occurs when staff members wonder but are not sure whether he really does suspect the worst. Or, they may wonder whether he "really knows" but is choosing not to reveal his knowledge. In either event they are careful

47

not to show their own suspicions, unless they specifically wish to make him suspicious or fully aware. These awareness contexts—where the patient covertly suspects his true status, or where staff only suspects that he may suspect or even know—will be touched on occasionally to highlight important features of "open" suspicion awareness context, in which staff is *certain* that the patient is suspicious.

CONTRIBUTING STRUCTURAL CONDITIONS

We indicated some of the structural conditions for this type of awareness in Chapter 3; here we shall discuss them in more detail. If any structural condition that ordinarily sustains a closed awareness context happens to be absent, the patient may begin to wonder about his real condition. For instance, as noted earlier, most patients are not very knowledgeable about the signs of terminality when they first enter the hospital, but a patient who is somewhat knowledgeable (a nurse, for example) may be much more alert to the implications of certain physical symptoms. Similarly patients who have been chronically ill not only may recognize genuine and alarming bodily changes when they occur, but also may be extremely shrewd about the significance of new procedures to which they are introduced. Especially in the county hospitals, where the impoverished aged are sent to die, terminal patients frequently if not indeed characteristically recognize their condition when not too far gone to note it. And physicians often admit to cardiac patients before last-chance operations how slim are the chances for their survival; so that during "intensive care" after the operation, their suspicions of terminality are high—and often accurate—despite reassuring statements by staff members.

Closed awareness is usually sustained by the physician's doing nothing that will arouse the patient's suspicion of terminality. But he may quickly decide not to withhold telltale information altogether but to hint at the truth, so that his patient begins to "catch on." And because the very names of certain diseases—notably cancer—are so alarming to laymen, a physician who names such a disease, even though he disclaims its fatality, may sharply arouse the patient's suspicions. In Japan, one of the authors once interviewed a patient at the Tokyo Cancer Hospital. This patient explained that he did not know what was wrong until he was brought to the hospital; then, seeing its name carved above the entrance, he realized with horror that probably he had a fatal disease.

The structural conditions that ordinarily maintain closed awareness may change during the patient's hospitalization, and so change the context to one of suspicion. One change lies in a failure of organizational efficiency—such as inadequate communication among daily shifts—so that the patient begins to understand that something is more radically wrong than he, in his innocence, had thought. In addition, the interaction itself may bring him to the brink of suspicion: family or staff members may unwittingly flash cues, or adequate answers may not be forthcoming when his symptoms begin to grow frightening. And of course, after spending some days in the hospital, the patient may become more knowledgeable about what is going on around him, either because he is now more alert physically, less dazed; or because he is now better acquainted with staff and hospital. For instance, he may realize that he is on an "intensive care unit" for very sick patients. Besides, the very structure of the institution tends eventually to arouse the patient's suspicion (especially if he recognizes his bodily deterioration) so far as he comes to understand, if he did not already, that the hospital is organized not to give him information but rather to withhold most of it—or to dole it out in carefully measured amounts.[1]

The difficulty—we do not say the impossibility—of keeping the patient in the dark about his terminality is recognized in American hospitals, in a myth to which hospital personnel

[1] Hans O. Mauksch, "Becoming a Nurse: A Selective View," *The Annals of the American Academy of Political and Social Science* (*Medicine and Society*), March 1963, pp. 88-98.

commonly subscribe: they believe that most terminal patients "really know" that they are dying, whether or not they openly display that knowledge. They reason that patients *must* know because, given a combination of alarming symptoms, the hospitalization itself, and the many telltale cues afforded by various institutional arrangements, it is impossible to keep the knowledge from them. Add to this that the physician may tell the patient indirectly, by his tone of voice or his lack of optimism. So staff members reason that even if a patient does not talk about his impending death or "test" bystanders to validate his suspicions, nevertheless he recognizes that he is dying. This myth is supported by a quasi-psychiatric common sense notion that the patient knows "way down deep" even if he doesn't know consciously.

Just because personnel apply this line of reasoning to certain patients does not mean that they apply it to all—and by no means all patients do suspect their terminality. But when the hospitalization period is long enough and the patient sufficiently sentient, continued interaction with others is likely to lead to suspicion of terminality if not, indeed, to full awareness. When he shows this suspicion, either by conversation or less explicitly and deliberately by gesture, then an open suspicion context exists.

THE CONTEST FOR CRUCIAL INFORMATION

Once a patient's suspicions of terminality have been aroused, for whatever reason, his problem is to confirm them.[2] We shall ignore for the present the situation in which the terminal patient is so determined to avoid confirming his suspicions that

[2] Sometimes patients suspect or believe themselves terminal when they are not. Then the staff tries to dispel the error by direct statements and disconfirming evidence. In one instance we observed, the patient remained suspicious, and continued "testing" the staff members long after they flatly told her she was merely ill. This kind of case highlights the difficulty a patient can have because of his relative ignorance of medicine, and when he believes he cannot trust his physician or nurses. The difficulty, of course, is heightened when his illness necessitates medical procedures which he finds frightening or threatening.

he refuses to read correctly even very clear signs. But when a patient defined as terminal begins to suspect that definition, ordinarily he attempts to obtain some confirming evidence. His major problem comes down to this: he must either *detect* or *elicit* signs that will confirm his suspicions. He needs crucial information, but how can he get it?

The patient's actual resources are exceedingly slim. Contrast his situation with two "suspicion" situations that commonly occur outside hospitals. Consider a wife who suspects that her husband has a mistress. She too must either detect or elicit confirming signs. Among her resources are the following: To begin with, she usually knows her husband far better than the patient knows his nurses, aides, and physician. She has more right, and certainly more occasion, to engage him in lengthy conversations during which she may detect or elicit confirming cues. Also she is physically mobile, so she can "shadow" his movements. She may pay someone else to follow him and question other people about him, or she may ask those questions herself. She may also enlist the efforts of informal teammates—she has friends who may observe his movements or seek cues through conversation with him. And though she may desperately want the truth immediately, her need is actually much less urgent than that of many terminal patients.

Another situation, where the stakes for suspected and crucial information are high, is that of organized espionage. In the real world of international relations, one spy system plays against many others, but for simplicity's sake let us say that one system is matched against a single other. Among the well-known tactics for getting ordinarily inaccessible information are the following: Either you must get men inside the other system, or people inside must betray information to you. Some insiders may voluntarily and freely offer their services because of animus against their government, as did Czechs within Austrian officialdom during World War I. You may have to buy insiders' services; then you must contact them or they must contact you. Important officials may reveal confidences to your spies, not recognizing their true identity. Also the use of "shadows" is usual: put your men inside the country if not actually within its government. You also set traps for the enemy, whereby he reveals information, whether unwittingly or with belated recognition. Some trapping strategies are based on yielding enough minor information to catch the enemy off guard; other methods of lowering his guard involve implementing a policy that conveys your lack of suspicion of his own line.[3]

It is interesting that Erving Goffman, writing about the problems of informational control faced by teams in work establishments, such as restaurants and stores, has noted that the audience (clients) for the team's performance "must not acquire destructive information about the situation that is being defined for them . . . a team must be able to keep its secrets and have its secrets kept."[4] Goffman suggests some types of person who are privy to the team's secrets, listing precisely the types that are potentially dangerous to any spy system. Among them are "the informers," the "spotters," the "go-betweens" and "the confidantes."

Now, compare the dying patient's situation with the spy system. He has no team and no allies, but he faces an organized team. Except under unusual circumstances, he must rely on his own senses and actions—and often his movements are quite restricted—to detect crucial signs or to discover outright confirmation. He cannot plant allies within the hospital staff, and only rarely can he purchase information from staff members. Of course, occasionally someone will consciously betray the secret out of sympathy for him, but not because he wants to betray the staff. (The teen-ager who was told about his

[3] For illustrations of such methods, cf. Richard Collier, Ten Thousand Eyes (New York: Dutton and Co., 1958); Allen Dulles, The Craft of Intelligence (New York: Harper and Row, 1963); Sanche de Gramont, The Secret War (New York: G. P. Putnam's Sons, 1962); and Oreste Pinto, Spy Catcher (New York: Harper and Bros., 1956).
[4] The Presentation of Self (Edinburgh, Scotland: University of Edinburgh Press, 1956), in Chapter 4, "Discrepant Roles," pp. 87, ff.

terminality by his friend is a nice example of an informal team member not kept in line by his own commitment to silence.) The patient, then, has to use his own eyes and ears. He does not even have the great resources available to any spy system for properly interpreting such bits of information as he is able to obtain. Furthermore, he must outwit the staff's countertactics, if he is to compete efficiently in this contest. Otherwise he will have to depend principally on sheer accident to bring him crucial information.

THE PATIENT'S INQUIRY AND TACTICS

The patient's objective is to get true indicators of his suspected status; that is, he wants validating cues that tell him "for sure." He may attempt to obtain the crucial information firsthand, by sneaking a look at his medical charts or by trying to overhear staff conversations. He may also directly query his physician or the nurses, "Am I going to die?"—not necessarily expecting an honest answer but hoping that his earnest desire to know will elicit at least a revealing one. Nurses find themselves confronted from time to time with these queries, which may be asked suddenly to catch them off guard.

But if a patient receives a negative answer, or if he chooses not to ask directly, then he may make various kinds of indirect queries. A simple approach is to announce that he is dying in order to see how staff members react. A patient may hint that he is dying without making a straightforward announcement, again seeking to elicit significant cues. He may engage a nurse or physician in conversation about his symptoms, pressing very hard, then listening intently for the meanings around the edges of their answers and comments. In certain illnesses, as in cancer, a great many medical tests may be given; these test situations afford opportunity for conversational gambits. Shrewdest of all are the conversational snares a patient can set for unwary personnel, to get them unwittingly to reveal what they know or contradict implicitly what someone else has told him. Those slips and contradictions can turn out to be important bits of information.

All these tactics are predicated on the assumption that the patient is purposely trying to elicit validating cues about his true status. Frequently, however, the suspicious patient acts spontaneously, without conscious design, and accidentally happens to bring out the cues. Unwittingly, he can ask embarrassing questions, or cry or complain or get angry, or spontaneously announce he thinks he's dying, and the way personnel respond to these may help to confirm suspicion.

Much of the patient's success, however, stems from pouncing on cues not elicited at all but flashed accidentally. The hospital milieu continually manufactures potential cues that arouse and sustain, and perhaps eventually confirm, the patient's suspicion. Once he imagines that others are in collusion to keep something from him, their every word or gesture can become significant. For instance, on services where people work in close quarters, as on intensive care units, a patient often sees staff members huddled in conversation, and he may overhear something that touches off, maintains, or confirms, his suspicion. Similarly, a patient who has had surgery may anxiously scan the staff's gestures and actions for revealing messages about his possible terminality. The very intensity with which a nurse cares for him, or the fact that emergency procedures are later performed on him, may further stimulate his suspicion. The amount of time the physician spends or does not spend with him; the nurse's silence, or her chattering: even these opposite cues may be read identically and pessimistically. Spatial cues, as when a patient is moved to another room, can be read with increased suspicion. So can temporal cues, as for instance, when a patient remains long hospitalized after having expected an early discharge.

But the important point about these cues is that the patient must *interpret* them, just as he must interpret those he gains by design. Here lies his big problem. Unless a remark or an action is so clear that it tells the true story immediately, the patient must construct his own version of its meaning. Ordinarily a suspicious patient does not have sufficient medical knowledge to read the many signs that may be available. He must put two and two together. In more technical language, he must build his cues into a systematic assessment, putting together a variety of indicators, which together represent an accurate and complete answer to his basic query. A patient cannot escape this problem of assessment unless the physician ends his wondering with an explicit announcement, or unless the equivalent confirmation is obtained from medical charts (but these rarely signify impending death with certainty) or from an overheard staff conversation. To make the matter even more complicated, the patient's inquiry has two parts: Am I dying, and if so, when? Consequently, even when he becomes certain he is dying, the patient still has to discover how much longer the medical authorities expect him to live. We shall, however, reserve the temporal aspects of the inquiry for Chapter 6.

THE STAFF: TACTICS AND COUNTERTACTICS

When a patient conceals his suspicions, so that the staff continues to believe him unaware, staff members are at a greater disadvantage in controlling potentially confirming cues than when they have some inkling of his suspicions.

The first problem for the staff, then, is to determine whether the patient *does* suspect. Ordinarily, this problem turns out to be simple, for a patient tends to reveal anxieties and conjectures through his actions. Still, occasionally staff members wonder, without knowing for certain, whether he might not suspect or even know the truth. After such a patient dies, especially if the staff was unusually devoted to him, debate about whether he suspected or knew can be endless and unresolved, sometimes continuing long after death.

Once staff members decide that a patient actually or probably suspects his terminality, then they must act accordingly.

The fact that personnel designate the patient's obvious confirmation-seeking tactics as a kind of "testing," bespeaks their own need for shrewd and careful stratagems. In general, the tactics are similar or identical to those in the closed awareness context, but the staff members now recognize the situation as more delicate. They are skating on thinner ice because the patient suspects his terminality.

If the suspicious patient asks why he is being moved to a room nearer the nursing station, or is subjected to a given procedure, the nurses give him reasonable answers. If the patient asks whether he is going to die, they inquire if he asked his physician, or remark bluntly, "I don't know, I'm not a doctor"—thus signaling that the patient should not ask them, at least. Accompanying such conventional managements is a controlled face and manner. Two nurses once spelled out how this is done; they happened to be speaking about managing the patient's suspicious relatives, but they might just as well have been talking about a patient:

> FIRST NURSE: A stern face, you don't have to communicate very much verbally, you put things short and formal. . . . Yes, very much the nurse.
> SECOND NURSE: Be tender but don't. . . .
> FIRST NURSE: Sort of distant, sort of sweet.
> SECOND NURSE: Talk about everything but the condition of the patient.
> FIRST NURSE: And if you do communicate with them, when you are not too much the nurse, you could talk about all kinds of other things; you know, carefully circling the question of death.

Confronted by the patient's more oblique references to his dubious future, a nurse may choose to ignore the conversational gambit, or deny that anything but a roseate future awaits him. As a general personal rule, she may evade the patient's conversational "testing" entirely, by paying strict attention to her chores and working attentively on the patient's body. She may divert the patient by chattering away, or when the going gets rough escape the room altogether.[5] But most of all, the nurses rely on acting as though the patient were ill but not dying, seeking to convey their impatience with his suspicions. Typically they conduct themselves in a cheerful, bland, or brisk manner. It is not surprising that some patients grow angry—or, from the nurses' viewpoint, ornery—accusing the staff of stringing them along, or giving them the "runaround."

In all of this, teamwork is essential. For example, the nurses customarily share some of the their observations about the suspicious patient, so that all can present more or less the same line to him. Nurses generally need to develop both common and personal tactics more than the physicians do, because they spend more time with the patient and are more likely to be asked extensive indirect queries. (Some patients, perhaps especially those of lower socioeconomic status, do not like to approach their physicians too directly, out of consideration for their high status.)

In their contests with suspicious patients, nurses are sustained by a number of resources. As noted earlier, the paucity of the patient's resources favors the staff members in keeping the secret. So does the hospital organization, both in its spatial arrangement and in more abstract ways, as when nurses invoke the hospital rules to counter a suspicious patient. Nurses also take advantage of the hospital organization when they avoid spending time with the patient by doing some other work, by spending time with other patients, or by charting back at the nursing station. Nurses also can call upon professional rules, as when they counter a direct query with "Have you asked your doctor?" or pretend that they are not "in" on his medical story. More subtly, they can also rely to some extent on rules of conventional tact: when a nurse indicates that she does not wish to converse because she is busy, the patient may be constrained simultaneously by the institutional requisite of "nurse's work"

---

[5] *Cf.* Jeanne Quint, "Institutionalized Practices of Information Control," *Psychiatry* (May 1965).

and the implicit imperative of "she's in no mood for talk." In short, personnel have various rights due their status which the patient may feel bound to honor.

Yet those rights are not always granted automatically. They must sometimes be enforced, at least for certain suspicious patients and at critical moments. Young nurses and new aides must not only learn the common tactics but also develop personal techniques for getting their rights honored. The common tactics are picked up relatively quickly from more experienced personnel, but the development of personal techniques can present problems. Young nursing students reveal this clearly as they work around suspicious patients. As students, nurses are taught how to care for patients, physically and sometimes "psychologically," but rarely if ever are they taught how to handle conversation about death with patients.[6] Young nurses have difficulty with a number of conversational gambits, questions, and topics. Suspicious patients can complain, ask embarrassing questions, indicate feelings of hopelessness, and be curious about diagnosis or prognosis. Like anyone, a young nurse may be more or less competent in such situations. Students commonly find the "testing" done by suspicious terminal patients very difficult at first; they have no professionally or personally satisfactory way to handle it. Rather quickly, however, they seem to develop the tactics described above, learning to control interaction largely by asserting their professional rights.

A CHARACTERIZATION OF THE INTERACTION

The concept of "rights" does not completely cover what transpires in this context of open suspicion. Perhaps one should say that each staff member may have to lay claim to his status during interaction with the patient. We use the term "claim" rather than "expectations," because expectations are more characteristic of highly structured interaction, especially

---

[6] *Cf.* Jeanne Quint, *The Nurse Student and the Dying Patient* (New York: Macmillan, forthcoming, 1966).

ceremonies and rituals. If you expect others to act appropriately toward yourself, but you and they share no firm understanding about this, then your expectation is more suitably viewed as a claim.[7] In the sometimes strenuous interactional contest between patient and staff, no clear rules express honored rights; the nurse (or aide or physician) must *claim* a given professional status (which includes working as she sees fit) and she must invite, persuade, or even force the patient to accept that claim. When an aide tells a patient who tries to probe about possible terminality, "Honey, just banish those morbid thoughts," she is saying, in effect, "Do not force me to talk about that subject;" she is telling the patient to behave himself in her presence by remaining silent about a subject she does not wish to discuss with him.

It is worth exploring the assertion that staff members must invite, persuade, and even force a patient to accept their claims, and that they must also deny *his* claim to be told about his terminality. They deny his claim by refusing his invitations to talk, to drop hints or even to disclose, and by rejecting his efforts to force them into unwanted interactional stances, as when he demands a straight answer or attempts to trap them into a revealing cue. In turn, the patient must either accept or attempt to deny the claims they make upon him. The stakes in this game involve not merely information or status in the hospital setting, but personal and professional identity.[8] For precisely this reason, staff members as well as patients tend to be under considerable strain.

The contrast with closed awareness interaction is immediately apparent, for then there is little contest in maintaining

[7] Anselm Strauss, *Mirrors and Masks* (New York: Free Press of Glencoe, 1958), p. 87.

[8] Nelson Foote has phrased this matter of stakes succinctly: "Fully to analyze and understand the participation of any person in an episode of interaction, account must be taken of what was authentically at stake for him in that situation. . . ." See his "Concept and Method in the Study of Human Development," in M. Sherif and M. Wilson (eds.), *Emerging Problems in Social Psychology* (Oklahoma City: University of Oklahoma Duplicating Service, 1957), p. 36.

the awareness context. It is precisely the contest aspect of the open suspicion context that calls for the strategems outlined above. This contest is in contrast with what happens when the suspicious patient determinedly attempts to deny rather than confirm his suspicions. Then he searches for, or elicits, denial cues rather than validating cues. If the staff members recognize that he is searching for denial cues, then ordinarily they play a supporting game rather than participate in the interactional contest described above.

CHANGES INTO OTHER AWARENESS CONTEXTS

The open suspicion context is a very unstable one. As we remarked earlier, patients may evince various degrees of suspicion. In general, the more suspicion, the fancier the footwork staff members must use to avoid final confirmation—at best they may only succeed in keeping him suspicious or perhaps lessening his suspicions. This suggests not only that the degree of suspicion can change over time but that change may fluctuate according to the nature of the cues the patient picks up from time to time and his interpretation of them. Unless, however, a patient can be kept oscillating between more and less suspicion, the open suspicion awareness context tends to be converted into other types. This tendency occurs even though patients have relatively limited resources available for confirming their conjectures; since the possibility that staff may unwittingly drop cues more than compensates for this deficiency.

A patient of course is sometimes lulled into believing that his suspicions were completely unfounded, and that he is going to get better or at least not worse. This interactional outcome (a closed awareness context) is not unknown to hospital personnel, especially when a patient earnestly wishes not to learn the truth about his condition or when they carry their collusive tactics to the point of sending him home, even though they really expect him soon to return to the hospital. A more common situation, however, is that staff members believe the patient has been fooled when in reality he merely refrains from voicing his partly or fully confirmed suspicions. (The first is a covert suspicion context, and the second a variant of the closed context.)

But the two awareness contexts into which open suspicion is most frequently transformed are open awareness (where everyone openly displays knowledge of terminality) and "mutual pretense awareness" (where both staff and patient know that the other knows, but nothing is said openly). We shall discuss these contexts in later chapters; here we wish only to note briefly that the patient can become aware through staff members' *purposeful* confirmation of his suspicions. There are occasions when someone knowingly engineers, or attempts to engineer, the patient's full awareness of his impending death. The rules pertaining to indirect disclosure are ambiguous enough to permit staff members not to disclose directly, but to drop sufficient cues for pretty fair confirmation when they feel the patient really should become aware. As we noted earlier, the staff members will sometimes wonder whether a patient suspects his terminality and will feed him subtle confirmatory cues, hoping he will signal back. Thus a chaplain told us he had intentionally read to a dying patient a psalm that referred to death. The patient, who was in a very weakened condition, seemed to press back slightly in return, but the chaplain did not know whether this response represented a genuine message.

Certain patients are probably more likely to get their conjectures confirmed in these indirect but intentional ways. Although we have no direct evidence on this point, certain patients undoubtedly can exert more powerful claims for disclosure on the staff—the very old, the well liked, the "VIP's," and certainly those who seem very eager to know about their terminality and seem of sufficiently strong character to "take" that knowledge. In any case, the circumstances under which patients' suspicions are confirmed intentionally supplement the more frequent circumstances of unwitting indirect disclosure.

CONSEQUENCES OF SUSPICION AWARENESS

The important consequences of the suspicion awareness context are easy to imagine. Concerning patients: they may become irrevocably comatose, or die, without confirming their suspicions. All the consequences of closed awareness noted in Chapter 3 then obtain, unless they are negated by prudent actions taken "just in case"—like drawing up wills. On the other hand, patients can be made frantic by the evasiveness of physician and nurses, when they suspect they are being given the "runaround." Oscillation between more and less suspicion can alternately lower the patient's spirits or raise them and affect his actions accordingly. The quality of nursing care given such patients—certainly the quantity, at least—is affected sometimes "adversely" and perhaps sometimes for the "better."

Concerning family members: as anyone who has participated in this collusive game of silence around the suspicious patient is aware, it may engender a fantastic psychological strain, especially if played for very long. Family members are also subject to the various advantages and disadvantages in dealing with a not fully aware relative, such as those associated with his open acceptance or fear of death.

The nurses, of course, bear the brunt of the hospital situation. Of course, they have more experience in this game than family members and usually are far less involved in the patient's fate; nevertheless they may experience considerable strain. Nurses tell us that they are often greatly relieved when the patient learns the truth, for then one need no longer be so gingerly in conversation nor keep one's guard so high. The nurses' reference to "testing" itself reveals how significant that activity of the suspicious patient is for their own work. Maintaining suspicion may protect the nurses from distressing scenes and embarrassingly graceless dyings; but when the patient is so well protected, when he recognizes very late—perhaps in the very last moments of life—that he is dying, then his behavior is all the more difficult for the nurses to cope with. At any rate, the nurses' supporting game does help the attending physician, since it relieves him of a good part of the interactional management of a suspicious patient.

A few consequences for the hospital itself should be noted.[9] A patient's open suspicion produces not only the division of labor between physicians and nurses we have already remarked upon, but also a collective mood of tenseness that quite literally gets built into the temporary structure of a hospital service. When the patient reacts against the "line they are handing me," that reaction also becomes part of the temporary structure. More permanent is the kind of informal training of new nurses and aides that a "rough" suspicious patient provides. And again, the general organization of work is affected by the need to handle the patient's open suspicions (often more than one patient at a time), to hold them at arm's length, as expressed in the tactic of being around these sometimes troublesome patients as little as possible.[10]

Finally, open suspicion awareness affects continued interaction. The way that staff members handle the patient's suspicions, whether they confirm or deny them, affects whether the patient will choose later to play a mutual pretense game or speak openly of his coming death. If he chooses the latter, there arises the question of his image of death and his reactions to it—these are the effects to which we shall devote the next two chapters.

[9] Here and elsewhere, we leave to the reader any judgments as to whether a particular consequence or set of consequences is "good" or "bad" for the hospital.

[10] Compare this situation, however, with one of *mutual* suspicion that sometimes existed in Chinese prison camps during the Korean War, when each American prisoner began to suspect each other of "informing" to the enemy. See Albert Biderman, *March to Calumny* (New York: The Macmillan Co., 1963), pp. 52-53.

5

The Ritual Drama
of Mutual Pretense

When patient and staff both know that the patient is dying but pretend otherwise—when both agree to act as if he were going to live—then a context of mutual pretense exists. Either party can initiate his share of the context; it ends when one side cannot, or will not, sustain the pretense any longer.

The mutual-pretense awareness context is perhaps less visible, even to its participants, than the closed, open, and suspicion contexts, because the interaction involved tends to be more subtle. On some hospital services, however, it is the predominant context. One nurse who worked on an intensive care unit remarked about an unusual patient who had announced he was going to die: "I haven't had to cope with this very often. I may know they are going to die, and the patient knows it, but (usually) he's just not going to let you know that he knows."

Once we visited a small Catholic hospital where medical and nursing care for the many dying patients was efficiently organized. The staff members were supported in their difficult work by a powerful philosophy— that they were doing everything possible for the patient's comfort—but generally did not talk with patients about death. This setting brought about frequent mutual pretense. This awareness context is also predominant in such settings as county hospitals, where elderly patients of low socioeconomic status are sent to die; patient and staff are well aware of imminent death but each tends to go silently about his own business.[1] Yet, as we shall see, sometimes the mutual pretense context is neither silent nor unnegotiated.

The same kind of ritual pretense is enacted in many situations apart from illness. A charming example occurs when a child announces that he is now a storekeeper, and that his mother should buy something at his store. To carry out his fiction, delicately cooperative action is required. The mother must play seriously, and when the episode has run its natural course, the child will often close it himself with a rounding-off gesture, or it may be concluded by an intruding outside event or by the mother. Quick analysis of this little game of pretense suggests that either player can begin; that the other must then play properly; that realistic (nonfictional) action will destroy the illusion and end the game; that the specific action of the game must develop during interaction; and that eventually the make-believe ends or is ended. Little familial games or dramas of this kind tend to be continual, though each episode may be brief.

For contrast, here is another example that pertains to both children and adults. At the circus, when a clown appears, all but the youngest children know that the clown is not real. But both he and his audience must participate, if only symbolically, in the pretense that he is a clown. The onlookers need do no more than appreciate the clown's act, but if they remove themselves too far, by examining the clown's technique too closely,

[1] Robert Kastenbaum has reported that at Cushing Hospital, "a Public Medical Institution for the care and custody of the elderly" in Framingham, Massachusetts, "patient and staff members frequently have an implicit mutual understanding with regard to death . . . institutional dynamics tend to operate against making death 'visible' and a subject of open communication. . . . Elderly patients often behave as though they appreciated the unspoken feelings of the staff members and were attempting to make their demise as acceptable and unthreatening as possible." This observation is noted in Robert Kastenbaum, "The Interpersonal Context of Death in a Geriatric Institution," abstract of paper presented at the Seventeenth Annual Scientific Meeting, Gerontological Society (Minneapolis: October 29-31, 1964).

let us say, then the illusion will be shattered. The clown must also do his best to sustain the the illusion by clever acting, by not playing too far "out of character." Ordinarily nobody addresses him as if he were other than the character he is pretending to be. That is, everybody takes him seriously, at face value. And unless particular members return to see the circus again, the clown's performance occurs only once, beginning and ending according to a prearranged schedule.

Our two simple examples of pretense suggest some important features of the particular awareness context to which we shall devote this chapter. The make-believe in which patient and hospital staff engage resembles the child's game much more than the clown's act. It has no institutionalized beginning and ending comparable to the entry and departure of the clown; either the patient or the staff must signal the beginning of their joint pretense. Both parties must act properly if the pretense is to be maintained, because, as in the child's game, the illusion created is fragile, and easily shattered by incongruous "realistic" acts. But if either party slips slightly, the other may pretend to ignore the slip.[2] Each episode between the patient and a staff member tends to be brief, but the mutual pretense is done with terrible seriousness, for the stakes are very high.[3]

---

[2] I. Bensman and I. Garver, "Crime and Punishment in the Factory," in A. Gouldner and H. Gouldner (eds.), *Modern Society* (New York: Harcourt, Brace and World, 1963), pp. 593-96.

[3] A German communist, Alexander Weissberg, accused of spying during the great period of Soviet spy trials, has written a fascinating account of how he and many other accused persons collaborated with the Soviet government in an elaborate pretense, carried on for the benefit of the outside world. The stakes were high for the accused (their lives) as well as for the Soviet. Weissberg's narrative also illustrated how uninitiated interactants must be coached into their roles and how they must be cued into the existence of the pretense context where they do not recognize it. See Alexander Weissberg, *The Accused* (New York: Simon and Schuster, 1951).

INITIATING THE PRETENSE

This particular awareness context cannot exist, of course, unless both the patient and staff are aware that he is dying. Therefore all the structural conditions which contribute to the existence of open awareness (and which are absent in closed and suspicion awareness) contribute also to the existence of mutual pretense. In addition, at least one interactant must indicate a desire to pretend that the patient is not dying and the other must agree to the pretense, acting accordingly.

A prime structural condition in the existence and maintenance of mutual pretense is that unless the patient initiates conversation about his impending death, no staff member is required to talk about it with him. As typical Americans, they are unlikely to initiate such a conversation; and as professionals they have no rules commanding them to talk about death with the patient, unless he desires it. In turn, he may wish to initiate such conversation, but surely neither hospital rules nor common convention urges it upon him. Consequently, unless either the aware patient or the staff members breaks the silence by words or gestures, a mutual pretense rather than an open awareness context will exist; as, for example, when the physician does not care to talk about death, and the patient does not press the issue though he clearly does recognize his terminality.

The patient, of course, is more likely than the staff members to refer openly to his death, thereby inviting them, explicitly or implicitly, to respond in kind. If they seem unwilling, he may decide they do not wish to confront openly the fact of his death, and then he may, out of tact or genuine empathy for their embarrassment or distress, keep his silence. He may misinterpret their responses, of course, but for reasons suggested in previous chapters, he probably has correctly read their reluctance to refer openly to his impending death.

Staff members, in turn, may give him opportunities to speak of his death, if they deem it wise, without their directly or obviously referring to the topic. But if he does not care to act or talk as if he were dying, then they will support his pretense. In doing so, they have, in effect, accepted a complementary assignment of status—they will act with pretense toward his pretense. (If they have misinterpreted his reluctance to act openly, then they have assigned, rather than accepted, a complementary status.)

Two related professional rationales permit them to engage in the pretense. One is that if the patient wishes to pretend, it may well be best for his health, and if and when the pretense finally fails him, all concerned can act more realistically. A secondary rationale is that perhaps they can give him better medical and nursing care if they do not have to face him so openly. In addition, as noted earlier, they can rely on common tact to justify their part in the pretense. Ordinarily, Americans believe that any individual may live—and die—as he chooses, so long as he does not interfere with others' activities, or, in this case, so long as proper care can be given him.

To illustrate the way these silent bargains are initiated and maintained, we quote from an interview with a special nurse. She had been assigned to a patient before he became terminal, and she was more apt than most personnel to encourage his talking openly, because as a graduate student in a nursing class that emphasized psychological care, she had more time to spend with her patient than a regular floor nurse. Here is the exchange between interviewer and nurse:

> INTERVIEWER: Did he talk about his cancer or his dying?
>
> NURSE: Well, no, he never talked about it. I never heard him use the word cancer. . . .
>
> INTERVIEWER: Did he indicate that he knew he was dying?
>
> NURSE: Well, I got that impression, yes. . . . It wasn't really openly, but I think the day that his roommate said he should get up and start walking, I felt that he was a little bit antagonistic. He said what his

condition was, that he felt very, very ill that moment.

INTERVIEWER: He never talked about leaving the hospital?

NURSE: Never.

INTERVIEWER: Did he talk about his future at all?

NURSE: Not a thing. I never heard a word. . . .

INTERVIEWER: You said yesterday that he was more or less isolated, because the nurses felt that he was hostile. But they have dealt with patients like this many many times. You said they stayed away from him?

NURSE: Well, I think at the very end. You see, this is what I meant by isolation . . . we don't communicate with them. I didn't, except when I did things for him. I think you expect somebody to respond to, and if they're very ill we don't . . . I talked it over with my instructor, mentioning things that I could probably have done; for instance, this isolation, I should have communicated with him . . .

INTERVIEWER: You think that since you knew he was going to die, and you half suspected that he knew it too, or more than half; do you think that this understanding grew between you in any way?

NURSE: I believe so . . . I think it's kind of hard to say but when I came in the room, even when he was very ill, he'd rather look at me and try to give me a smile, and gave me the impression that he accepted . . . I think this is one reason why I feel I should have communicated with him . . . and this is why I feel he was rather isolated. . . .

From the nurse's account, it is difficult to tell whether the patient wished to talk openly about his death, but was rebuffed; or whether he initiated the pretense and the nurse accepted his decision. But it is remarkable how a patient can flash cues to the staff about his own dread knowledge, inviting the staff to talk about his destiny, while the nurses and physicians decide that it is better not to talk too openly with him about his condition lest he "go to pieces." The patient, as remarked earlier, picks up these signals of unwillingness, and the mutual pretense context has been initiated. A specific and obvious instance is this: an elderly patient, who had lived a full and satisfying life, wished to round it off by talking about his impending death. The nurses retreated before this prospect, as did his wife, reproving him, saying he should not think or talk about such morbid matters. A hospital chaplain finally intervened, first by listening to the patient himself, then by inducing the nurses and the wife to do likewise, or at least to acknowledge more openly that the man was dying. He was not successful with all the nurses.

The staff members are more likely to sanction a patient's pretense, than his family's. The implicit rule is that though the patient need not be forced to speak of his dying, or to act as if he were dying, his kin should face facts. After all, they will have to live with the facts after his death. Besides, staff members usually find it less difficult to talk about dying with the family. Family members are not inevitably drawn into open discussion, but the likelihood is high, particularly since they themselves are likely to initiate discussion or at least to make gestures of awareness.

Sometimes, however, pretense protects the family member temporarily against too much grief, and the staff members against too immediate a scene. This may occur when a relative has just learned about the impending death and the nurse controls the ensuing scene by initiating temporary pretense. The reverse situation also occurs: a newly arrived nurse discovers the patient's terminality, and the relative smooths over the nurse's distress by temporary pretense.

THE PRETENSE INTERACTION

An intern whom we observed during our field work suspected that the patient he was examining had cancer, but he could not discover where it was located. The patient previously had been told that she probably had cancer, and she was now at this teaching hospital for that reason. The intern's examina-

tion went on for some time. Yet neither he nor she spoke
about what he was searching for, nor in any way suggested
that she might be dying. We mention this episode to contrast
it with the more extended interactions with which this chapter
is concerned. These have an episodic quality—personnel enter
and leave the patient's room, or he occasionally emerges and
encounters them—but their extended duration means that
special effort is required to prevent their breaking down, and
that the interactants must work hard to construct and maintain
their mutual pretense. By contrast, in a formally staged play,
although the actors have to construct and maintain a performance, making it credible to their audience, they are not required
to write the script themselves. The situation that involves a
terminal patient is much more like a masquerade party, where
one masked actor plays carefully *to* another as long as they
are together, and the total drama actually emerges from their
joint creative effort.

A masquerade, however, has more extensive resources to
sustain it than those the hospital situation provides. Masquer-
aders wear masks, hiding their facial expressions; even if they
"break up" with silent laughter (as a staff member may "break
down" with sympathy), this fact is concealed. Also, according
to the rules ordinarily governing masquerades, each actor
chooses his own status, his "character," and this makes his
role in the constructed drama somewhat easier to play. He may
even have played similar parts before. But terminal patients
usually have had no previous experience with their pretended
status, and not all personnel have had much experience. In a
masquerade, when the drama fails it can be broken off, each
actor moving along to another partner; but in the hospital
the pretenders (especially the patient) have few comparable
opportunities.

Both situations share one feature—the extensive use of
props for sustaining the crucial illusion. In the masquerade,
the props include not only masks but clothes and other cos-
tuming, as well as the setting where the masquerade takes

place. In the hospital interaction, props also abound. Patients dress for the part of not-dying patient, including careful attention to grooming, and to hair and makeup by female patients. The terminal patient may also fix up his room so that it looks and feels "just like home," an activity that supports his enactment of normalcy. Nurses may respond to these props with explicit appreciation—"how lovely your hair looks this morning"—or even help to establish them, as by doing the patient's hair. We remember one elaborate pretense ritual involving a husband and wife who had won the nurses' sympathy. The husband simply would not recognize that his already comatose wife was approaching death, so each morning the nurses carefully prepared her for his visit, dressing her for the occasion and making certain that she looked as beautiful as possible.

The staff, of course, has its own props to support its ritual prediction that the patient is going to get well: thermometers, baths, fresh sheets, and meals on time! Each party utilizes these props as he sees fit, thereby helping to create the pretense anew. But when a patient wishes to demonstrate that he is finished with life, he may drive the nurses wild by refusing to cooperate in the daily routines of hospital life—that is, he refuses to allow the nurses to use their props. Conversely, when the personnel wish to indicate how things are with him, they may begin to omit some of those routines.

During the pretense episodes, both sides play according to the rules implicit in the interaction. Although neither the staff nor patient may recognize these rules as such, certain tactics are fashioned around them, and the action is partly constrained by them. One rule is that dangerous topics should generally be avoided. The most obviously dangerous topic is the patient's death; another is events that will happen afterwards. Of course, both parties to the pretense are supposed to follow the avoidance rule.

There is, however, a qualifying rule: Talk about dangerous topics is permissible as long as neither party breaks down. Thus, a patient refers to the distant future, as if it were his to talk about. He talks about his plans for his family, as if he would be there to share their consummation. He and the nurses discuss today's events—such as his treatments—as if they had implications for a real future, when he will have recovered from his illness. And some of his brave or foolhardy activities may signify a brave show of pretense, as when he bathes himself or insists on tottering to the toilet by himself. The staff in turn permits his activity. (Two days before he returned to the hospital to die, one patient insisted that his wife allow him to travel downtown to keep a speaking engagement, and to the last he kept up a lively conversation with a close friend about a book they were planning to write together.)

A third rule, complementing the first two, is that each actor should focus determinedly on appropriately safe topics. It is customary to talk about the daily routines—eating (the food was especially good or bad), and sleeping (whether one slept well or poorly last night). Complaints and their management help pass the time. So do minor personal confidences, and chatter about events on the ward. Talk about physical symptoms is safe enough if confined to the symptoms themselves, with no implied references to death. A terminal patient and a staff member may safely talk, and at length, about his disease so long as they skirt its fatal significance. And there are many genuinely safe topics having to do with movies and movie stars, politics, fashions—with everything, in short, that signifies that life is going on "as usual."

A fourth interactional rule is that when something happens, or is said, that tends to expose the fiction that both parties are attempting to sustain, then each must pretend that nothing has gone awry. Just as each has carefully avoided calling attention to the true situation, each now must avert his gaze from the unfortunate intrusion. Thus, a nurse may take special pains to announce herself before entering a patient's room so as not to surprise him at his crying. If she finds him crying, she may ignore it or convert it into an innocuous event with a skillful comment or gesture—much like the tactful gentleman who, having stumbled upon a woman in his bathtub, is said to have casually closed the bathroom door, murmuring "Pardon me, *sir.*" The mutuality of the pretense is illustrated by the way a patient who cannot control a sudden expression of great pain will verbally discount its significance, while the nurse in turn goes along with his pretense. Or she may brush aside or totally ignore a major error in his portrayal, as when he refers spontaneously to his death. If he is tempted to admit impulsively his terminality, she may, again, ignore his impulsive remarks or obviously misinterpret them. Thus, pretense is piled upon pretense to conceal or minimize interactional slips.

Clearly then, each party to the ritual pretense shares responsibility for maintaining it. The major responsibility may be transferred back and forth, but each party must support the other's temporary dominance in his own action. This is true even when conversation is absolutely minimal, as in some hospitals where patients take no particular pains to signal awareness of their terminality, and the staff makes no special gestures to convey its own awareness. The pretense interaction in this case is greatly simplified, but it is still discernible. Whenever a staff member is so indelicate, or so straightforward, as to act openly as if a terminal patient were dying, or if the patient does so himself, then the pretense vanishes. If neither wishes to destroy the fiction, however, then each must strive to keep the situation "normal." [4]

THE TRANSITION TO OPEN AWARENESS

A mutual pretense context that is not sustained can only change to an open awareness context. (Either party, however, may again initiate the pretense context and sometimes get

---

[4] A close reading of John Gunther's poignant account of his young son's last months shows that the boy maintained a sustained and delicately balanced mutual pretense with his parents, physicians and nurses. John Gunther, *Death Be Not Proud* (New York: Harper and Bros., 1949). Also see Bensman and Gerver, *op. cit.*

cooperation from the other.) The change can be sudden, when either patient or staff distinctly conveys that he has permanently abandoned the pretense. Or the change to the open context can be gradual: nurses, and relatives, too, are familiar with patients who admit to terminality more openly on some days than they do on other days, when pretense is dominant, until finally pretense vanishes altogether. Sometimes the physician skillfully paces his interaction with a patient, leading the patient finally to refer openly to his terminality and to leave behind the earlier phase of pretense.

Pretense generally collapses when certain conditions make its maintenance increasingly difficult. These conditions have been foreshadowed in our previous discussion. Thus, when the patient cannot keep from expressing his increasing pain, or his suffering grows to the point that he is kept under heavy sedation, then the enactment of pretense becomes more difficult, especially for him.

Again, neither patient nor staff may be able to avoid bringing impending death into the open if radical physical deterioration sets in, the staff because it has a tough job to do, and the patient for other reasons, including fright and panic. Sometimes a patient breaks his pretense for psychological reasons, as when he discovers that he cannot face death alone, or when a chaplain convinces him that it is better to bring things out into the open than to remain silent. (Sometimes, however, a patient may find such a sympathetic listener in the chaplain that he can continue his pretense with other personnel.) Sometimes he breaks the pretense when it no longer makes sense in light of obvious physical deterioration.

Here is a poignant episode during which a patient dying with great pain and obvious bodily deterioration finally abandoned her pretense with a nurse:

There was a long silence. Then the patient asked, "After I get home from the nursing home will you visit me?" I asked if she wanted me to. "Yes, Mary, you know we

could go on long drives together. . . ." She had a far-
away look in her eyes as if day-dreaming about all the
places she would visit and all the things we could do
together. This continued for some time. Then I asked,
"Do you think you will be able to drive your car again?"
She looked at me, "Mary, I know I am daydreaming;
I know I am going to die." Then she cried, and said,
"This is terrible, I never thought I would be this way."

In short, when a patient finds it increasingly difficult to
hang onto a semblance of his former healthy self and begins
to become a person who is visibly dying, both he. and the staff
are increasingly prone to say so openly, whether by word or
gesture. Sometimes, however, a race occurs between a patient's
persistent pretense and his becoming comatose or his actual
death—a few more days of sentience or life, and either he or
the staff would have dropped the pretense.

Yet, a contest may also ensue when only one side wishes
to keep up the pretense. When a patient openly displays his
awareness but shows it unacceptably, as by apathetically "giving
up," the staff or family may try to reinstate the pretense.
Usually the patient then insists on open recognition of his own
impending death, but sometimes he is persuaded to return to
the pretense. For instance, one patient finally wished to talk
openly about death, but her husband argued against its
probability, although he knew better; so after several attempts
to talk openly, the patient obligingly gave up the contest. The
reverse situation may also occur: the nurses begin to give the
patient every opportunity to die with a maximum of comfort—
as by cutting down on normal routines—thus signaling that he
should no longer pretend, but the patient insists on putting up
a brave show and so the nurses capitulate.

We would complicate our analysis unduly if we did more
than suggest that, under such conditions, the pretense ritual
sometimes resembles Ptolemy's cumbersomely patched astro-
nomical system, with interactants pretending to pretend to
pretend! We shall only add that when nurses attempt to change

the pretense context into an open context, they generally do this "on their own" and not because of any calculated ward standards or specific orders from an attending physician. And the tactics they use to get the patient to refer openly to his terminality are less tried and true than the more customary tactics for forcing him to pretend.

CONSEQUENCES OF MUTUAL PRETENSE

For the patient, the pretense context can yield a measure of dignity and considerable privacy, though it may deny him the closer relationships with staff members and family members that sometimes occur when he allows them to participate in his open acceptance of death. And if they initiate and he accepts the pretense, he may have nobody with whom to talk although he might profit greatly from talk. (One terminal patient told a close friend, who told us, that when her family and husband insisted on pretending that she would recover, she suffered from the isolation, feeling as if she were trapped in cotton batting.) For the family—especially more distant kin— the pretense context can minimize embarrassment and other interactional strains; but for closer kin, franker concourse may have many advantages (as we shall discuss further in Chapter 6.) Oscillation between contexts of open awareness and mutual pretense can also cause interactional strains. We once observed a man persuading his mother to abandon her apathy—she had permanently closed her eyes, to the staff's great distress—and "try hard to live." She agreed finally to resume the pretense, but later relapsed into apathy. The series of episodes caused some anguish to both family and patient, as well as to the nurses. When the patient initiates the mutual pretense, staff members are likely to feel relieved. Yet the consequent stress of either maintaining the pretense or changing it to open awareness sometimes may be considerable. Again, both the relief and the stress affect nurses more than medical personnel, principally because the latter spend less time with patients.

But whether staff or patient initiates the ritual of pretense, maintaining it creates a characteristic ward mood of cautious serenity. A nurse once told us of a cancer hospital where each patient understood that everyone there had cancer, including himself, but the rules of tact, buttressed by staff silence, were so strong that few patients talked openly about anyone's condition. The consequent atmosphere was probably less serene than when only a few patients are engaged in mutual pretense, but even one such patient can affect the organizational mood, especially if the personnel become "involved" with him.

A persistent context of mutual pretense profoundly affects the more permanent aspects of hospital organization as well. (This often occurs at county and city hospitals.) Imagine what a hospital service would be like if all terminal patients were unacquainted with their terminality, or if all were perfectly open about their awareness—whether they accepted or rebelled against their fate.[5] When closed awareness generally prevails the personnel must guard against disclosure, but they need not organize themselves as a team to handle continued pretense and its sometimes stressful breakdown. Also, a chief organizational consequence of the mutual pretense context is that it eliminates any possibility that staff members might "work with" patients psychologically, on a self-conscious professional basis. This consequence was strikingly evident at the small Catholic hospital referred to a few pages ago. It is also entirely possible that a ward mood of tension can be set when (as a former patient once told us) a number of elderly dying patients continually communicate to each other their willingness to die, but the staff members persistently insist on the pretense that the patients are going to recover. On the other hand, the prevailing ward mood accompanying mutual pretense tends to be more serene—or at least less obviously tense—than when open suspicion awareness is dominant.

[5] For a description of a research hospital where open awareness prevails, with far-reaching effects on hospital social structure, see Renée Fox, *Experiment Perilous* (New York: Free Press of Glencoe, 1959).

6

The Ambiguities
of Open Awareness

Whenever both staff and patient know that he is dying, and acknowledge it in their actions, the context is one of open awareness. (We have touched several times on the structural conditions that contribute to the existence or appearance of open awareness.) But openness does not eliminate complexity, and, in fact, certain ambiguities associated with two properties of the open awareness context are inevitable. The first—the time and manner of death—will occasionally be relevant to our discussion. The second property, however, will be central because it pertains directly to awareness of death itself.

First, even when he recognizes and acknowledges the fact of terminality, the patient's awareness is frequently qualified by his ignorance or suspicion about other aspects of his death. Thus, a patient who knows that he is dying may be convinced that death is still some months away. Staff members may then conceal their own knowledge of the time that death is expected to occur, even though they may refer openly to the fact that it is expected. Similarly, they may keep secret their expectation that the patient is going to deteriorate badly, so long as he is unaware of this contingency. Only rarely will staff members attempt to make the patient fully aware about time or mode of death if they judge the time to be sooner than the patient expects or the mode unpleasant.

Of course certain structural conditions may occasionally be present to make the patient more aware of these subsidiary aspects of his impending death. He may be a physician who is familiar with the course of his disease, for example. And patients who have the same disease are often kept together, so that each may observe a kind of rehearsal of his own fate by watching others who are closer to death. American patients, however, can seldom negotiate successfully enough with their physicians to obtain good information directly about the mode of dying when it is likely to be unpleasant; indeed, sometimes they find it difficult to secure an understanding that the physician will ever be candid about the probable time of death.

The awareness, therefore, of subsidiary features of terminality may be of different types than the openness about death itself. Those other types can change, or be maneuvered, in various directions: for instance, closed awareness about time of death can be transformed into suspicion about time of death; or suspicion about mode of death can be transformed into closed awareness about mode of death. Open awareness about terminality itself, however, stays quite stable. Although patients may think of the time of dying as farther away than indicated by the warnings they have received, or they may choose to ignore the prospect of living as "a vegetable" before finally dying, they display little tendency to forget or "repress" the knowledge that they are going to die.

The second ambiguous property of the open awareness context is another new uncertain element which exists even though both parties can refer relatively openly to the patient's terminality. The patient may wish to die in certain ways: without pain, for instance, with dignity, or perhaps in private. At the same time, the staff has its own ideas about the way patients ought to die, involving not merely the physical aspects of dying, but also its moral and stylistic aspects. Much of the consequent interaction depends on the initial congruence of their respective ideas, as well as on the congruence that may develop before the patient's death occurs. But the existence of open awareness about *terminality* makes this confrontation of persons possible, and so makes important the discrepancy between their ideas on how to die.

Divergent expectations about "appropriate" ways of dying

reflect in part the common tendency, in American hospitals, for staff and patients to come from different class and ethnic backgrounds. Although the patients may come from various strata, and the staff may also be heterogeneous in both class and ethnic membership, the majority of the staff is frequently unlike the majority of patients. In city and county hospitals, for instance, the patients are relatively impoverished, while nurses and physicians are "middle class." In hospitals supported by wealthier patients, the nurses are lower in socioeconomic origin and often ethnically different from most patients. Although the degree of difference between patient and staff backgrounds varies in various hospitals, probably it is often great enough to produce rather incongruent perspectives on dying. An additional source of discrepancy is that deeply inculcated professional and institutional norms separate staff from patients. To the extent that dying is a medical phenomenon, doctors and nurses necessarily have a view of death unlike the layman's.

An example from Malaya illustrates, though in rather an extreme form, the kind of divergence possible. Malayan hospitals are staffed almost exclusively with Chinese and Indian professionals. When a Chinese patient is near death, his kinfolk flood the space around his bed—and no staff member is surprised by their ritual preparations for his death or by their loud lamentations after death occurs. But the Malayans' special beliefs about death and the body make them highly suspicious of hospitals and the non-Malayans who run them. On the somewhat unusual occasions when Malayans permit a very sick kinsman to enter a hospital, they are quick to whisk him from the strangers' hands when he seems to be dying. Naturally, the medical staff greets this action with disapproval or paternal amusement. The staff's reaction is based predominantly on professional attitudes but also upon ethnic perspectives. In Japan, however, where the population is culturally homogeneous, the norms affecting mode of dying seem more uniform than in either Malaya or the United States, and there is probably less divergence between patient and staff perspectives.

STYLES OF DYING

Once a patient has indicated his awareness of dying, the most important interactional consequence is that he is now responsible for his acts as a *dying* person. He knows now that he is not merely sick but dying. He must face that fact. Sociologically, "facing" an impending death means that the patient will be judged, and will judge himself, according to certain standards of proper conduct. These standards, pertaining to the way a man handles himself during his final hours and to his behavior during the days he spends waiting to die, apply even to physically dazed patients. Similarly, certain standards apply then to the conduct of hospital personnel, who must behave properly as humans and as professionals. The bare bones of this governed reciprocal action show through the conversation between a nurse and a young dying girl. The nurse said, "Janet, I'll try as hard as I can"; and then when the youngster asked whether she was going to die, the nurse answered, "I don't know, you might, but just keep fighting."

At first glance, staff members' obligation to a dying patient (regardless of specific awareness context) seems simple enough. If possible, they must save him; if not, then they must give proper medical and nursing care until he dies. But so simple a conception of their obligation ignores the fact that the patient *deserves* their obligation because he has been defined as dying. Generally he need not actively seek definition of this status, but need only be defined medically as dying (though on rare occasions a patient may have to convince his physician that he really is dying). On the other hand, ethical and social as well as medical judgments enter into questions such as when to try to save a patient and when to give up, how much to prolong life when death is certain or the patient is already comatose, and so on. If such nonmedical judgments are relevant, then logically some patients must act so that they do *not* deserve as much care as do patients who behave properly.

Consequently, certain patients may receive "better" medical and nursing care, not because the staff's obligation is greater, but because they are defined implicitly as more deserving.

In an open awareness context, patients defined as less deserving risk the additional judgment that they are acting with purpose. Since they know that they are dying, their improper behavior cannot be interpreted as a consequence of ignorance. Patients known to be aware of death have two kinds of obligation: first, they should not act to bring about their own deaths. Second, there are certain positive obligations one has as a dying patient. Let us examine these two aspects of acceptable behavior in the face of death.

Occasionally patients who discover that they are about to die attempt suicide. The staff takes a relatively charitable attitude toward suicidal acts if the patient has suffered a great deal. Otherwise they view such an act as either incomprehensible or requiring additional explanation of a psychiatric kind. (In fact, if the attempted suicide survives he is likely to be sent—as at an emergency service where we observed—to a psychiatric service. The presumption is that such a person is mentally ill; patients who attempt suicide while hospitalized also get psychiatric attention.) The American attitude that suicidal persons do not deserve respect or extensive care is rather starkly expressed on emergency services in our hospitals. If the suicide arrives already dead, staff members may display little sympathy for him. If he is alive, they will try to save him, but with traces of contempt and disgust. When they fail to save him, the absence of sadness and dismay is conspicuous. Sometimes, when a suicide seems rather far gone, the staff may sharply curtail its efforts to save him.

In addition to suicides, other types of relatively undeserving terminal patients arrive at our emergency services: accident cases known to have caused the accident by carelessness or drunkenness, drunkards picked up dying from the streets, and the stabbed, slashed, or battered victims of brawls. Staff members tend to express distaste and even enmity for all these, whether they are dying or not. From the staff's perspective, these patients are in the hopsital only because they have acted improperly. Those who die have broken an implicit pact with society not to die "this way"—or perhaps a pact to live properly so as not to die this way. Where the majority of such patients are drawn from lower socioeconomic strata, or are Negroes, Puerto Ricans, or other minority group members, then the staff tends to disapprove of their style of life generally, which reinforces staff attitudes toward suicide, drunkenness and violence.

More subtle instances of this judging of "impropriety" include a patient's failure to validate his suspicion that he is ill. Thus, two interns indirectly berated an undeserving mastectomy (breast cancer) patient after her operation by standing outside her door and talking, in deliberately loud voices, about her foolishness in not visiting a physician earlier. Other patients who, after hospitalization, "give up" by not struggling to stay alive are guilty of the same kind of lapse. Surrender is justifiable if death is certain, or if suffering is intense and the battle for life almost hopeless. But sometimes the staff can find no justification for the patient's "giving up." One nurse said about a cancer patient, "Oh, that patient, I still think he didn't have to die." She saw no good physiological reasons for the patient to have died just then—he simply went ahead and did it. This particular patient was "difficult" anyway, even pretending to fall into comas, so that the nurse understandably found his behavior, including his dying, quite unjustifiable.

But such patients are considered far less reprehensible than the suicides or the fatally careless automobile drivers. It is also instructive to compare them with an 81-year-old woman found half dead on the street. She was resuscitated in the hospital but she wished to die, and when the physicians insisted on blood transfusions, she kept the nurses on the run by repeatedly attempting to remove the transfusion tube from her arm. The nurses were upset about her doing this, although they

were also disturbed by the physician's insistence on rather
"senselessly" prolonging her life.

Geriatric patients like this woman have almost earned the
right to die. Indeed, staff members almost literally say so. Truly
deserved deaths are designated by such statements as "It is
just as well he died," "It's a blessing he died," or "He had
nothing to live for." These comments are applied to very worn-
out geriatric patients, terribly deteriorated patients, and premature infants who might be brain-damaged, to inescapably
comatose patients, and those who are fully sentient but quite
painfully dying. These patients all have a right to die quickly,
and if sentient cannot be blamed for not struggling against
death. Even their occasional acts of suicide may elicit sympathy
rather than adverse moral judgments.

The second aspect of dying improperly is failure to fulfill
one's obligations as a dying patient. People are supposed to
live correctly while dying, providing they understand that they
are dying, but Americans have no clear rules for this behavior.
No script has been carefully laid out for the *dramatis personae*.
Structural reasons why the script is unclear include lack of
specific training in ways to die; Americans generally have had
few opportunities to observe death firsthand. (Unlike most
European and Asian countries, the United States in this century has had no war on home territory, which has drastically
reduced the likelihood of civilians seeing actual scenes of
death.) The recent trend toward dying in hospitals and other
institutions, away from home, has further reduced opportunities
to see people die. In addition, the heterogeneity of the American
population mitigates against consistent and clear-cut societal
directives: even the standards that pertain to the more ritual-
istic aspects of death—whether the body should be on display
at the funeral parlor or whether burial or cremation is preferable—are somewhat hazy. Such standards as exist for behavior
in the face of death are even more conflicting and vague. Hospital personnel, as we have noted, have had little or no explicit

training for their roles in the drama of death, and like other Americans they have differing opinions as to exactly how a patient should face death.

Nevertheless, in our hospitals staff members do judge the conduct of dying patients by certain implicit standards. These standards are related to the work that hospital personnel do, as well as to some rather general American notions about courageous and decent behavior. A partial list of implicit canons includes the following: The patient should maintain relative composure and cheerfulness. At the very least, he should face death with dignity. He should not cut himself off from the world, turning his back upon the living; instead he should continue to be a good family member, and be "nice" to other patients. If he can, he should participate in the ward social life. He should cooperate with the staff members who care for him, and if possible he should avoid distressing or embarrassing them. A patient who does most of these things will be respected. He evinces what we shall term "an acceptable style of dying," or, more accurately, "an acceptable style of living while dying."

An example of this style was described by the nurse who said: "Until he became unconscious he was always cheerful. He'd have a smile for you and never complained. While he was still able to he'd help out on the ward, doing work. This case was especially hard on all of us. . . . His mother was like him, never complaining." Staff members are also familiar with the typical "grandmother" of the service: the wonderful elderly lady who is so cheerfully reconciled to death, and who is so nice to talk with that even the interns and residents drop in to spend time with her. A psychiatrist might point out that the grandmothers teach the youngsters how to banish anxiety about their own deaths; to a sociologist, the significance of the grandmothers is that their style of dying approaches the ideal.

The contrasting pattern—what the staff defines as unacceptable behavior in aware dying patients—is readily illustrated. For instance, physicians usually honor requests for additional (or consultants') opinions, but object to "shopping around" for impossible cures: as one physician warned a wife about her dying husband, "faced with death. . . .He might want to find quacks to tell him they could cure him." [1] Other types of unacceptable behavior emerge vividly from our field notes. Thus, the next quotation involves a patient's serious failure to "cooperate" in his medical care, and it shows the extremes to which a physician will go to get such cooperation:

> The patient had been moving his arm around a lot so his intravenous needle was in danger of coming out; he is very testy at all such rigmarole. The doctor got irritated, apparently, at his lack of cooperation and said that if he took that needle out of his arm, he'd die. The nurse: "That's what the doctor said to his face—that this is what is keeping you here; you pull it out and you'll die."

There are less dramatic instances of unacceptable dying. Thus:

> Miss Jons mentioned that Mr. James was giving a great deal of trouble today. They had been trying everything on him, and nothing had worked. He was refusing all kinds of things, such as medication, pills, and food, and having trouble getting him to take his temperature. They had tried to be persuasive and now there was a nurse who was trying just the opposite. Miss Jons giggled and said it wasn't getting her anywhere either. . . . To this other nurse I said, "Tough customer, isn't he?" She looked stolid and said, "He just wants to be ornery." Then added, "He's been ornery all day."

Then there are patients who do not face dying with fortitude but become noisy or hysterical:

> Miss Smith came into the nursing station saying, "I'm sick of insight." According to her, this woman patient gets scared and there's nothing you can do, and then

[1] Lael T. Wertenbaker, *Death of a Man* (New York: Random House, 1957), p. 56.

she gets more scared. . . . At the staff meeting, Miss Smith said that this lady gags more and belches, and the nurse finally decided there was no physical reason for this. The nurse put on a big dramatic act as she said this because in a big stew about it. She had spoken to the patient and told her it was just doing her harm and would hurt her more. Later I heard this lady belching pretty loudly, and the nurses just looked at each other.

Other patients are defined as making excessive demands—and it does not especially help the nurses to know that patients can make those demands precisely because they know they are dying.

She finally came back [to the hospital] for the last time and knew that this was the end and kept saying, "I'm getting closer and closer; I'm dying, dying. Do something for me." She wanted somebody by her all the time as a security. . . . She'd praise us and things like that. Then if we'd say something to the opposite effect, or not answer right away, then she'd turn against us. She was just scared all the time. . . . She was a great mental strain on me. . . . My reaction to her was quite hostile at times because I didn't know how to handle her and I got angry with her. I felt she should accept a lot of these things and she didn't. . . . I guess some feel that in their life they have things that they set out to accomplish more or less, so that death is easier for them than others.

The nurse's last comment clearly enunciates the doctrine that people ought to face their deaths properly, though some do not. In addition, her remarks help to clarify why nurses may feel anger as well as guilt when a patient emphasizes their inability to give adequate care or comfort while he is dying.

Crying or sobbing is one thing but when patients wail, cry out in terror, complain, accuse you of doing nothing, or refuse to cooperate in their medical or nursing care, that is something else again. Perhaps most unnerving to some staff are patients who become apathetic; they sometimes seem "hostile" and even reproachful. A change of this kind is particularly disturbing in a patient who previously has been cheerful and likable. We remember a young cancer patient who returned to the hospital in just such an apathetic condition, thereby causing widespread consternation among the nurses. When one day he recovered his spirits slightly and started to fight with the nurses over minor matters, as he had previously, they were delighted. Apathy in such a patient is perceived by the staff not merely as "giving up" but also as an implicit message that he is finished with everything and everyone—including the staff. For instance, a previously mentioned courageous woman who finally gave up, signifying this by permanently closing her eyes, so distressed her family, as well as her private nurses, that a son finally flew in from across the country. He persuaded his mother to open her eyes again, because her withdrawal was "hurting everybody so."

In general, then, the staff appreciates patients who exit with courage and grace, not merely because they create fewer scenes and cause less emotional stress, but because they evoke genuine admiration and sympathy, as well as feelings of professional usefulness. It is difficult to admire a patient who behaves improperly even though one can sympathize with his terrible situation. When a patient *knows* he is dying, he must present some kind of dying self to the world. People cannot help judging him, even if by diverse and not altogether explicit standards. Occasionally a patient provides such a model of courage and fortitude that the staff remembers him with admiration long after his death. In the reactions of staff members is not only respect for a great human being but gratitude for being allowed to participate in the near-perfect drama of his dying.

THE MANAGEMENT OF ACCEPTABLE DYING

Patients who already know how to die—by reasoned judgment, or by intuition, or by sensing the staff's implicit standards

—make life easier for the staff. Staff members need not work at getting these patients to behave properly, since they take considerable responsibility for dying properly—if not with dignity, then with minimal loss of self-control. (For instance, one American nurse described an old-world patient who closed off his life with great ceremony: he called his family to his bedside, so that he could say farewell, then thanked the nurse for all her care, and finally closed his eyes to sleep and die.) The staff members need only align their own conduct with the patient's particular but acceptable style of facing death.

Patients who do not die properly, on the other hand, create a major interactional problem for the staff. The problem of inducing them to die properly gives rise, inevitably, to a series of staff tactics.[2] Some are based on the patient's understanding of the situation: staff members therefore command, reprimand, admonish and scold. Thus one nurse spoke firmly to patients, or relatives, when they began to make too much noise at the approach of death. Another scolded a patient, "If you can do all that, why you can drink fluids too. If you'd eat and drink, then the doctor wouldn't have to stick needles in your legs." And patients are told to stop incessant crying, "It doesn't help you and it doesn't make me feel any better." Threats are also used:

> I asked what they did about such patients generally, and she went into a lovely imitative act: she put on a firm voice and appearance and told the imaginary patient just what would happen to him if he didn't take whatever he was supposed to take, or do whatever he was supposed to do. If you don't do this, then these conse-

[2] Getting the patient to die properly is, of course, also a problem in the suspicion awareness and mutual pretense contexts. In the latter situation, however, the tactics characteristic of open awareness can also be used; or the staff can occasionally shatter the pretense, but then quickly return to it. When a patient is suspicious of his terminality, inducing him to die properly is managed less directly and fully than when the patient is aware. Consequently, we have chosen to discuss "acceptable dying" mainly in connection with the open awareness context.

quences will follow, physically and medically, is what she got across, saying also "and then we'll have to put a tube down your stomach."

But these negatively toned tactics—commands, reprimands, threats—are supplemented, and often overshadowed, by others through which personnel attempt to teach patients how to die properly. In effect, the nurses signal what they define as unacceptable behavior and point out what is acceptable. Sometimes, when she is angry enough or intimate enough with the patient, a nurse can talk at some length with him, and this talking, perhaps by accident rather than design, may help teach the patient how to die. But generally the teaching process consists of fragments of interaction—coaxing, brief coaching, and the like—rather than extended coaching sessions. Teaching usually consists of something like this: "Well, you just have to have patience for a while, we just can't do everything all at once that you want us to. You've got to try, Mrs. Smith," rather than this:

Another time I got the feeling the patient wanted her children to cry about it because she'd moan and groan in front of them. . . . I got rather angry with her because I had talked to her so many times before about dying . . . and she was beginning to accept a lot of it; and she was trying to prepare her daughters for it, and then she would turn around and want them to feel sorry for her. I missed my chance that one day. I was going, really, to tell her.

Nurses may call on higher authority or on allied forces to remind or help teach the patient what is required. Thus the physician may be asked to command the patient to complain less or cry less loudly. In one hospital we observed that the nurses gladly delegated to a skillful chaplain the task of "breaking through" to frightened, hostile or silently apathetic patients. Psychiatrists sometimes perform similar functions. Where open awareness is the prevailing context, the other patients as a group can also be relied on to exert implicit and sometimes explicit controls on unacceptable dying.[3]

Of course, staff members may ask the patient's relatives to help manage their dying kinsman, but in most cases their unsolicited cooperation is depended on for encouraging acceptable dying. For instance, one man actually did some of the nurses' work because he was not sympathetic to his wife's withdrawal. He made her get out of bed and walk; he jollied her, or ordered her to eat when she didn't want to eat. A nurse described another patient who spoke angrily to her; his wife would intercede: "Don't be like that, don't talk to the nurses like that." Another nurse remarked: "I encourage the relatives sitting there—holding their hand—it *may* help."

When the patient's kinsmen visit the hospital they too, of course, are expected to behave properly in the face of dying and death. Although we shall consider the family's reactions at some length in later chapters, we will note here that kinsmen who fail to conform to the staff's notions of propriety are likely to be coached, reprimanded or even subjected to disciplinary measures. A rather extreme instance of this was observed once on the cancer service of a teaching hospital. Family members spoke loudly and clearly to each other about a dying adolescent in his presence; they laughed often, and "carried on" generally. The nurses felt that this was causing the boy great distress, and, unable to control the situation, they finally appealed to the physician. He banned everyone but the parents from the room, explaining his action to the parents.

Visiting nurses sometimes comment unfavorably on the households they visit in terms of the members' behavior in the face of death: the family may behave worse than the patient, or vice versa. Thus one harassed nurse exclaimed: "I had another case that was just the opposite—the patient was very nice and the person taking care of her, her daughter, was awful." Another nurse who had genuine problems of manage-

[3] Renée Fox, *Experiment Perilous* (New York: Free Press of Glencoe, 1959), pp. 139-181.

ment remarked that: "The mother was irritable and swore at both the daughter and the RN's." Hospital personnel do not usually have to contend with "difficult" families as often or as directly as visiting nurses, but when they do, they may encounter the same problems of management.

Our discussion of the style of dying would be incomplete if we failed to note that the patients' own conceptions of the proper way to die may contradict staff expectations. When a patient has his own clear conception of propriety, staff members may have difficulty inducing him to accept or conform to their ideas. Occasionally, for example, a patient displays so much composure as to seem unnatural: "The hospital staff reacted to Wert's behavior, which changed in no particular from his normal behavior, with awe and awkwardness. I had hoped they would react with easy frankness toward him. Instead the opaqueness of the relationship between patient and medical attendants seemed to increase. . . . One . . . young nurse . . . said to me, 'But he's so *natural.*' " [4]

One patient we observed greatly unnerved the nurses because he insisted upon signing his own autopsy permit. Others, as already noted, simply want to die in private, alone with themselves and perhaps with their God. In fact, some patients would rather die at home, not because of the familiar surroundings, but because then they can minimize interference with their own management of death. In the hospital, the nurses tend to see gestures toward privacy as a rejection of themselves, and find them difficult to understand or tolerate. And when a hospital patient commits suicide, he represents at its widest the potential gulf between staff and patient conceptions of the proper approach to death, for suicide epitomizes the possibilities for rationally managing one's own death so as to remove it from staff control altogether. Thus, staff members may sometimes condone a suicide but rarely can fully approve of it.

[4] Wertenbaker, *op. cit.*, p. 66.

THE PATIENT NEGOTIATES

The interaction between patient and staff members is also greatly affected by the patient's negotiations with them. Every sentient patient, whether terminal or not, wants to get certain things or to have certain events occur; he coaxes, wheedles, bargains, persuades, hints, and uses other forms of negotiation. A patient who is aware that he is dying may attempt to negotiate explicitly about matters pertaining to his own dying.[5] For what he gains, he can, in return, offer specific cooperation with the staff, or a generally acceptable style of dying; or even, negatively, threaten a less acceptable style if they will not negotiate properly.

Much of the daily negotiation centers around the pacing and minimizing of such routines as bathing, eating, taking medication or undergoing treatments. Understandably, a nurse wants these routines scheduled, and if they are medically important, she wants them done properly. But a weary or depressed patient may wish to delay or completely avoid some routines. Thus, when a cancer patient suggests later cooperation, the nurses may not urge him to eat or bathe or have his temperature taken; or they may cater to his wishes to the extent of offering to do something for him ("How about a bath now?") rather than announcing that something will now happen.

A patient sometimes rejects a nurse's offer, perhaps by saying that he is not going to get out of bed anymore and thus implying clearly that his end is near. Or, foreseeing his end, a patient may bargain to avoid some routine. ("He kept telling me he doesn't need a bath, he's not going to be around very long anyway, and 'I don't care what you do to me,' and 'I'm going to die anyway.' ") He may negotiate for a delay in pro-

---

[5] Negotiation about dying may occur also in the suspicion awareness or mutual pretense contexts. We have chosen to discuss negotiation, however, in relation to open awareness contexts because their negotiations are especially explicit.

cedure. ("The nurse said he's at a stage where he's slowing certain procedures. She wanted to give him a bath and he said, 'Well, wait 'til after the doctor comes and examines me,' and then he pleaded for another half hour.") A patient who died shortly thereafter was described by a nurse: "I sympathized with him when he said, 'Don't feel like eating,' and said, 'It's not gonna make that much difference.'" In general, then, a considerable amount of daily negotiation occurs around the pacing, minimizing and the avoiding of routine.

Negotiation may also involve the time that nurses spend with the patient and the amount of talk that occurs. Again, the nurses tend to take their cues from the patient. If they feel he doesn't want to talk, they do not force him to do so: "There were times when I knew that he just didn't want to talk. We kind of sensed it, so we talked when he felt like talking, and we didn't when he didn't want to." This assessment of the patient's desire to talk may not always be correct but it is based on a reading of cues from the patient. A patient may, of course, declare openly whether he wishes to talk. A social worker noted that some patients are quite verbal about dying and openly discuss, for example, "What can I do about my wife?" On the other hand, some patients say quite plainly that they are finished talking forever and turn their faces to the wall. Staff members may respect that wish spontaneously or, feeling that the patient has rejected their good intentions, retreat in despair or hostility.

The death scene itself may be the subject of negotiation. Sometimes a patient wants a staff member to stay with him, perhaps because he simply desires not to be alone, or perhaps because he is afraid to die alone: "He talked to me the day he died. He wanted me to stay there by him all the time, because he said, 'I'm going.' He got the attention, even though we were busy." Patients may beg personnel to call relatives when death is imminent, just as relatives may wring that same promise from personnel. A patient may also negotiate with his physician for permission to die at home. He may try to elicit the physician's promise not to let him live needlessly long, not to permit him to die in excessive pain, and to let him know when death is quite near. And of course patients negotiate—principally with kinsmen—to have things done after death has taken place.

It is worth noting also that a person who is dying in an unacceptable manner faces difficulties when he attempts to gain his ends through negotiation. Staff members understandably have less patience for the negotiation and altogether less empathy with him. One woman, for instance, behaved so "badly" for so many weeks that the nurses gradually took to spending as little time with her as possible. Shortly before she died, the chaplain entered her room and found her in considerable pain. She said, "I'm looking for the nurses." The chaplain, when later describing the scene, remarked that "I'd been pushing the nurses on this just as hard as I could and was wondering how far I could go" on pushing them. He helped to rearrange the patient's body on the bed so as to reduce her pain. Then he and she prayed together. As he left the room, he asked, "Is there something else you would like the nurses to do for you?" She said, "Yes, see that one comes immediately." The chaplain thought to himself that he wasn't sure whether he could manage that particular feat. In the hallway he found a nurse and, putting his arm around her, he asked, "How about doing me a favor? Would you go in and take care of Mrs. Plum immediately?" She answered, "Yes, I'll do it for you as a favor."

NON-MEDICAL NEGLIGENCE AND PRIDE

From the staff's point of view, negotiation involves much more than simply deferring to patients' wishes. If the staff "plays ball" with a patient, of course, then he is more likely to die in a manner acceptable to them. Less obvious in the negotiation is that they may develop an emotional commitment to fulfilling their end of bargains made with patients. If they succeed, they can remember the patient, after his death, with pride, but if they fail or perceive themselves as having failed him, then they are likely to feel "negligent."

This kind of negligence is not the same thing as medical or procedural negligence. The professional canons that prescribe reasonably effective medical and nursing care also encourage professional pride when a job is well done, and feelings of negligence when the job is badly done (whether or not negotiation is involved). Patients who might have been saved by more skillful surgery, or whose lives might have been usefully extended by better nursing care, stimulate feelings of medical and nursing negligence. This phenomenon is quite different from what happens when personnel reckon that they have failed patients in human, not technical, ways.

There are, of course, many possibilities for failure in meeting human needs of patients who are unaware of their terminality. One nurse, for instance, remarked, "Something that bothers me is the lack of prayers for the [unaware] dying. The chaplain sees them when they are put on sick list, but not at the end. . . . I'm wondering if maybe we get hard and callous." Inherent in the open awareness context, however, are certain additional possibilities for failing or succeeding in these human responsibilities—including those related to negotiation. An aware patient can make certain demands involving humane considerations that he would not make if unaware. For example, a patient who, sensing one evening that he would die that very night, tried to persuade the evening nurse to call his wife. Believing that he was wrong, she refused. Pressed, she called a staff physician, who sustained her opinion. When the patient would not yield, she got additional backing from her supervisor; but finally, she called the wife. The patient died soon after his wife arrived. The nurse's assent saved her from feeling negligent because of failure to render human assistance, though had she continued to deny his request she would not have been negligent because of any professional error.

A nurse may make an explicit promise—that she will be there when the patient dies—and if she fulfills the promise, then she can feel that she has done her human duty. If she fails him, she is likely to feel somewat negligent. Promises may be extended to relatives also. One nurse sent a husband to the coffee room, promising that if his wife began to die, he would be notified in time, but she failed to notify him quickly enough, and afterwards felt very badly.

Negotiations need not take such an explicit form as exacting and giving a promise. Nurses, thus, sometimes feel negligent when they cannot converse adequately with patients who wish to talk about their impending deaths, whether the desire to talk is announced or only signaled. Here is an unusual but illuminating example:

> We had a man on a pacemaker. We had him in intensive care for five weeks. We were probing his chest, four times a day; he was arresting. . . . He developed an infection. As long as they keep draining it, he'll live. But it's deep and eventually going to get him. I ran out of things to say. I had to sit and watch him and pound his chest for five weeks. . . . I was very awkward because he was very intelligent and very much aware of what was going on. . . . Every day I had to come in and say "Good morning, how are you today?" We talked, we used to read, it was just terrible. I was never so much involved with a patient.

Even physicians sometimes betray similar feelings of negligence or unease by the very brusqueness with which they reject invitations to talk while making medical examinations of patients who are fully aware of their own terminality.

A chaplain, whom we observed, derived great satisfaction (because of having few feelings of negligence) from his ability to converse with dying patients about their oncoming deaths as well as about their post-death affairs. His satisfaction is highly instructive for two reasons. He could respond to patients' invitations to talk and, indeed, draw them into conversation better than could the nursing and medical personnel. And he was wonderfully able to wed his professional standards, with their emphasis on giving spiritual and psychological comfort rather than medical care, with his sense of the humane—of what was a proper human death. The same unity of professional and human standards occurs when physicians and nurses are able to meet patients' requests for human rather than purely medical assistance. The special hazard of an open awareness context is that the patient can make requests pertaining to his dying. Not only does this possibility add to the number of possibilities for human failure, but it also presents intrinsic difficulties, for, as we have indicated, personnel may prefer to avoid references to death.[6] They may sometimes feel negligent because they cannot manage this aspect of terminal care.

One of the complicating features of the open awareness context is that negotiations instituted by the patient may catch staff members in crossfires of professional and human responsibilities, with consequent inescapable feelings of negligence. The instance noted earlier of the patient who begged the nurse to call his wife also illustrates how a nurse may be required to choose between satisfying a patient's request and following ordinary institutional and professional practice. Even medical and human responsibilities, however, may sometimes be incompatible.

A patient may request his physician not to prolong his life in the event that he becomes comatose, but the physician, guided by the medical canon that life should be preserved as long as possible, may ignore that request, or even renege on his promise to the patient when the time comes to honor it. But the physician cannot make such decisions without some turmoil. Nurses whom we have observed have also often reflected considerable strain, not always knowing whether it was better

[6] We predict that the strong trend in nursing education toward inculcating standards of nursing care based on greater attention to "interpersonal" relations, and to the patient's "psychological needs," will make nurses increasingly vulnerable when they work with patients who are aware of terminality. We have observed this increased vulnerability in young nurses, but even more so in graduate student nurses who were learning the intricacies of giving psychological care to patients who happened to be aware of their own impending deaths.

that the patient be kept alive or allowed to die. When a physician can gain enough support from a professional rationale, he may escape internal conflict, and consequent feelings of negligence, over his medical decisions. For instance, once we observed medical and human standards in especially sharp conflict—between a mother, pleading that her child be allowed to die, on humane grounds, and a physician, who made his decision on medical grounds to keep the infant alive under oxygen just as long as was possible. The physician bluntly told the mother that a physician's job was to keep life going as long as possible, and that the decision to do so was his alone, not her's.

AWARENESS OF CONTINGENCIES

We noted earlier that an open awareness context might be "qualified," because though the patient may know about his terminality he may not know about or suspect other features of his impending death, such as its time or mode. Of course, the staff members may not be any better informed, since some contingencies—such as a lingering death or terrible bodily deterioration—may be quite unpredictable. On the whole, however, the staff members have a much better chance of knowing or suspecting these matters than the patient, and certainly earlier than he does. The patient's dawning suspicion or final awareness of such contingencies noticeably affects interaction in the open awareness context.

When the staff members judge that the contingencies will not seem unduly unpleasant, then they may reveal them to the patient, especially if he asks about them specifically or envisions less pleasant contingencies. For instance, if he queries anxiously and repeatedly whether his death will be painful, they may assure him that it will not, emphasizing that his kind of disease generally does not entail great suffering. If he presses his physician for approximate time of death and suggests an earlier date than the physician believes is probable, then the physician may assure him that he is grossly underestimating how long he may yet live. Naturally if the patient remains suspicious, the physician may have to redouble his efforts to convince him, that is, to make him truly aware of the real, or probable, contingency.

A patient who becomes aware of these contingencies may take them into account in managing his own dying. He need not panic long before his death, but, knowing he has some months to live, prepare to meet death with fortitude. He need not have fantasies about terrible bodily deterioration, but can prepare for death assured he will be in relative control of his faculties and limbs. He need not fear that he will pass from life screaming with pain (which might tempt him to seek an earlier and easier way out).

But when the staff judges that contingencies associated with a patient's death *will* seem unpleasant or upsetting, they ordinarily attempt to conceal what they know about them. They find it more difficult, however, to conceal their knowledge from a patient who is already cognizant of his terminality than from one who is not. For instance, the staff commonly paces the medication given to a dying patient so that his increasing pain can be kept under control, but a patient awaiting his own death is sometimes likely to become aware of his increasing medications and wonder about them in connection with his impending death. Similarly, a patient aware of his terminality is likely to read signs of bodily deterioration in terms of such possibilities as: Will I go completely and disgustingly to pieces physically before I die? Will I go to pieces sufficiently to disgrace myself as I lie dying? Will I become a vegetable before I die?

When a patient suspects such contingencies, or begins to recognize their passage into actual fact—his pain increases, or he is obviously close to death since his strength is ebbing rapidly—then this additional awareness may greatly affect his behavior. He may become terrified at the prospect of increasing pain. He may berate the physician who assured him that pain could be kept under control, but who has long since realized his inability to do so. Indeed he may fear actual desertion by the physician if and when the physician believes "nothing more can be done" for him. The patient may also utilize his new knowledge to manage his dying according to his own conceptions of proper dying. For instance, one patient drove her physician into suggesting a last-ditch operation that might relieve her increasingly intolerable pain. Yet she herself had to decide whether to endure the pain or to risk an operation that she visualized as possibly making her into a brainless vegetable. She chose to undergo the operation, preferring the latter alternative to dying with unendurable pain. Another elderly patient, previously mentioned, who knew she was being kept only temporarily alive "on machinery," kept the nurses hopping because she insisted on removing the blood transfusion tube leading into her arm. She had chosen to die sooner rather than later, if she could manage the earlier death.

Physicians and nurses are usually prepared to contend with the patient's eventual suspicion or recognition of contingencies, since they have long since seen them as probabilities or certainties. For many of the patient's responses they may have routine tactics. Thus, nurses may attempt to reassure him that his deterioration will not get much worse, or they may urge the physician to "snow" the patient with drugs when death is imminent and the patient is screaming with pain or fear. But just as the patient's expectations of his own behavior may go awry in the face of the actual contingencies, so may the staff members' behavior. There are no routine reactions when a patient, recognizing that he is dying, right now, from suffocation, pleads with the nurse to "save me!"

Often the patient, however, prefers to initiate mutual pretense about contingencies of which he is aware. Although speaking openly about his terminality, he does not make reference either to the time or mode of his death. And he may prefer to keep silent about his own reactions to that known time or mode of death. One patient we observed, for instance, was so frightened about his obviously imminent death (obvious both because of his deterioration and the nurses' reactions to it) that his chin could be observed quivering. A nurse was asked about the quivering: "Well, he's that way all over, inside." Do the nurses talk to him about it? "No, but we've given drugs for it, so we didn't talk about this." In short, the man's reactions to his immediately expected death were understood by the nurses, but by mutual consent neither they nor the patient referred to them.

CONSEQUENCES OF OPEN AWARENESS

A few points about the consequences of open awareness, though already noted in previous chapters, are worth emphasizing here. Awareness of impending death gives the patient an opportunity to close his life in accordance with his own ideas about proper dying. He may finish important work, make satisfying farewells, give gifts to his friends, and leave detailed plans for his family and estate. The advantages of openness are also implicit in a chaplain's account of how he and a patient together had reconciled the wife, the children, and the patient's parents to his inevitable death. With or without staff intervention, a wife and husband may achieve more amicable relations when both know that he is dying and can talk about themselves in light of that event. In addition, the aware patient who dies "acceptably" stands a good chance of getting staff members to cooperate with him in the management of his dying.

But open awareness has disadvantages for the patient too. Other people may not approve of the patient's way of managing his death, and may attempt to change his ideas or even subvert his management. Also, a patient may not be able to close off his life usefully, and with dignity, either because he cannot face death itself or because he suspects or knows its associated features. An aware patient, therefore, may be unable to face death with equanimity, dying with more anguish and less dignity than he might if he were unaware of his terminality.

He may question, with anguish, "Why must it be me who must die?" Some patients even question what their lives were all about as they lie dying. And some must decide whether to accept imminent death or perhaps to prolong their lives somewhat through surgery. Such decisions are often agonizing for the patient, and his agony while deciding will affect his family and the hospital personnel.

A patient who makes it easy for himself also makes his death easier for his family. So far as awareness is accompanied by acceptable dying, it reduces the strain that would otherwise be imposed on kinsmen by closed or suspicion awareness. If the patient is able to attain a kind of psychological closing for his life before he dies, his kinsmen may be able to share his satisfaction at the close, and they may treasure their experience for the remainder of their lives.[7] On the other hand, some people cannot sustain conversation with a patient who knows that he is going to die. And if the patient dies in agony or terror, or otherwise unacceptably, his family would doubtless have preferred to have kept him unaware of his terminality.

Many staff members, especially nurses, prefer the open awareness context. As one nurse said, "I like . . . it best. I'm more comfortable when I can talk about it with the patients." Nurses may derive genuine gratification from "working with" a patient who allows them to participate in his confrontation of death. Many a nurse remembers with satisfaction how she sat with a patient a few hours before his death, as he talked about his past life. She has not only provided him with an empathetic listener, but she has been brought into his ceremonial preparation for passing out of life. Whether or not they are present during the final hours, many nurses do derive pleasure from actively helping a patient "face death" properly. While they cannot always give much help to patients who are recoiling from thoughts of death, they can take comfort from their own small, and sometimes impulsively compassionate, actions: "The patient reached out to the night nurse.

---

[7] Cf. Wertenbaker, *op. cit.*, and Maurice Goudeket, *Close to Colette* (New York: Farrar, Straus and Cudahy, 1937).

She instinctively moved away. The patient said, 'I want some-body to love me.' The nurse realized what was happening, so she took the patient in her arms and let her cry. It was the crying of real despair."

Of course, patients who do not die acceptably make staff members' work more difficult than it would have been in a closed awareness situation, creating, in addition, an emotional strain, particularly for the nurses. The open awareness context, in fact, does increase the probability that nurses will be sub-jected to stressful sessions with patients who wish to talk about their deaths, and openly bemoan their dying. Most nurses we have observed cannot "take" these sessions. They develop tactics for minimizing their impact and the probability of their occurrence; for instance, a nurse who has a knack for talking with dying patients is drafted to work with those who wish to talk about their deaths.

What about the hospital itself, how is it likely to be affected by open awareness? The answer depends on several matters discussed in this chapter. For instance, when patient's and staff's ideas about proper dying are congruent, and where both can act in accordance with those ideas, then maximum condi-tions exist for what might be called "graceful" dying. The research hospital described by Renée Fox, where doomed patients cooperated manfully with physicians in their usually hopeless efforts to check progressive deterioration, was char-acterized by high morale and graceful dying. Even patients cooperated in each other's dying dramas.[8] In this case, there actually seemed to develop at least implicit norms for how to help one another die properly. Also negotiation by both pa-tients and physicians was perhaps exceptionally governed by fairly explicit agreements developed between them. On most hospital services, a lower proportion of patients will, in the staff's eyes, die with acceptable style; that is, there will be a greater discrepancy between patients' ideas and staff members' ideas about proper dying.

At most hospitals there also tends to be less openness about

[8] Renée Fox, *op. cit.*

the subsidiary features of dying—time and mode—than at the hospital described by Renée Fox. Consequently, the organization of patient care will be affected by the staff's attempts to keep those secrets. The staff's work must also be organized to face the consequences that appear when the patient who finally becomes aware of them then grows angry at being kept in the dark, or wishes then to engage in a ritual of mutual pretense about the circumstances of his dying.

7

Discounting
Awareness

In each of the foregoing chapters, we have described ways in which others consider a patient's actual or potential awareness of his impending death, in combination with their own awareness. But imagine, now, certain situations in which the patient's awareness might be discounted. The hopelessly comatose patient, of course, comes most quickly to mind, but awareness is also discounted in less obvious cases. Our discussion in this chapter is intended to highlight, by contrast, the behavior that occurs because people *usually* must take awareness into account.

CATEGORICAL DISCOUNTING

With certain categories of patients, staff members may act without taking awareness into account. We shall consider four such categories, beginning with premature babies.

Most "premies" who die are recognized as doomed at time of birth, or even before. Because an infant cannot know that it is dying, the nurses on premie services need not take awareness into account. They can talk, in the infant's presence, about the time it is likely to die, or how its parents feel about its death, or say that they themselves feel "it's just as well" the infant will die. They can act as if they neither wanted nor expected it to live, because of its physical immaturity. With other premies, who at first are expected to live but then "take a turn for the worse," nurses work desperately to prevent death, sometimes becoming very devoted to the dying baby. Again the nurse's behavior can be quite open, rather than

107

masked, as with a sentient adult; what is said and done in any infant's presence need not be affected by consideration of his awareness. Similar discounting of awareness can occur in the presence of very young children.

With the parents, of course, awareness must be taken into account. When the parents openly expect their baby to die, the nurses can play openly into that expectation, but when the parents express the hope that the baby will survive, then parental awareness creates the same problems for nurses as that of sentient adult patients. Thus, uneasy parents may telephone the head nurse, who has to handle their suspicion that the baby's condition has become worse than was initially reported to them. The death of a baby who has been frankly expected to die is usually announced to its mother, who then tells the father; but when death is unexpected, the psysician often tells the father.

A second class of patients with whom awareness can be discounted is the hopelessly comatose. Personnel are warned against talking freely in the presence of any patient who is only temporarily unconscious or has recently become comatose, since the unconscious one may "come to" sufficiently to understand conversation, and the comatose may remain sentient enough to understand its drift. Only when comatoseness is unquestionably permanent can staff members completely discount awareness. Then they tend to act in the patient's presence as if he were a "non-person," [1] talking freely even about things that would matter to him if he were sentient, just as if he were not there. This does not mean that the patient's body does not receive excellent medical and nursing care; but even though the patient is regarded as if he were still somewhat of a person, perhaps once liked or respected, considerations of awareness no longer affect the interaction around him. After all, he can no longer know, or discover, that he is dying. Socially he is already dead, though his body remains biologically alive.

[1] For a discussion of the "non-person," see Erving Goffman, *Presentation of Self* (Edinburgh, Scotland: University of Edinburgh, 1956), pp. 95-96.

Because a socially dead person cannot be aware, some rather peculiar behavior may occur in his presence. For example, a comatose terminal patient, who happened to be a young nurse herself, began to lose her hair because of her particular malady. The nurses, distressed by the way she would look at her funeral, began to prepare the living corpse for its later public appearance. They worked assiduously on her hair but finally, after giving up that task as hopeless, swathed her head in a turban. Another instance of unusual discounting behavior, one we have mentioned before in another context, occurred because of admiration for the patient's husband. Refusing to accept his wife's comatoseness, he treated her at each visit as if she were socially alive. The empathetic nurses took to preparing the patient's body for his visits. They fixed her hair and face so that she would look as pretty as possible. They dressed her properly. And when they were in her room with the husband, they acted as if she were not what they knew her really to be. (Their methods of sustaining this odd pretense with the husband, as well as their reasons for doing it, were very different than if they had been trying to persuade a sentient patient to dress nicely, so that she would feel more like a woman. Then the patient's awareness is directly taken into account.)

A third category of terminal patients with whom awareness is discounted includes those who are senile rather than comatose. Where there are many such patients, as in state mental hospitals and in nursing homes for the aged, death is not noticed by the senile patients because of their senility. The dying patient himself can be treated by the staff as if he were ignorant of his own impending death, although he may be completely conscious, or alive, about such matters as bathing and eating. No additional discounting takes place when such a dying patient also becomes comatose, though the staff now has the additional burden of bathing and feeding him. Another point: although the hospital personnel may be very fond of certain senile patients, or of patients who later become senile, and may treat them as if they were much alive, this can be done without acting as if the patient could ever become aware of his terminality.

When senile patients are consigned to such homes and hospitals, family members, too, sometimes tend to treat the patients as if they were already dead—as socially dead as if they were hopelessly comatose—and do not bother to visit them. Other families treat the senile as being alive but perhaps not "all here." These families periodically visit their unfortunate kinsman (just as parents visit children who were never "all here"), but even they do not act as if the dying patient were aware of his forthcoming death.

A fourth group of dying patients whose awareness may be discounted is those whose awareness matters little to the staff because of the way they view the patients' characteristics. Staff members respect these patients so little that they give less thought to the control of cues that might disclose terminality. Most strikingly, this kind of discounting occurs on the emergency wards of city or county hospitals where, as we have already observed, middle class professionals confront lower class patients under conditions encouraging the staff to view patients as inexcusably negligent in the preservation of their own lives. Partly because so many lower class patients are brought in as accident cases, or as victims of razor slashings or other forms of violence, staff members tend frequently to disapprove of them. When such patients are brought dying to the emergency ward, staff members talk about them without much regard for what they may see, hear, or sense. Staff disregard for awareness is particularly evident in the way suicide cases are handled, for suicides, regardless of social class origin, are especially likely to arouse anger and tendencies toward overt disrespect. A genuine effort to save the suicide's life may be accompanied by talking to him, or in his presence, as if he deserved to die.

SITUATIONAL DISCOUNTING

Three types of situations also exist in which awareness is often discounted. The first involves the conscious use of space to prevent the changing of suspicion or closed awareness into open awareness, so that staff members can ignore the patient, as when they talk about his terminality beyond the range of his hearing. This use of space can be hazardous, since the patient accidentally may overhear the conversation or take special pains to overhear it. Yet a spatial barrier very often allows personnel to discount the patient's awareness.

A second type of situation occurs when patients who are fully aware of their own terminality behave acceptably and permit others partly to discount their awareness. Conversation can flow easily because they do not make death the sole topic of conversation. Not every word and gesture need touch on the mutual awareness of the impending death, though after a few minutes the matter of terminality may emerge again, entering directly or obliquely into the interaction. Even when a patient who does not accept his death easily converses with a staff member, terminality can be on the far edge of the patient's consciousness and not appreciably intrude into their conversation. And, of course, many tasks that staff members perform in the patient's presence are so remote from matters of terminality that any incidental conversation taking place at the same time can be commonplace or related to the tasks themselves.

Under these rather ordinary circumstances, the discounting of awareness is optional; staff members may either ignore awareness or take it into account. But in the third type of situation, awareness *must* be ignored because other more important matters are at stake. For instance, if a patient's heart suddenly stops beating, staff members must ordinarily take "heroic measures" to keep him alive. These measures usually convey to a patient, whether or not he was previously aware of danger, that he is about to die, or that he is very likely to die soon afterwards. The staff has no option but to bring him into awareness; the gravity of the situation forces them to ignore whether he is aware or unaware. Emergency measures of any kind often are highly visible to a sentient patient, so that staff members are forced to discount awareness. Personnel on emergency and intensive care services engage rather constantly in this type of discounting.

Similarly, when a physician decides that certain procedures, tests, or even diagnostic surgery is necessary to determine accurately the patient's condition, then he risks permitting the patient to become suspicious about, or know of, his terminality, but the stakes are so high that the risk is run. A man who later died of cancer in France makes this point vividly in his published diary:

> He prescribed a fluoroscopic examination and X-rays and I was examined by Dr. Cartier himself and by the radiologist. . . . The examination was incomplete; I could not retain the barium, fed from below. . . . This indicated to me that something was badly wrong . . . as did the muttered conversation of the two doctors, the conversation of technical men over a technical problem. . . . But when . . . I came out with the word cancer to Dr. Cartier, he put his hand on my arm and assured me that it was most unlikely; there were no signs right up to the very edge of the suspicious spot, which barium couldn't reach.

Later, Dr. Cartier said, "You'll have to have an operation," heartily assuring him that many tumors weren't cancerous but that:

> It was necessary to hurry, to take this while it was young; he advised me to wait no more than three or four days . . . I asked him point-blank: "If I do nothing about this, how long will I live?" A look of shock passed over his face . . . he took my arm. "But that

would be foolish," he said. I told him that I was only trying to consider all the possibilities. After another moment, he answered: "Perhaps a year, perhaps two years—if it is *mauvaise*." [2]

In short, this physician had to risk alerting the patient, first through the X-ray procedure and later by advising a diagnostic operation. This particular patient forced the issue by direct questioning, but not until after the phyician had aroused his suspicion. Regardless of whether the patient questions him directly, a doctor's medical responsibility often forces him to discount the patient's awareness.

FAILURE TO DISCOUNT

Curiously enough, people sometimes *fail* to discount when they should—because the patient is dead. But if he is dead, how can his awareness sensibly be taken into account? If we seem to be stretching the limits of credibility here, it is only to illuminate the ordinary instances of discounting while patients are still alive.

When a patient has just died, people who see the corpse rather soon thereafter tend, under certain conditions, to behave almost as if the patient were alive and aware of his imminent death. Temporarily the deceased is regarded virtually as a sentient *person*. For instance, nurses who have gotten deeply involved with a patient will sometimes back away from post-mortem care of his body. Their avoidance can be interpreted in many ways: our interpretation is that he is not quite a corpse to them but still a person, under whose gaze they would have to make funeral preparations. Relatives, immediately after the patient's death, often speak to him or caress him as if he were alive. Although they know he is dead, they act as if he knew what they were saying and doing, because his death is so recent. Staff members rarely speak to or caress the corpse,

[2] Lael T. Wertenbaker, *Death of a Man* (New York: Random House, 1957), pp. 6-7.

but in a lower key they sometimes act much like kinsmen. The tendency to treat a recently deceased kinsman as if he were still alive is reinforced by the nurses' or physicians' efforts to protect family members against the shock of making symbolic farewells to a disfigured corpse, arranging appearances so that the deceased person resembles his former self. When they are successful, the effect is not only to fix a more normal image in the kinsmen's memories, but permit them temporarily to regard and act toward the patient as not quite dead.

Persons who are present when a death actually occurs are often struck by the remarkably thin line that stretches between life and death. Momentarily, the person now dead seems hardly dead because he was so recently alive. As long as this mystic illusion persists, the onlooker tends to act as if he were *not* discounting the awareness of a living person. Again, even hospital personnel are subject to this brief illusion.

Staff members who give post-mortem care are open to another kind of experience as well. General rules of decency, and institutional instructions, prescribe that the corpse be treated with respect. One should not handle the corpse roughly, or make any disrespectful gestures toward it; in fact, nothing should be done to the body that is not required by post-mortem care. These rules may be neglected because personnel become callous or because they are in too great a hurry to complete the post-mortem tasks. Young nurses who witness such disrespectful handling may become physically sick, or at least irate, primarily because they feel that humans ought not to be treated thus. They react not only to what they consider inappropriate behavior, but also to their sense that this person (the corpse) would have been horrified had he foreseen what would happen to him after his death. The deceased person's awareness is thus taken into account, in a strange way, by the living, even though, realistically, that problem should disappear after the patient has died.

Our interpretation of post-mortem reactions may seem farfetched, but it does highlight our main point in this chapter.

Under most conditions, people's actions are very much affected by the problems associated with the patient's awareness, or lack of it. Only under relatively special circumstances do people ignore these problems, and the circumstances under which they *must* ignore them are even more unusual. Thus the natural impulse is, ordinarily, to continue acting as if awareness were still a crucial issue when it no longer is.

Part Three

Problems of
Awareness

8

Direct Disclosure of Terminality

One of the most difficult of doctor's dilemmas is whether or not to tell a patient he has a fatal illness. The *ideal* rule offered by doctors is that in each individual case they should decide whether the patient really wants to know and can "take it." However, 69 to 90 per cent of doctors (depending on the study) favor not telling their patients about terminal illness,[1] rather than following this "ideal" individual decision. So it appears that most doctors have a general standard from which the same decision flows for most patients—that they should not be told. This finding also indicates that the standard of "do not tell" receives very strong support from colleagues.

Many conditions reduce a doctor's inclination to make a separate decision for each case. Few doctors get to know each terminal patient well enough to judge his desire for disclosure or his capacity to withstand the shock of it. Getting to know a patient well enough takes more time than doctors typically have. Furthermore, with the current increase of patient loads doctors will have less and less time for each patient, which creates a paradox: with more patients dying in hospitals, more will not be told they are dying. Even when a doctor has had many contacts with a particular patient, class or educational differences, or personality clashes, may prevent effective communication. Some doctors simply feel unable to handle themselves well enough during disclosure to make a complicated illness understandable. If a doctor makes a mistake, he may

[1] Herman Feifel, "Death," in Norman L. Farberow (ed.), *Taboo Topics* (New York: Atherton Press, 1963), p. 17.

be liable for malpractice. Some doctors will announce an impending death only when a clear-cut pathologist's report is available. Others do not tell because they fear the patient might become despondent or mentally ill or commit suicide, because they do not want him to "lean" on them for emotional support, or because they simply wish to preserve peace on the ward by preventing a scene.

At the same time, a number of other conditions encourage disclosure regardless of the individual patient's capacity to withstand it. Some doctors disclose to avoid losing the patient's confidence if he should find out through cues or accidentally. Telling also justifies radical treatment or a clinical research offer; it also reduces the doctor's need to keep up a cheerful but false front. Some tell so that the patient can put his affairs in order and plan for his family's future, or reduce his pace of living; others, because family members request it. Of course, if the chances for recovery or successful treatment are relatively good, a doctor is naturally more likely to disclose an illness that is possibly terminal; disclosing a skin cancer is easier than disclosing bone cancer.

The combined effect of these conditions—some of which may induce conflicting approaches to the same patient—is to make it much easier for doctors to apply to all patients a flat "no, he should not be told." For when people are in doubt about an action, especially when the doubt arises from inability to calculate the possible effects of many factors about which there is little information, it is almost always easier and safer not to act.[2]

A doctor who does decide to say "yes, tell the patient he is probably going to die," has in effect decided to transform a closed awareness context into an open one (or possibly into a suspicion context). Our intention in this chapter is to develop a model for this transformation; *i.e.*, a model combining the

[2] For a conceptual analysis that applies to why there is less risk for doctors in not disclosing terminality, see Thomas J. Sheff, "Decision Rules, Types of Error, and Their Consequences in Medical Diagnosis," *Behavioral Science*, 8 (April 1963), pp. 97-107.

stages typically present in the response process stimulated by direct disclosure of terminal illness, with the characteristic forms of interaction between the patient and staff that attend each stage of the response process (starting off with how the disclosure was made). Thus our focus is just as much upon how the staff initiates and attempts to guide and control the response process through interaction with the patient as it is upon the patient's responses *per se*.

Many of the standard arguments given by doctors both for and against disclosure anticipate a single, permanent impact on the patient.[3] He is expected to "be brave," "go to pieces," "commit suicide," "lose all hope," or to "plan for the future" and such. But the impact is not so simple. Disclosing the truth sets off a generalized response process through which the patient passes. To base the decision about disclosure on a single probable impact is to focus on only one stage in the response process; not only does it neglect the other stages, but also it omits how each stage may be controlled by the staff through appropriate forms of interaction. For example, to predict that the patient will become too despondent is to neglect the possibility that he might overcome this despondency and, with the aid of a chaplain or social worker, prepare adequately for his death and for his family's future. But to expect a patient simply to settle his affairs is to fail to evaluate his capacity for overcoming an initial depression, as well as the capacity of the staff to help him at this stage.

The generalized response process is stimulated by a doctor's *disclosure* to the patient. The patient's initial response is almost invariably *depression*, but after a period of depression he either *accepts* or *denies* the disclosure; and his ensuing behavior may be regarded as an affirmation of his stand on whether he will, in fact, die. Acceptance of the doctor's disclosure may lead to active preparation, to passive preparation, or to fighting the

[3] For an illustration of this kind of argument, see the discussion between two doctors in "How Should Incurably Ill Patients Be Dealt With: Should They Be Told the Truth," *Parent's Magazine,* 71 (January 1963), pp. 196-206.

illness. A particular patient's response may stop at any stage, take any direction, or change directions. The outcome depends first on the manner in which he is told, and then on his own inclinations combined with staff management.

A doctor deciding whether to tell the patient, therefore, cannot consider a single impact, but how, in what direction, and with what consequences the patient's response is likely to go; as well as what types of staff are available and how they will handle the patient at each stage. A doctor who says "no" to disclosure because the patient will "lose hope" need not be in conflict with one who says "yes" to give the patient a chance to plan for his family. Each is merely referring to a different stage of the same process. For both, the concern should be with judging whether the patient can achieve the acceptance-active preparation stage.

Our conception of the stages characteristic of a patient's response to direct disclosure is based largely on our interviews with patients, doctors and nurses in the cancer wards of a Veterans' Administration Hospital. In this hospital the normal procedure is to tell every patient the nature of his illness; as a result, many patients are told of a fatal illness.[4]

By and large the patients in these wards are in their middle or late years, of lower class status, and in destitute circumstances. Since their care is free, they are captive patients— they have little or no control over their treatment, and if they do not cooperate their care may be stopped. If a man goes "AWOL" the hospital is not obliged to readmit him, or if it does readmit him, it can punish him by denying privileges. Because the patients lack financial resources, they typically have no alternative to their current "free" care, and lower class status accustoms them to accepting or to being intimidated into following orders from people of higher status. Since these captive lower class patients cannot effectively threaten the hospital or the doctors, the rule at this hospital is to disclose

---

[4] This norm may be considered an aspect of "batch" treatment of inmates of a total institution. See Erving Goffman, "The Characteristics of Total Institutions," in Amitai Etzioni (ed.), *Complex Organizations* (New York: Holt, Rinehart and Winston, 1961), pp. 312-340.

terminality regardless of the patient's expected reaction. These patients seemed to exhibit the full range of responses to disclosure of terminality which it is our purpose to set forth here. (We cannot say how the distribution of these patients throughout the range of responses would differ, if at all, for higher socioeconomic patients.)

So many cases of direct disclosure, and the consequent variety of response patterns, made this hospital a highly strategic research site for studying disclosure. In other hospitals we found only a few cases of direct disclosure, and their general aspects were the same as those of the VA cases.

DISCLOSING FATAL ILLNESS

Disclosure of fatal illness to patients in this hospital has two major characteristics. First, the patient is told that he is certain to die, but not when he will die. As we indicated in chapter 2, expectations of death have two dimensions: certainty and time of demise, with the first more readily determined in advance. As one doctor put it: "In my opinion, however, no doctor should take it upon himself to say to a patient, 'You have ten weeks to live'—or three months, or two years or any time whatsoever." And another doctor said: "Doctors simply do not know when patients are going to die." Stopping short of full disclosure tends to soften the blow to the patient and reduces chances of error for the doctor.

Second, the doctors typically do not give details of the illness, and the type of patient under consideration usually does not ask for them. Primarily, this is a problem of communication: a doctor finds it hard to explain the illness to a working class patient, while lack of familiarity with the technical terms, as well as a more general deference to the doctor, inhibits the patient's impulse to question him. In addition, not giving details is a tactic doctors use to avoid or cut down on talk with the patient and to leave him quickly. Thus (as referred to in Chapter 6) transforming the closed awareness context to open does not make *all* important issues open to discussion.

Issues such as time of death and mode of dying may be left relatively closed, or on the level of suspicion over which the contest for information and control will be waged.

In combination, these two characteristics of disclosure often result in short, blunt announcements of fatal illness to the patient. Even the nurses are often shocked by the doctors' bluntness. Nevertheless, they often feel that the patient is better off for being told "because, as one nurse put it, he becomes philosophical in a day or two."

A short, blunt announcement may be softened, however, in various ways. One way is to add a religious flavor: "You've had a full life now, and God will be calling you soon." This manner is perhaps most appropriate for older patients. Another is to muffle the language. To the patient's question, "Is it cancer, Doc?" the doctor responds, "We don't call it that . . ." and then gives it a technical name that the patient can understand only vaguely. The "suspicion" announcement also dulls the blow: "There is a high clinical suspicion that the tumor removed was cancer. However, we won't have a pathological report on it for ten days." The announcement that there is "nothing more to do" (to cure the patient) can be muffled with a hopeful lie, such as "but then who knows, next week, next month or maybe next year there may be a drug that will save you," or by suggesting to the patient that he join an experimental program that may help him, as well as mankind.[5] Finally, there is the important statement that softens any form of disclosure: "We can control the pain."

In some forms, the blunt announcement *sharpens* the blow of a disclosure by forcing a *direct confrontation* of the truth with little or no preamble. Some doctors are quite aware of this directness and favor their colleagues' use of this approach. One doctor says, "With average patients, we tell them what they've got." Another says, "I don't think the staff as a whole

[5] If the patient takes the experimental drug, he continually checks his condition by asking the doctor: "What next, Doc?" "What now?" "Am I better?" Am I getting well?" When the experiment is over and the patient is still going to die, he must start through the response process again with a depressing "now what" feeling.

goes along with the hard-boiled approach, but me, I try to tell them the truth." The "hard-boiled" announcement is often linked with a report to the patient of the results of his surgery. In this hospital, patients are customarily told, two or three days after surgery for cancer, whether they will die. For example, one doctor walks into the patient's room, faces him, says, "It's malignant," and walks out. To be sure, this tactic also eliminates having to answer the patient's questions. Another rather direct confrontation is, "We weren't able to get it [the malignant tumor] all out." Another form of sharp announcement is the *direct retort*: when a patient asks, "Doctor, do I have cancer?" the doctor replies, "Yes, you do." (One doctor commented, "If they ask directly, we answer as directly as possible.") Lastly, the *implied,* but sharp, confrontation of fatal illness is exemplified by the doctor who met a returning patient with the order to sell her house and all her things, for she would not leave the hospital again.

In this group of doctors who generally favor the short, blunt disclosure there is one who does not. He refuses to disclose in this fashion because he has had previous experience with errors due to changing pathology reports, and because he tries, through surgery, to make the patient's last weeks more comfortable. Other doctors tend to disagree that his "comfort surgery" is useful, but he continues because sometimes he actually saves the patient for years. This doctor continually maintains a cheerful and optimistic manner, never directly disclosing to the patient that he will die, but actually giving *silent disclosure* by his offer of comfort surgery or participation in a clinical experiment. Silent disclosure initiates the mutual pretense awareness context: both doctor and patient know of the latter's fatal illness, and both know the other knows, but they do not talk to each other about it. The doctor reveals the patient's fatal illness by oblique reference to it in proposing comfort surgery or experimental participation, the meaning of which the patient clearly understands. The patient thus begins his process of response-to-disclosure without the customary stimulus of direct disclosure.

DEPRESSION

The initial response of the patient to disclosure is depression. The large majority of patients come to terms with their depression sufficiently to go on to the next stage of the response process. A few do not. They withdraw from contact with everyone and remain in a state of hopelessness. In this limiting sense they become non-interacting, non-cooperative patients; the nurses can not "reach" them. Depression is usually handled by sedation until the patient starts relating to the staff. In one case a nurse observed that a patient visibly shortened his life because of his period of anxiety and withdrawal.

ACCEPTANCE OR DENIAL?

After an initial period of acute depression, the patient responds to the announcement by choosing either to accept or to deny the imminence of his death. In effect, he takes a stand on whether and how he will die, and this stand profoundly affects his relations with the staff from that time on.

In general, sharp, abrupt disclosure tends to produce more denial, than dulled disclosure.[6] When the disclosure is sharp, the depression is more immediate and profound, and denial begins immediately as a mechanism to cope with the shock.[7] To predict an individual's response, however, one needs the kind of intimate knowledge of the patient that doctors would prefer to have. Without it, it is very difficult to say which path to death a patient will take, or for how long. In some cases, the patient's response changes; he cannot hold out against

[6] This hypothesis complements the discussion by Feifel (*op. cit.*) on the importance of "how telling is done."

[7] For another discussion of denial of illness upon disclosure, see Henry D. Lederer, "How the Sick View Their World," in E. Gartly Jaco (ed.), *Patients, Physicians and Illness* (New York: Free Press of Glencoe, 1958), pp. 247-250. Denial of dying is characteristic of our society as shown by Robert Fulton's data: see "Death and the Self," *Journal of Religion and Health*, 3, No. 4 (July 1964), pp. 359-368. See the analysis of denial of death in American society by Talcott Parsons, "Death in American Society," *American Behavioral Scientist*, 6 (May 1963), pp. 61-65.

accumulating physical, social and temporal cues. The usual change is from denial to acceptance, though short-term reprieves sometimes occur, when patients improve before growing worse, or when a new drug helps for a few days; and in such cases acceptance may change, for a time, to denial. The direction an individual takes depends not only on how he is told, but also on a variety of social and psychological considerations impinging on the passage from life to death.

Acceptance: Patients may demonstrate acceptance of impending death by actively preparing for death, passively preparing, or fighting against it. *Active preparation* may take the form of becoming philosophical about dying, death, and one's previous life; with family, nurses, social workers and the chaplain, patients review and discuss how full their life has been. They may pose the destiny question: "Why me?" and try to work through it with the philosophical help of others. This approach leads the patient to draw the nurses into a discussion which can be very difficult for them, since nurses are trained by and large to help motivate patients to live, not to die. But if a nurse is to help a patient prepare himself, she too must accept his impending death and refrain from chastising him for not fighting to live. Otherwise she is likely to consider the patient "morbid" and tend to avoid his invitations to help him face death squarely. She will usually try to transfer the burden to the social worker, nun, or chaplain when they are available.

Some patients start immediately to prepare themselves for death through religion. For others it is an easy transition to slip from philosophical to religious terms, a transition often aided by the chaplain, who then helps the patient prepare himself.

Another form of active preparation for death is to *settle social and financial affairs,* perhaps linking this effort with philosophical or religious preparation. The typical helpers in settling affairs are family members and social workers. For example, upon learning that he was going to die, the patient turned to his wife and said, "Well, we've got to get everything lined up; I promised [so-and-so] my. . . ." This immediate getting down to the provisions of a will was considered abnormal by one nurse who said, "I've never seen a reaction like that, it was almost morbid." Another patient began discussing with the social worker the various veteran's benefits they could obtain for his wife, and another tried to get his wife, who was emotionally very dependent on him, married to a hospital corpsman. One patient gave up his pain medication long enough to put his financial affairs in order with the aid of a social worker, for he knew that as soon as he was too drugged to operate effectively, his family would try to take over his estate.

To give the patient a chance to settle his affairs and to plan for the future of his family, is, of course, an important consideration when a doctor decides whether to disclose fatal illness.[8] He can seldom be sure, however, that the patient's response will take this direction or advance so far. Moreover, some affairs to be settled are less important than others; still, patients have a chance to pick up loose ends or accomplish unfinished business. For example, before entering the hospital for cancer surgery one woman said, "I am going to do three things before I enter the hospital—things I've been meaning to do for a long time. I'm going to make some grape jelly. I've always dreamed of having a shelf full of jelly jars with my own label on them. Then I'm going to get up enough nerve to saddle and bridle my daughter's horse and take a ride. Then I'm going to apologize to my mother-in-law for what I said to her in 1949." Another patient with leukemia quit work and bought a sailboat. He planned to explore the delta region of the Sacramento and San Joaquin Rivers until his last trip to the hospital.

Another form of active preparation is to attempt a *"full*

---

[8] A study by Dr. Donald Oken showed that MD's are more likely to disclose to businessmen because they needed to wind up business matters; *i.e.*, MD's perceived this matter as important: Donald Oken, "What to Tell Cancer Patients: A Study of Medical Attitudes," *The Journal of the American Medical Association*, 175 (April 1961), pp. 1120-1128.

life" before death.[9] This pattern is characteristic of younger patients (in contrast to older patients who review the fullness of the life they have had), like the twenty-two-year-old man who, when told he had between three months and three years to live, married a nurse. "If we have only two months," she said, "it will be worth it." The patient lived two years and had a son. Faced by certain death he had achieved the most he could from life.

Auto-euthanasia (suicide) is another way of actively preparing for death.[10] It eliminates the sometimes very distressing last weeks or days of dying. One patient, who had no friends to visit him, felt that he was very alone and that no one in the hospital cared, so he tried to hasten his death by suicide. Some patients try to end their lives while they are physically presentable, not wanting their families to see their degeneration. Other stresses that encourage auto-euthanasia are unbearable pain and the discipline imposed by a clinical experiment to which one may be irrevocably committed. Others decide to end their life when they can no longer work.[11] Still others prefer auto-euthanasia as a way of controlling their dying as they controlled their living, thus wresting this control from the hands of the staff and the rigors imposed by hospital routine.[12]

Passive preparation for death, among patients who accept

[9] This form of active preparation is appropriate in American society which stresses the value that death is unacceptable until one has had a full life; see Parsons, *op. cit.*

[10] Shneidman feels a question deserving of research is "why so many cancer patients *do not* commit suicide," Edwin S. Shneidman,"Suicide," in Farberow, *op. cit.*

[11] For an account of a cancer patient who planned to commit auto-euthanasia after he could no longer work, see Lael Wertenbaker, *Death of a Man* (New York: Random House, 1957).

[12] A growing problem that medical staff and hospitals must face is that people wish to control their own way of dying; they do not want it programmed for them by medical staff and hospital organization. To achieve this end, many patients also wish to die at home; Fulton, *op. cit.*, pp. 363-364. See the analysis of this problem in Jeanne C. Quint, "Some Organizational Barriers to Effective Patient Care in Hospitals," paper given at the American Medical Association convention, June 24, 1964.

their terminality, also has some characteristic forms. One is
to take the news in a nonchalant manner, which nurses sometimes find disturbing. One put it: "But some take it quite
nonchalantly. We've had several very good patients—right to
the end. One that upset me was here when I came. He was
the hardest for me to see die—he was young and not only
that—such a wonderful fellow. Even as sick as he was, he was
always kind and courteous." Apart from the social loss factor
—"young" and "wonderful"—which usually upsets nurses,[13]
this nurse also found such a passive outlook on death rather
disquieting. As we noted in Chapter 6, the patient's passivity
tends to be judged as an unacceptable style of dying.

Nurses, however, are grateful to patients who approach
death with *calm resignation*. This response not only relieves
them of the responsibility for cheering up the patient, but also
improves their own morale. Since it would not do for a nurse
to be less calm or resigned than her patient, a patient who
responds in this fashion raises and supports the nurse's morale.
The non-verbal patient who simply accepts his fate and does
not talk about it also relieves the nurses of the stress of discussing it, as she often must do with the more actively preparing
patient. The calm patient makes few or no demands on nurses
or social workers. A disquieting aspect of this response is the
loss of contact with the patient: "It is very hard for us 'well
people' to really grasp how they feel." One social worker
bridges this gap by sitting with the patient for a time each day.
She reports, "Sometimes it's a matter of just touching their
hand—whatever is natural—to make them feel that you understand and care." Another disquieting version of the passive
response is expressed by the patient who emerges from his depression only to turn his face to the wall, "the spirit drained out
of him," and "passively wait to die."

Some patients accept their fatal illness but decide to *fight*
it. Unlike denial behavior, this fight indicates an initial accept-

[13] Barney Glaser and Anselm Strauss, "The Social Loss of Dying
Patients," *American Journal of Nursing,* 64 (June 1964), pp. 119-121.

ance of one's fate together with a positive desire to somehow change it. Three forms of fighting behavior are *intensive living, going to marginal doctors or quacks,* and *participating in an experiment.* One patient, for example, started going out on passes and living it up, asserting, "I'll beat it," as if he could hold death off by living life to the full. He kept getting thinner and eventually died. This mode of resisting death can be readily transformed into active preparation for death if it increases the patient's fullness of life before he dies.

Taking an outside chance with quacks or marginal doctors [14] gives some patients a feeling that they are actively combatting the disease. A regular physician may permit his patient to go to a marginal doctor, since that visit keeps the patient hopeful and busy while letting the physician see that the marginal treatments do not injure his patient. Denied this permission, a patient who wants to fight his disease in some way may break off relations with his physician, so that the physician loses control over both the patient and the marginal doctor. A rupture like this makes it difficult for the patient to return to the original doctor after the marginal treatment fails.[15]

The search for a way to fight the fatal illness can also lead a patient into a clinical experiment. If he does not win his own battle, he at least may help future patients with theirs. The chance to contribute to medical science does not, however, sustain the motivation of *all* research patients.[16] Some, realizing things are hopeless for themselves and finding the experimental regime too rigorous to bear, try to extricate themselves from the experiment. If the doctors decide to carry on anyway, these patients sometimes interfere with the experiment by

[14] In this connection see Beatrix Cobb, "Why Do People Detour to Quacks?" in Jaco, *op. cit.*

[15] For an illustration of how the doctor allowed, hence could control a dying patient's submission to the rigorous treatment of a marginal doctor, see John Gunther, *Death Be Not Proud* (New York: Harper Bros., 1949).

[16] *Cf.* Renée Fox, *Experiment Perilous* (New York: Free Press of Glencoe, 1959). One gets the feeling that patients in Fox's sample were all highly motivated to go on with the experiments to the bitter end.

pulling tubes out, by not taking medicine, or by taking an extra drink of water. Some attempt auto-euthanasia. (See Chapter 11.)

Denial: Some patients deny they are approaching death and proceed to establish this stand in their interaction with staff members. Typical denying strategies are juggling time, testing for denial, comparing oneself to others, blocking communication, becoming intensely active, emphasizing a future orientation, and forcing reciprocal isolation. These strategies result in a tug-of-war between staff and patient, with the staff trying to institute an open awareness context, and the patient trying to keep the context closed, or at least institute one of mutual pretense.

In the cancer ward, it is relatively easy to deny impending death by juggling time, for disclosure, as we have noted, implies certainty that death will occur but no assurance as to *when* it will occur. Patients can therefore invent a time, and this becomes a way of denying that one is truly dying.[17] Some literally give themselves years. But even when a denying person is given a time limit, he is still likely to start thinking, as one nurse said, "in terms of years, when it really is a matter of a month or two."

A patient can *test* the staff in various ways to establish his denial. A negative way is by *not* testing, or failing to ask the expected questions. For example, the doctor who tells the patient he has a tumor adopts a grave manner which indicates that the tumor is malignant, and expects the patient to try to verify it. But the denying patient never asks the doctor or anyone else. Other patients do test the nurses indirectly, by asking, "Why aren't I gaining weight? Why aren't I feeling better?" Since these patients can be assumed to know why, the nurse understands that they want these physical cues interpreted in

[17] That in the case of dying, patients will tend to give themselves *more* time than they actually have, contrasts with studies of recovery which show that patients are likely to give themselves *less* time than it takes to recover. See Fred Davis, *Passage Through Crisis* (Indianapolis: Bobbs-Merrill, 1963) and Julius Roth, *Timetables* (Indianapolis: Bobbs-Merrill, 1963).

such a way as to deny that they indicate impending death. Patients often ask nurses to manage temporal cues in the same way, by interpreting their extended stay in the hospital or slow recuperation in ways that point away from death.

Another form of testing for denial is the *polarity game*. By questioning a nurse or social worker about the most extreme life-or-death implications of his illness, the patient forces her to give a normalizing answer, which usually locates him a safe distance from death. For example, focusing on the dying implications, the patient asks, "Am I getting worse? The medicine isn't helping." The forced answer is, "Give yourself a chance—medicine takes a long time." Or, focusing on the living implications, a patient replies to a social worker trying to figure out his VA benefits for his family, "Well, all right—but it won't be for long, will it?" Since the social worker cannot confront the patient with coming death if he "really doesn't know," she in effect denies it for him by classifying him with the living but disabled: "This is what welfare is for—to help the families of men who are disabled and can't work." Here, the social worker understood the patient's words as a request "for assurance that he wasn't going to die," and she responded appropriately.

Patients may deny their fate by using other patients as *comparative references*. Two common types of comparison are the exception and the favorable comparison. A patient using the first approach becomes very talkative about other patients with the same disease. He adopts a manner, or style, like that of staff members; that is, people who do not have the illness. In the end this borrowed objectivity and immunity lead him to conclude that he is an exceptional case, that somehow the illness that caused so many others to die will not kill him: he will be cured. The favorable comparison is a distorted effort to include one's illness in a nonfatal category: one patient said, "The doctor says I only have a [severe illness]." Another literally dying patient said, "Thank God, I am not as bad off as [another patient near death]."

Some patients try to prove they are not terminal by *engaging in strenuous activities*. One patient, having been told he had a bad heart, left the hospital and started spading up his garden to prove the doctor wrong (and his own denial right). Another patient wouldn't stick to his diet. The death impending in the present can also be denied through *future-oriented talk* with the nurses. One patient began making plans to buy a chicken farm when he left the hospital—as soon as he learned he was going to die. *Communication blocks* of various sorts aid denial. Some patients simply don't hear the doctor, other refuse to admit it, others cannot use the word "cancer" in any verbal context, and still others avoid any discussion of the nature of their illness or the inevitability of death.

As a result of the contest between staff and patient, with one trying to open the awareness context and the other trying to close it, a denying patient can start an accumulating process of reciprocal isolation between himself and nurses, doctors, family members and social workers. After disclosure, others expect him to acknowledge his impending death, so they attempt to relate to him on this basis. Doctors speak to him and nurses give treatment on the understanding that his impending demise can be mentioned or at least signaled. Family members and social workers may refer to plans for his burial and his finances. A patient who avoids the subject when he is not expected to avoid it forces others to avoid it too, which makes them unable to help or prepare him. One social worker said, helplessly, about a denying patient, "There was nothing I could do for him." At this first stage of the isolation process, the patient forces an implicit agreement between himself and others that the topic of his terminality will not be discussed, thus instituting a mutual pretense context. In the next stage, some of these people may avoid all contact with the patient because he has frustrated their efforts to help him. Nurses, doctors and social workers tend to spend their time with patients they can help, to prevent the feeling of helplessness that often overcomes them while engaged in terminal care. As a result, the patient finds himself alone, apart from receiving the necessary technical care to insure painless comfort, and his isolation is complete.

Avoidance of the denying patient occurs because he refuses to act as a dying patient, although it has been clearly pointed out to him that this is exactly what he is. In contrast, an unaware patient, who is not expected to act like a dying patient, will not be avoided on these grounds. Rather he is likely to attract others who will gather around him in silent sympathy, wishing they could help and perhaps tell him. In the end, both the denying patient and the unaware patient may die without preparation for death. But a denying patient still has a chance to accept his impending death and prepare himself, usually with the help of others, while the unaware patient's chances for preparation are mostly dependent on his doctor.

Once again, the benefits and liabilities of unawareness (nondisclosure), as opposed to disclosure and its possibilities for acceptance or denial, depend on the nature of the individual case. But on the whole, there is much to recommend giving the patient an opportunity actively to manage his own dying. As a strong controlling factor, staff members who interact with the patient could consciously soften the disclosure, handle the depression so as to encourage acceptance, and guide the patient into active preparations for death. Perhaps they could even find interaction strategies that would in the tug-of-war convert a patient's denial to acceptance. Yet staff members often hesitate to tamper with a patient's choice of passage to death. For example, one social worker said of a denying patient: "I'm loath to play God on this. Unless it could serve a useful purpose—would it really be helpful? Where a man shies away from something—maybe you should let him—why make him face this most terrible reality?" To help staff members overcome this reluctance, readily ascertainable and unambiguous general criteria are needed for deciding when to disclose terminality and when to keep the patient unaware of it. Criteria that require "intimate knowledge of each patient" offer no better a solution to the doctor's dilemma than does a universally applied rule of telling or not telling.

9

The Unaware Family

A dying patient's family creates a chronic problem for nurses. Family members are relatively easy to handle one at a time, but as a group they can join forces to put pressure on the nurse to give them better visiting hours, more information, special treatment, and so on. Nurses must control the family so as to keep disturbing scenes at a minimum, and to maintain family composure, so that family members can make crucial decisions, visit the patient, and help with patient care, without disrupting hospital routine.

The nurse's problem is compounded, for she often has to handle many family groups in the course of her day. In the cancer ward, for example, a nurse may be in charge of a number of long-term dying patients; she has to cope with all their families through their long ordeal. And of course her task is doubled or even tripled for any patient who has two or three independent, sometimes hostile families (in-law groups, two wives—one divorced—and their children, children's families, etc.).

Another condition that increases this aspect of a nurse's work is the rotation of patients under her care. Rotation confronts the nurse with new, unfamiliar families, while at the same time the family of a previous patient may still be drifting around the ward, asking her for information or help whenever they pass each other. In addition, on wards with long-term patients, nurses become acquainted with the families of other nurses' patients, and these families come to make demands on her too. (A compensating feature in dealing with the families of long-term patients is that the nurse can use her familiarity with them as a source of control.)

Short-term dying patients generally require more constant care, so a nurse is usually assigned fewer of these patients and thus has fewer families to contend with. But the higher turnover of short-term patients means that she does not get to know their families as well and constantly has to deal with new people. On some wards (operating room, intensive care units, premature babies) nurses are well screened from the families by doors, walls and rules and can avoid being distracted from constant attention to their patients.

Thus, depending on the nature of the patient's illness and on the way the ward is organized, the family handling required of nurses varies greatly throughout the hospital. Many of the staff tactics in coping with family members are standardized; others are of an ever-changing interactional nature, determined in part by the awareness context surrounding the patient and his family.

A family may be involved in a closed as well as an open awareness context. A family involved in a closed awareness context must collaborate with the staff to keep the patient unaware, and staff members must handle the family members accordingly, making sure they do not leak information to the patient. When the family members are outside a closed awareness context; that is, when *they* are also unaware, the staff must keep them out so as to keep the patient unaware. Of course, family members (except young children) are seldom outside an open awareness context; and those that are outside, because they have not been in touch with typical medical sources of information, are usually brought into awareness as soon as they arrive on the scene.

In this chapter we shall consider, for the most part, the unaware family of an unaware patient (that is, a family outside a closed awareness context), and the interaction tactics staff members use to cope with problems generated by these conditions. In the next chapter we shall consider the aware family.

CONDITIONS FOR KEEPING THE FAMILY UNAWARE

Several conditions encourage the staff to keep the family unaware of the patient's impending death. Although the doctor may be fairly sure the patient is dying, he may not want to go on record with this information in the early stages of a disease. In long-term illness he will have plenty of time to verify his prognosis before telling the family. Reversals, though usually temporary and seldom complete, do occur, and if the doctor's early prognosis seems to be contradicted, the family may begin to question his judgment. Short-term reprieves of even a few hours can cause an ever hopeful family to distrust the doctor. And a doctor loses an element of control over the family when it stops believing in his expertise. A distrusting family often starts searching for new doctors—often somewhat marginal ones if not outright quacks—and new cures.

Telling the family members at the beginning of a long-term illness may also put them under stress for a longer time than they need to prepare adequately for the patient's death. Should a reversal occur, the family's relief is balanced by a certain amount of resentment at having been subjected to stress in the first place. With too much advance warning, family members could prepare themselves so well that they give the patient up before he dies, and may therefore not be sufficiently available to help during the last stages of dying.

Putting family members under stress by telling them about the patient's true condition brings the ward staff new problems of family control. As we shall see in the next chapter, once family members learn the patient is dying they put pressure on the staff for visiting privileges, more information, special treatments, and help in preparing for their loved one's death. The ecology of the dying situation is also disturbed. Feeling that their circumstances justify their disdain for hospital regulations, the family members drift into unauthorized areas, not content to remain in waiting rooms gleaning information as best they can. En route they may disturb staff and patients by breaking down and sobbing, asking questions and so on. Also the staff may have to prevent family members from passing the news on to the patient, usually unwittingly through cues, say, of grief. And if the closed context changes to either a suspicion or mutual pretense context, the family must be supported and guided in the art of either not validating suspicions or maintaining pretenses.

When there is enough time, then, these reasons for keeping the family in the dark are likely to outweigh any pressure to tell them the truth. Even when time is short, family members may be kept unaware if the doctor suspects they are psychologically incapable of bearing up under the news. And though time is usually short on an emergency ward, staff doctors will prefer not to tell the family that a patient is dying, if they expect a private doctor to take over, because it is considered his prerogative to disclose or not.

In many cases, of course, especially in veterans' hospitals and state hospitals, there is no family to tell. The patient may be without kin, or perhaps no one in his family cares enough to visit the hospital or maintain sufficient contact to be reached by the "seriously ill, come at once" telegram. A nurse, a fellow patient, or a friend may stand in for family, and indeed many people in this position feel strongly that they are the only "family" the patient had before death.

CLOSED AWARENESS AND THE SUSPICIOUS FAMILY

Keeping the whole family outside a closed awareness context creates, for nurses, the problem of managing family members' suspicions to forestall their growing realization that the patient is dying. Of course, if the family is not suspicious, or does not press for validation of any suspicions it might have, then the nurse has only to cope with a relatively self-composed group that is likely to obey visiting-hour rules, not to ask for exceptions in treatment, to wait patiently in prescribed areas, and to be reasonably satisfied with standard statements about the patient's condition. In short, the nurse whose patient's family is both unaware and unsuspicious can rely on the ordinary hospital procedures used for families of patients who are not dying.

If a suspicious family is to be kept unaware, however, staff members must allay suspicions based on either physical or temporal cues given by the patient's condition. Since a basic property of suspicion is doubt as to one's accuracy in judging a cue, family members will ask the nurse or the doctor to verify their readings of the patient's condition. The staff member, in his role as an expert cue reader, thus has considerable control over the credence that family members will give their own suspicions. And since families would rather hope than know the worst, staff efforts to keep the family unaware often succeed, unless the patient's condition is clearly "bad."

Nurses have many available interaction tactics to forestall growing awareness. When several family members begin to suspect the worst, each suspicious member may hide his suspicions from the others, because each believes he is the only one who thinks the patient may die; not yet certain of his belief, he wishes to spare the others. In hiding their suspicions, they mutually sustain their faith in the recovery of the patient; thus all of them remain outside the closed awareness context.[1] No one wants to lose his own faith (as one nurse said, "I think she was afraid we might tell her."), or jeopardize the faith of other family members by asking nurses or doctors the questions

---

[1] This may be termed a "misperceived pretense" awareness context within the family unit. Unlike the mutual pretense context in which all know and share a truth but pretend not to, in the misperceived context each thinks he knows the truth but that the other does not, and so he pretends he does not know the truth either. The misperception on each person's part is that he does not share the truth with others, whereas if he dared to check he would find out he does. Then, they might find out either that it is not necessary to pretend they do not know the truth, or that it is necessary to engage in mutual pretense. For a good example of a "misperceived pretense" awareness context whose force generates a subculture, see David Matza, *Delinquency and Drift* (New York: John Wiley and Sons, 1964), Chapter 2.

really necessary to verify suspicion. Staff members can take advantage of this situation simply by staying out of family interaction, or, if called upon, by lending their weight to the family's pretenses which support their faith in recovery.

A variation of this procedure is to make one family member aware of the patient's true condition and let him help keep the other members unaware. Usually the "strongest" member of the family is told even if he is not the closest relative or must even be brought in from out of town. A relatively detached cousin would be preferred over a mother or a wife who is on the verge of complete breakdown. A grown son may be told rather than the wife of a dying man. A father of an unexpectedly dying premature infant is usually told first, and he tells his wife when, in his judgment, she can "take it." When the strong member is told, it becomes his responsibility to decide whether others in the family—and which others—should also be made aware. If he decides not to tell anyone else, his burden is doubled, for not only is he unable to share his grief with other family members but also he must collaborate with the staff to allay their suspicions. At a time of great sadness he is forced to appear relatively cheerful.

In larger families, a group aware of the patient's impending death may form, its members supporting each other to keep the others unaware. Again, the family takes care of itself; under these circumstances, the staff can rely on the family members who are "in" on the secret to control those left out. These are but two varieties of the general tactic—letting family members control each other—which is used in many other situations, as we shall have occasions to note.

Other tactics, involving more staff intervention, are not as easy to apply. An event that typically raises the suspicions of even the most hopeful family members is a sudden change in the patient's location—to a private room, nearer the nursing station, to a pre-operation ward, or (worse still) to an intensive care unit. The staff is immediately asked *why?* And if the family is still to be kept unaware, the nurse must counter a suspicion that may be very close to certainty. She immediately ushers the family into a room and shuts the door to insure a private discussion. Invariably, her first explanation is that there is no cause for concern, the move to the new location is only to provide the patient with better care. But this may not reduce suspicions, because patients *are* put in single rooms to die, *are* taken to the intensive care units for access to special equipment with which to forestall a possibly impending demise, *are* put near the nursing station so as to be under constant surveillance by all nurses on the floor, and *are* taken to the operating room for a last effort to prevent death. So additional tactics are needed.

The next one is to give the family all available *favorable* information on the patient's condition and to suggest that his changed location indicates nothing so drastic as dying, or that, with the information available, nobody could possibly be sure that he is dying. Then, both to discourage a recurrence of any suspicious, morbid thoughts and to get the family out of the way and avoid a scene, the nurse suggests that they go home and rest or go out for food, promising to notify them if the patient's condition should change. Sometimes she assures them that anyone who becomes anxious again may call her at any time for more information. The nurse's strategy, in other words, is to reduce suspicion with expert information and then try to prevent its recurrence by making additional expert information readily accessible to the family. In this way the family continues to depend on the nurse as a readily trusted source of expert news, and the nurse in turn maintains control over their awareness.

Now and then a patient who is expected to recover will turn "bad" while relatives are present! This requires fast action on the nurse's part, to keep the family unaware at the same time they are responding to the striking change in the patient's condition. Her best strategy is to show concern in her words and facial expressions without expressing undue alarm. If she fails, thereby revealing the gravity of the situation, the relatives may become aware so suddenly that panic is highly probable. In this situation, then, the nurse's main concern is to prevent an emotional upheaval and all the repercussions that could follow. The family can be eased into awareness later, if the patient is surely dying.

A standard tactic in normal situations, "role switching," has implications for the whole staff. To handle questions and probes in a way that will not force her to bring the family into awareness, a nurse may first counter a request for information with "I don't know" or "I'm not allowed to say." The family member is then switched to a person at the next higher level of authority, who may be empowered to state the patient's true condition. This staff member's role *vis-à-vis* the family member may be more appropriate for dispensing information. In extreme cases the family member is referred from an aide up through various levels of the nursing staff, with perhaps a few side trips to an orderly, social worker, nun, chaplain, or ward clerk, and ends by asking the doctor, the very person who still feels it is best to keep the family out.

To be sure, role-switching is stimulated in part by the fact that a nurse has no right to disclose a patient's terminality to a relative unless the doctor explicitly permits it. Professional ethics thus become involved in keeping the family unaware, and for nurses this sometimes creates a dilemma, for they may have no other reason to keep the family out and many good reasons to bring it in. Only when the family is aware, for example, can its members help with the intense, constant physical and emotional care a dying patient requires, or understand new or complicated treatments, or begin to prepare for the patient's death.

In one case, neither a father nor his son knew that the father would die soon. The attending nurse felt strongly that both should know, so the father could give the son some last words of encouragement and support and "bequeath" the many activities that would soon be the son's responsibility. Yet, because doctor's orders forbade disclosure, she was forced against her own feelings seemingly to approve the "meaningless" talk between the pair. Although she had the power to keep the family members out, she could not bring them in even to help the patient. Her helplessness had to be muffled in her interaction with the patient and family member. In this situation, as in many others, nurses would often find it much easier to be honest with the family. It would help them maintain their own composure and better achieve the "comfort" goals of nursing care.

Another common situation that makes it possible to control the family's awareness occurs when family members demand information on the patient's condition. Perhaps one of the crudest techniques, certainly one that does not work well if family suspicion is running high, is to "hem and haw" with vague or very general statements. The very worried relative will then probe for the nurse's meaning of what she is trying to say; and at this point she must use one of the many "escape strategies" in her repertoire. She can invoke some highly legitimate and compelling reason for being elsewhere, for example: "Another patient needs me," or "The doctor is expecting me right back," and so on. In many situations the nurses can simply evade contact with questioning relatives, without even rejecting them too blatantly. Nurses have back rooms to hide in, and a legitimate running gait with which to breeze past family members. Wards like the intensive care unit or premature baby ward have doors to be kept shut, and glass and screens to hide behind; requirements for sterility can be used to prevent contacts; and a ward clerk can answer the phone and give a pat statement on the patient's condition—"no change today," "ate well" or "doing fine," and so on.

In desperation for information, family members may even turn to other patients who seem to have been around long enough to know what is going on. Of course, the doctor cannot hold these other patients responsible for keeping the awareness context closed. But often, especially if they have been helping in the care of the dying, they can be depended upon to collabo-

rate in keeping the secret from the patient and will be reluctant
to reveal it to his family. (In their search for information on
the patient's status, relatives may even accost the sociologist
doing field work, since he seems nice enough to approach, looks
intelligent, and is hanging around seemingly not doing much of
anything. If he does respond, the staff may use him to absorb
the relative's anxiety, knowing that he will not jeopardize his
research position on the ward by leaking closed information.)

CONDITIONS FOR MAKING THE FAMILY AWARE

The previous discussion illustrates that, at best, staff success
in keeping the suspicious family unaware is very tenuous. In
the ever-developing interaction between staff and family, it
is only a matter of time before suspicions are confirmed by
the patient's obvious condition, and by the family's increasing
skill in piecing together information and trapping or "testing"
the staff (this is a *contest*, just as in Chapter 4). The tactics
we have described, then, lose their meaning and fade into other
patterns of interaction based on conditions for making the
family aware.

Even before the patient's moribund status is obvious, other
conditions may initiate the transition to confirmed awareness
among family members. When staff members are certain that
the patient will soon die, they feel that "someone must be
told," that at least one family member has the right to know.
If none seems strong enough, then a close friend is selected,
who discusses with the doctor when various family members
should be told. At the other extreme, when disclosure is direct,
the patient is told first, and he tells the family. The general
procedure, however, is to disclose first to the closest or most
intimate family member deemed strong enough to take the
blow. This person sooner or later tells others, and the news
spreads through the family.

Another factor encouraging disclosure is that family members can help with terminal care, and thus facilitate the ordeal associated with dying. Linked with this factor is an important one we have already mentioned—disclosing to family members gives them time to prepare themselves for the patient's death. Hopefully, this preparation also renders family members composed enough to help during the final ordeal.

Immediate contingencies, especially for short-term and emergency dying patients, often make it essential to tell family members quickly, so that they can authorize a treatment or an operation, take leave of the patient, and make social, financial, and emotional preparations. Sometimes a relative must make a lengthy journey if he is to see the patient before he dies. Under these emergency conditions, relatives may feel cheated if they are not told promptly enough to give them a chance to participate in the patient's last days or hours. Participation may not only be a personal need of a family member, but also may be expected of him by friends and other relatives. A general norm in American culture is that no one should die alone; preferably, death should be attended by a close relative.[2] Telling the family too late may mean that the patient's life may have to be unduly prolonged while awaiting the arrival of a relative. On the other hand, too sudden a disclosure may leave the family ill prepared to cope with these last-minute activities, and results can be traumatic indeed. Other factors that affect disclosure to the family are its ethnic status, language, religion, and education, as well as the degree of rapport with the doctor. These are among the criteria that a doctor uses to judge whether the members want, and can take the news, and whether he will be able to make them understand the nature of the patient's illness.[3]

  [2] See Robert Fulton, "Death and Self," *Journal of Religion and Health.* 4 (July 1964), p. 364, for properties of this norm.
  [3] The relationship of social factors such as ethnic status, social class, language, religion, education to properties of disclosure to the family (particularly if, when, and how) is an important research problem. The research should also develop the intervening interaction process that links the relationship of a social factor to a kind of disclosure.

TRANSITIONS TO AWARENESS

Staff members use a great many special tactics to ease the family's transition to awareness. Most of these tactics are relatively purposeful variations on the general procedure for disclosing terminality to the family.

The customary assumption that "someone must be told" has resulted, in some hospitals, in formal procedures for gradual disclosures to families. At some point in the patient's progress toward death—this point varies, but typically it occurs when uncertainty becomes firm certainty—he is put on a critically or seriously ill list. This action, usually ordered by the doctor, sets in motion many activities designed to bring at least one family member into awareness. If none are on the scene, a wire is automatically sent to the closest kin: "Your (wife) has been put on the seriously ill list, please come at once." Or a phone call is made: "You'd better come over here, your little boy is injured." These communications, while short of full disclosure of terminality, create suspicion and prepare a family member for full disclosure as soon as he reaches the hospital. Once on the ward the family member is ushered into the privacy of a room or office and is gently told by the doctor, "Unless he takes a turn for the better, I'm afraid he won't pull through." The doctor then answers questions, while other staff members come to complete the process of making the relative aware of the impending death. A nurse, social worker, nun, clerk or chaplain may take over the last stages of the transition in an effort to avert a possible breakdown or a scene.

The same process of disclosure is also followed when the expectations of an aware family member must be altered in a direction closer to death; for example, from "uncertain" and "time unknown" to "certain" and "time imminent." When the hospital has no formal procedures, the doctor may initiate the process on his own, or a nurse may initiate it by reminding the doctor that the patient has reached a stage that warrants

making the family aware or changing their death expectations.
For family members who are continually asking for information,
this disclosure process need only be made part of answering
their latest questions by telling them the new diagnosis. For their
part, some family members simply refuse to believe the patient
will die, "no matter what any of those doctors say."

Gentle disclosure. When the patient's condition, especially
the rate at which he is dying, permits it, gentle disclosure to
the family is preferred. Gentleness may be accomplished by
delegating disclosure to the nurse; although the impact of the
doctor's authoritative presence is then absent, disclosure is
softened by the woman's touch. One nurse reported: "Sometimes they do not realize—I gently try to say 'He's not improving' and then 'He's failing a bit.' " She was trying to coax
the family into awareness. Another nurse waits until the family
seems ready before disclosing: "I let the lead come from them
[parents]—I have some personal feelings that some people
aren't ready to talk about this, that people have to work something through before they can talk about it or are even ready
to talk."

The nurse may be a bit more brusque if she has been
trapped into bearing sad tidings by a doctor who wants to
evade the task by delegating it to her. The doctor in this
situation tells the family that "they" are not sure yet and to
check back with the nurse who will be authorized to give the
diagnosis. The nurse, in turn, may express her resentment of
this strategy by dealing rather harshly with the patient's family.
In this case the doctor's higher status permits him to saddle
the nurse with the "dirty work," even though ethics call for
disclosure to come from the higher status person.[4]

Doctors too often make disclosure gentle by saying, "We're

[4] For properties of "dirty work," see Everett C. Hughes, *Men and
Their Work* (New York: Free Press of Glencoe, 1958), pp. 49-52,
70-72, 122, 137. Hughes sees "dirty work" as a task of a professional
that is physically, socially and morally beneath his dignity. While
disclosing to a family is not beneath the doctor's dignity, it is simply
a difficult task that his superior status may allow him to delegate
nurses.

doing all we can," or "It's out of our hands now," and then outlining what will come. This briefing tactic can be usefully interwoven with the known tendency of family members to take care of each other. In one case a doctor faced seven family members, including the patient's wife, who was on the verge of collapse. The doctor first briefed the whole group together, then took the wife to the patient's bedside. When she was ready to leave the patient, obviously close to breaking under the strain, the doctor returned her to the waiting family, who immediately gathered around her in close collective support. At this point the doctor disappeared, signaling the nurses to stay away. Thus the weakest family member was brought into awareness, without imposing on the staff the burden of "picking up the pieces." In addition, the doctor could phrase his briefing in fairly technical language because the family provided its own emotional support and control for the wife. Had the wife been alone this would have been too harsh an approach. The presence of stronger family members protected the doctor by permitting him to keep the wife at a safe distance, emotionally. The social distance imposed by the use of technical language made it doubly appropriate for the family to gather round and help the wife; it also released the doctor from the need to express much sympathy, so that he could better maintain his own composure during the strain of instigating the transition to awareness.

A prime means of softening disclosure to the family is to leave out the temporal dimension of the impending death, which makes the event itself appear less certain than it is. By saying, "It's out of our hands now," the doctor implies that he is helpless, unable to stop the illness or to ascertain when death will come. As death approaches, and it becomes appropriate to reveal the time it is expected to occur, a doctor may either be very vague—"It will be a short time"—or abandon his effort to soften the blow, making his announcement precise enough to enable the family to pace its preparations more correctly, if not comfortably.

Gentle disclosure can have negative effects on both family

and staff; these must always be weighed against the possible positive effects of a harsher disclosure. A gentle disclosure may be too weak to stimulate adequate family preparation. Leaving out the temporal dimension in disclosure also risks lack of preparation by the family, for family members invariably give their loved one more time than he actually has.[5] If they are not completely ready for the death they may miss the opportunity to participate in the patient's last hours. In addition, unprepared family members are still prone to surprises and shock. Thus they are more likely to trouble the staff at the time of death, with breakdowns that might have been forestalled. They are also less able to decide upon and attend to such matters as autopsy, disposal of the body, dispersing the patient's personal effects and meeting his obligations to the hospital.

Harsher disclosure. Accident, suicide attempts and sudden onset of critical illness may require a relatively abrupt, surprising disclosure to the family, if death is very likely to occur immediately. The harshness with which a surprise disclosure is made depends both on how near the patient is to death, and on the family's physical proximity to the patient. When the family is not on the scene, the phone call or telegram "to come quickly" will create an expectation strong enough to prepare them to accept confirmation of their suspicions on arrival. The suspicion preceding full disclosure ameliorates the shock of suddenly learning that a member of the family is dying. Sometimes suspicion is raised by an event such as the infamous church bombing in Birmingham—for one Negro mother whose daughter was killed in the explosion, the announcement of death merely confirmed a realization that occurred as soon as she heard the bomb explode. The family on the scene whose relative has yet a day to live may also be eased quickly into

[5] In contrast, the family tends to give a relative in the recovery status *less* time than it takes to get well. See Fred Davis, *Passage Through Crisis* (Indianapolis: Bobbs-Merrill, 1963), Chapter 4.

awareness this way, with a suspicion announcement to be confirmed later in the same day.

Often, however, the patient's condition changes so fast that there is simply no time to prepare family members in advance or to indulge in the comparative luxury of a gentle disclosure. A non-terminal patient may suddenly turn "bad" while a family member is visiting, or a patient's heart may stop beating while his family is waiting for him to come out of the operating room. In these cases family members are practically present at a death for which they are totally unprepared. Someone must tell them, and if a doctor is not present—as is often the case when the patient was not expected to become terminal so suddenly—a nurse may disclose without doctor's orders. One nurse told a son and his wife during a visit, "Your mother is barely breathing. I don't expect her to last the hour"—a direct disclosure with both dimensions of the death expectation put clearly and succinctly. The nurse realized that she had no time for a preliminary suspicion announcement; she had to give the family a chance to prepare and participate as soon as they could collect themselves. Aware of her breach of normal ethics, she said, "I *had* to tell them. You couldn't say please step outside. I had to tell them."

Because they prefer to announce an *impending* death, however rapidly it may be approaching, rather than an *unexpected* death, which may occur while the family steps outside, nurses may feel forced to disclose dying on the spot in an abrupt manner. If a nurse must announce a death—which she must if the family faces an obviously dead patient—even before the patient is officially pronounced dead by a doctor, the strain on both nurse and family is great, and a scene is almost sure to follow. An announcement of this kind is also a more serious breach of professional announcement ethics than an unauthorized statement that the patient is dying. Quick action is often essential, too, for if the nurse, in asking the family to step outside, permits the family members to suspect that death will be immediate, she may lose control over their behavior. In one case, a relative, asked to step outside, became suspicious and ran back into the room to find the patient dead; she grabbed his hand and wouldn't let go. In another case the relative tried to revive the patient by rubbing his cheek. In both cases the relatives had to be removed from the room by the staff. In short, it is generally much less disruptive for all concerned if the nurse can announce unexpected, sudden dying instead of unexpected, sudden death.

The shock for the family is most harsh, of course, when death is so sudden that no disclosure of immediately impending death is possible. In this limiting case the notion of a *non-awareness* context applies to staff, patient, and family; all normal sentiments surrounding the patient are abruptly shattered. Everyone involved is surprised, but of course the family is hardest hit. (Victims of sudden heart attacks typically die with a look of complete surprise on their faces. A doctor called in for such an emergency reported that this surprised look was mixed with hatred for the regular physician who had, only a few days before, pronounced him in perfect condition.)

Staff members too can be so shaken by the surprise that they make untoward gestures and indelicate announcements. In one case friends had surrounded the wife of a stricken man to protect her from unduly blunt disclosure, but the doctor in desperation and helplessness said loudly, "There is nothing I can do. The man will die in a few moments." The friends judged that the impact on the wife was harsher than it would have been had the disclosure been less abrupt.

In an emergency ward case, just after a surprise death, staff members discovered the patient's mother in the waiting room. The doctor was so involved in the technical aspects of the death, since its details were somewhat threatening to his self-confidence and medical competence, that he simply went over to the mother, told her the son's fate, and walked off in a state of preoccupation. The public nature of this unexpected announcement was devastating to the mother. Other people in the room, including staff members, were highly indignant at the "absolute cruelty" of the doctor. Finally realizing what he had done, the doctor took the woman into a private room to smooth over the situation.

Disclosure space. As our description of the disclosure procedure suggests, management of space is a strategic factor in bringing families into awareness. Ideally it occurs in the privacy of a closed room. At the opposite extreme, space is disregarded, as in the case just described, and disclosure occurs through a blunt surprise announcement made in a public place filled with people. The less urgent the situation—for instance, uncertainty, with time unknown—the more likely a doctor is to disclose in the hallway instead of his office. Even in the hallway, privacy varies—some places are virtually private and others are full of heavy traffic. In a closed context, the patient's room is generally taboo for disclosure to the family, though the ends of larger ward rooms or rooms of comatose patients may not be.

Variations in the effort to manage space depend on the amount of time the doctor has available (as determined by the rate at which the patient is dying as well as the doctor's work load), and his relations with both the patient and his family. The spatial provisions the hospital has made for family members are also important. Some wards have their own waiting rooms. Some hospitals provide only a central waiting room on the ground floor, and others provide no facilities at all except perhaps a chair in the hallway. These various places may be used for less urgent disclosures that seem to require less than complete privacy. Invariably, however, all hospitals have near at hand a room or office where disclosure can be made privately.

No disclosure. Under certain conditions, the preferred strategy, or non-strategy, is simply not to make an explicit disclosure. When the doctor thinks that terminality is obvious, in view of the patient's visibly moribund condition, he feels that he need not initiate the disclosure process, expecting family members to realize what is happening, and to seek help from a chaplain, nurse or social worker for their preparations, or make an appointment with him if they need information. While in many cases his observation is correct, in others it is an avoidance strategy, when the doctor is not "up" to announcing an impending death. Doctors who do not like the "death-sentence" responsibility tend to force everyone to operate on a suspicion level until the patient's condition becomes obvious.

An important aspect of the physical arrangement of wards is the degree of visibility the family, not actually at his bedside, has of the patient. The physical arrangement of a ward which allows high visibility may encourage a doctor to conclude that the patient's status is obvious to family members. For example, in many emergency wards, family members need only look and listen through a door—usually open—beyond which staff members are frantically working on the patient, and they can confirm any suspicion they might have that the patient is dying. Some emergency wards have bedrooms, treatment rooms, and operating rooms arranged around a nursing station, with the waiting area for families nearby. Family members cannot help observing their relative as he is hustled from room to room, and usually this permits them to get a good idea of his chances —or even to see his death. And what is not seen is easily imaginable, or can be filled in by observing other visible patients who are in a similar condition.

On most types of hospital wards, however, the waiting family is completely segregated from the patient and from the areas in which treatment occurs. Under these circumstances, family members know only what they are told until they are permitted to see the patient. The patient's condition may by then be glaringly obvious. However, in this latter instance the staff has a chance to prepare the family and thus to avoid possible disruptive consequences of not disclosing.[6]

[6] In this chapter we did not consider what happens when the patient is aware and the family is not. If this occurs in the open context then the family members will be readily brought in except for those members who could obviously not take it. A more interesting situation, which bears research, is when the patient is aware and the context is closed—the staff do not know he is aware—and the family is unaware. The burden is on the patient to pretend to family members that all is going all right. This happens in heart cases when a patient knows he could go any time, but does not tell his family that he even is a heart case.

10

The Aware
Family

No clear line divides the family in transition to awareness from the fully aware family, but staff members can see the difference, and they change their tactics accordingly. Once a family is aware that the patient is dying, managing that family takes on new dimensions. Perhaps the most critical change is in its visiting patterns. The usual relaxation of visiting restrictions for an aware family creates for the staff new problems associated with maintaining family privacy, helping family members maintain their composure and prepare for the patient's death, and also coping with their intensified need for information.

VISITING

Relaxation of Visiting Rules. When they learn that the patient is dying, relatives usually increase their visits, coming more often and in larger numbers, and more of them visit on private schedules. (Sometimes, of course, particularly for the old, neglected patients in state hospitals, family members stop coming altogether after they become aware of the impending death; this may also happen sometimes to young patients who are estranged from their families.) If the awareness context is kept closed to the patient, these increased visits can become an obvious cue that must be managed by both staff and family to reduce the patient's suspicion of his true condition. Otherwise the increased visits may inadvertently transform the awareness context to an open one or to one of mutual pretense.

155

To accommodate these increased visits, hospital and ward rules are relaxed. Family members are allowed to visit patients at almost any time, and one member may be permitted to stay "around the clock." In the case of one woman, "as soon as the physician informed her family, the patient became the center of attention of several sisters and brothers, her own children and many grandchildren, nieces and nephews, all of whom crowded the small TV room every day, staying long beyond visiting hours, and hovering about her with affectionate attentions." [1] The family expects the rules to be relaxed or waived, "under the circumstances," and the nurse who does not relax visiting rules for at least some of the relatives risks a family protest that may be carried to top administrative levels for a decision. In contrast, the obstetrics ward of one hospital, which of course is not used to having dying patients, does not alter its visiting rules for the family of a woman who is "posted" as terminal. The work of the ward is geared only to the routine of taking care of healthy women and their babies.

Obviously this influx of family members creates many management problems for the staff. One problem is to see that the patient has enough rest. Sheer numbers of people can sap the patient's energy, and even when the nurse tries to limit unrestrained visiting to the intimate kin, there may still be too many people and visits. Another difficulty that interferes with rest is that some families "bother" the patient or "pick, pick, pick" just as they are used to doing at home. But since the nurse relaxes visiting rules at her own discretion, she can control a troublesome visitor by reinstituting the regulations for a good cause, and send him back to the waiting room or even out of the hospital.

The patient's domestic problems may follow him to his deathbed in another form: especially when visiting rules are relaxed, independent sets of family members may visit simultaneously. Hostile interaction at his bedside, between his first

[1] Rose Laub Coser, *Life in the Ward* (East Lansing: Michigan State University Press, 1962), p. 59.

and second wives, is hardly restful to a dying patient.[2] In one case an embarrassed nurse had to ask one wife and her children to leave the room and wait their turn. But in other cases, independent family groups, who might be unwilling to tolerate each other's presence under ordinary circumstances, join forces in this grave situation to make the patient's last weeks or days as comfortable as possible.

Weekend Leave-Taking. Another problem for the nurse, made more acute by the relaxed regulations, is that of the repeated weekend farewell. Aware family members who live out of town sometimes come every weekend during the last weeks, thinking each time that they may be taking leave of the patient forever. If the patient is not aware that he is dying, the nurse must try to allay the suspicion generated by all these tearful farewells. Ultimately this weekly scene may create a context of mutual pretense awareness between patient and staff, which the staff initiates, and which is potentially harmful to the patient's faith in the staff. And if the family lives a hundred miles away or more, the nurse cannot assure them that they will be notified in time if the patient takes a turn for the worse. They must come each weekend, not knowing which will be the last. In some hospitals these problems are maximized because a high ratio of terminal patients live out of town.

Attention Patterns. Stable family relations are built on many standard patterns which are broken only for special reasons. One such pattern—attention given and expected—is very often broken by aware families. Relatives not only visit more often when they learn that the patient is dying, but they bring flowers and candy; they kiss and reminisce, and so on. To the patient, these are unexpected, perhaps unprecedented, attentions. If he is to be kept unaware (often at the family's request), the nurse must control these revealing gestures. She can sometimes

[2] This is a problem on the increase for nurses with the increase both of dying in hospitals and of the divorce rate.

invoke rules to prevent some attentions—the patient must not be touched, relatives are not allowed on the patient's bed unless a staff member is present, flowers are not allowed except in private rooms, etc. She can also try to explain away the unprecedented attentions when the patient becomes suspicious. Family members also must explain away unexpected attentions, even so simple a one as a visit from a relative who ordinarily "wouldn't cross the street" to see the patient unless something was drastically amiss.

An aware family in the closed awareness context has many opportunities to disclose unwittingly to the patient. As the interaction continues, staff and family efforts to keep him at least only suspicious must eventually fail, altering the awareness context from closed or suspicion to mutual pretense, or causing it to vacillate between these states. For example: "The sister told me that on Thursday night before Alice died, all her family was sitting around her bedside and she was sleeping or pretending to be asleep, when suddenly she opened her eyes and in clear and angry tones said, 'What is this, a death watch?' "[3] Since no one made an explicit disclosure in this situation, no one ever knew whether the patient died in a state of suspicion, or pretense. Consequently, all interaction between family and patient had been designed to reduce suspicion and maintain the pretense.[4]

Status-Forcing Scenes. When nurses relax the visiting rules they raise the risk of having to face "status-forcing" scenes.[5] Giving the family relatively free access to the patient means that family members are always around to observe and judge

[3] Florence Joseph, "Transference and Counter Transference in the Case of a Dying Patient," *Psychoanalysis, and the Psychoanalytic Interview* (Winter, 1962).
[4] This is a good example of how an open awareness context would have saved family and patient much wasted effort, and would have allowed them to participate as a total family in preparing themselves for the death.
[5] On "status forcing" see Anselm Strauss, *Mirrors and Masks* (New York: Free Press of Glencoe, 1959), pp. 76-84.

the patient's care. All too often this untutored concern is focused on trivia, or it takes the form of demands for undue heroics. Relatives try to force staff members to make these unnecessary or extra efforts by reminding them of their obligations as medical-care experts; they force them to enact their official roles, perhaps with threats or reprisals if they do not.

In the "status-forcing" scene which ensues, the nurse must adopt tactics which vary by how much she can satisfy the family member without compromising her own position or harming the patient. If, for example, the treatment begged or demanded is not feasible, the nurse can give the family member an "expert" or technical reason, using a slightly rough manner to remind the relative that knowledgeable discipline is required in such a serious situation. Hopefully, the family member will submit to these technical exigencies; apart from being cowed by the nurse's brusque manner, believing that the restrictions are technical helps him to limit and control his own expectations. But if the family member does not subside, he can be insulated from staff by being put in a waiting room filled with people (in essence he is "drowned out" of interaction with staff) and told to await information on changes in the patient's condition.

When relatives beg for impossibly heroic measures, nurses make every effort to accompany their "reasonable" refusal with comforting measures such as sedation or a shoulder to cry on. One nurse told us that a woman who begged for heroics to save her husband, "rushed into my arms, crumpled on my chest, buried her face between my two little breasts, crying and wailing. I held her and let her cry." Meanwhile another nurse said, "Do we have any liquid amytol to make her drink, to calm her down?" On the other hand, when the patient's case is hopeless, the family may ask the staff to stop treatments that result in the "useless" prolonging of life so painful to all concerned.

Family members use status-forcing scenes also to motivate the staff to do everything possible, to the very end. As patients near death it often becomes evident that certain treatments are superfluous, and staff members may slack off a little. A family member who witnesses this may panic, accusing the staff of negligence and promising that "if a stone is left unturned," someone will pay. This forces the staff to continue the superfluous treatments, which can be very frustrating because they accomplish nothing. To overcome this frustration, nurses often switch their motivated involvement to the family, thinking of the treatment for the patient as if it were actually for the distraught relative. We have termed this tactic "object switching." It is a general tactic that nurses used to cope with their helplessness in giving superfluous or meaningless care to a dying (or any other kind) patient. In switching their involvement to another party to the situation, they feel they are actually working for this person and not for the patient. Switching involvement to another person both motivates the nurse to go on working and starts a new relationship with the person switched to, which has interactional consequences. We shall have occasion to mention this tactic again.[6]

If staff members are not careful, status-forcing scenes may produce conflict within the staff, as when a relative tries to enlist one staff member on his side in an argument with another. A relative may express various kinds of dissatisfaction with a nurse, for instance, to get the doctor to order superfluous treatment, and the doctor may very well comply, perhaps because he is concerned about his relations with the family (a problem common to private physicians), or perhaps because he believes the family member is right. In one case, a doctor "who was interested in little items of care" saw to it that the nurses turned the patient regularly, at least while he and the nurses were under pressure from the family. The clinical purpose of this requirement was unknown to the nurses, but they did it—"usually just before the relatives arrived."

[6] "Object switching" is a general strategy in all work that people use to keep up motivation for a task, the object of which they either have *no* involvement in (*e.g.*, assembly line work) or *too much* (*e.g.*, dying).

Normally, of course, nurses and doctors cooperate to keep the family happy, providing as much superfluous care as is harmless and not too time consuming. This collusion is to a certain extent a response to the family's power over the staff: [7] an irate relative can compromise the whole staff by seeking "a doctor who will do something!"—sometimes the "best doctor" at a university medical center, but also sometimes a marginal doctor, or an outright quack. Thus the power over the patient's care that staff members derive from their superior medical knowledge is partially offset by the family's power to search for another doctor or hospital. If present care does not meet expectations, this search becomes more urgent and less discriminating. This balance of forces between family and staff is implicit in every status-forcing scene.

Privacy versus Care. As long as visiting regulations are enforced, it is not difficult for nurses to respect the general social norm that family privacy should not be violated.[8] When the family is allowed only certain hours with the patient, staff members can care for the patient freely during the remainder of the day without worrying about whether they will interrupt a family gathering. But when family members are constantly present at the dying patient's bedside, the nurse must resort to interaction tactics. Her daily round takes her in and out of the patient's room periodically. When visiting rules have been waived, she must consider each time whether a family member is there, whether he requires privacy and whether her task overrules the demands of privacy. If her task cannot wait, then the relevant question is whether she can carry it out in front of a family member without grossly violating the normal

[7] The collusion plays of one team as a coping response to the power of another is intimated in Erving Goffman, *Presentation of Self in Everyday Life* (New York: Doubleday Anchor Books, 1959).

[8] On the societal structure of privacy see: Alan P. Bates, "Privacy—A Useful Concept?", *Social Forces*, Vol. 42 (May 1964). See also Arthur Stinchcombe, "Institutions of Privacy in the Determination of Police Administration," *American Journal of Sociology*, 69 (September 1963), pp. 150-160.

privacy expectations. Such tasks as feeding, taking blood pressure, marking charts, and giving arm shots can be accomplished in the presence of others, since these tasks at most merely suspend private conversation for a short time.

Certain nursing tasks cannot ordinarily be performed in front of family members however: those that require body exposure and manipulation for medication, bathing, changing bandages and the like. In American society a stranger, no matter how legitimate his purpose, cannot usually expose or touch certain areas of an adult's body in the presence of an intimate of the person, for this is considered an intrusion into their private relationship.[9]

Family privacy is often disturbed by the nurses' need to care for other patients in the same room. A way to handle this problem so that the family will not be disturbed, nor the nurse's routine disrupted, is to provide the family a room or section thereof, an office, an isolated part of the hall, or simply a curtain around the patient's bed, where family members can feel secure from interruptions not directly involved in their relative's care.[10] Nurses assure the visiting family that this region is entirely given over to their private contacts with the patient; by the same token, they assure themselves freedom from having to defer to ever-present relatives.

Management of Space. The private-region solution to the dilemma of privacy versus care depends, of course, on the availability of sufficient space. When family members are allowed to visit constantly, the general problem of distributing

[9] An American wife returning from France with her husband, who had to have an operation commented on this norm: "As was expected of me in the United States, I had gone out during the examination." (This examination was on the lower right side of the husband's body.) Lael T. Wertenbaker, *Death of a Man* (New York: Random House, 1951), p. 37. This norm of privacy is common knowledge to all husbands who have been with their wife in labor. Husbands are asked to leave the labor room when the doctor performs a rectal examination of the dilation of the cervix.

[10] In Asian hospital wards where there are up to 40-60 or more beds, a screen is usual—with other patients therefore cut out from the scene.

space, always present in hospitals, becomes critical. Increased visits from an entire family can inundate a waiting room or the patient's room. Status-forcing scenes absorb halls and waiting rooms, since these scenes tend to drive other people away, and a patient's room becomes too small when two or more independent family units are present. At one hospital, a gypsy family with its twenty-plus members overflowing everywhere caused confusion throughout the ward. To maintain order in the ward, and especially to protect the space around the patient, family members must be carefully distributed throughout the ward, or even the hospital.

Certain criteria emerge for distributing family members. The members who obviously cannot be helpful, who are on the verge of collapse, or who are likely to create a scene, may be insulated from the staff and patient by being directed to offices, to waiting rooms or "treatment rooms" on the ward or to the hospital lobby. In cases like this, visiting rules may be reinvoked with the implication that they will be relaxed again later.

Another criterion for distributing the family throughout the hospital is the visitor's relation to the patient. To prevent inundation of the patient's room by many family members, the nurse may restrict close contact with the patient for any length of time to the closest relatives (usually children, parents, or spouse). Relatives in the immediate family (cousins, aunts and uncles) are allowed to come less often; they are put in waiting rooms on the ward and told when they can approach the patient for a brief visit. Distant relatives may be asked to wait in the main lobby of the hospital; they are permitted to come to the ward waiting room only during regular visiting hours, and then they must wait their turn for a few minutes with the patient.

This criterion for distribution dovetails neatly with the tactic of letting family members take care of each other. Often the strongest or most dependable member is in the immediate family and is therefore likely to be readily available in the ward waiting room, to help console an intimate family member who breaks down at the patient's bedside. The strong family mem-

ber can then, if needed, take the sobbing one down to the lobby
to receive the support of the whole family. Keeping the intimate
family members close at hand also allows them to spell each
other at the patient's bedside, thus reducing the strain on any
one member.

Under the stress of waiting, however, family members may
develop "drift routes," the more distant relatives trying to get
closer by slipping back up the scale of distance the staff has
put between them and the patient. They drift up elevators, out
of waiting rooms, and past the nursing station to the patient's
door and in to his bedside. When they are noticed and challenged, they obligingly return to their assigned waiting space
but soon they start drifting back again. Nurses do have some
control over this tendency, especially in the intensive care wards
where space is at a premium. Once at the door the family member usually stops and peeks through a window or otherwise
attracts a nurse's attention. She may either invite him in or
give him a time to return for a legitimate visit. As long as
relatives acknowledge this "door norm," nurses have a means
of control that they can use to redistribute the family members
to their appropriate waiting places.

The Relative as Worker or Patient. A hospital visitor cannot remain at his dying kinsman's bedside for very long without
taking on a role—other than that of relative or visitor—suggested by the situation, one that integrates him with the staff's
daily work. Since the "kinsman" or "relative" role is external
to and often interferes with hospital routine, it is useful to
classify the relative in such a way that he becomes a dependable
participant in the work context. The two major roles adopted
by family members are "patient" and "worker," both of which
link them directly to daily activity.

A less frequent alternative is to turn the constant visitor
into a "non-person." Completely ignored and discounted, "non-
person" relatives are least disturbing to staff work. In state and
county hospitals for the aged, and in VA hospitals and on
emergency wards, where family visits are less common, few

provisions are made for them, and the non-person alternative is frequently used. Often under these conditions, however, staff members have so little time and interest for individual patients that they prefer to convert relatives to workers instead.

Of the two major roles, the preferred role is usually that of *worker*. If the relatives are going to be around all the time they might as well help, so the rationale goes, and the simple fact that many dying patients require more than the normal amount of attention prompts the nurses to ease their burden by taking advantage of family members' constant presence. A relative may help without being clearly cognizant of it, merely by watching the patient. A nurse can leave a patient who must be watched with a family member who does not know that he is actually doing a job, because she can depend on him to notify her if something happens. Or, she can ask the family member to watch for a specific change or even for death and call her immediately; in return, the relative is left in privacy with the patient. Sometimes the family member is clearly aware of being part of the medical team and is grateful for the chance to help. Help can vary from such tasks as keeping a cool cloth on a patient's forehead to taking over most nursing care, as when the relative is also a nurse. Of course, as we have indicated, the family member must usually be aware that the patient is dying before he can be an effective helper. An unaware relative may very well become confused and panicky if the patient's condition changes, and hence he is not dependable enough to be used as a worker in an emergency.

In the hospitals we studied, family participation is not institutionalized, and the nurse who initiates and permits it is held responsible for what the family worker does. But in two hospitals described in the literature, the family is worked into the daily round and therefore bears responsibility.[11] Not only does this give the nurse more time for other patients, but it

[11] See K. M. Carpenter and J. M. Stewart, "Parents Take Heart at City of Hope," *American Journal of Nursing*, 62 (October 1962), pp. 82-85; and Leonard Reissman and John H. Rohrer, *Change and Dilemma in the Nursing Profession* (New York: G. P. Putnam's Sons, 1957), pp. 28-48.

means that the family shares any imputation of negligence in the care of a dying patient. Family helpers were used, in the hospitals we studied, most extensively by nurses who could accept sharing their work, but not their responsibility. In the City of Hope Hospital, nurses in the "parent participation program" on the pediatrics ward were chosen for their ability to share both work and responsibility; but in Charity Hospital, staffing was so difficult that nurses or aides had no choice but to work with "visiting attendant" family members.

As we shall see in more detail in the next chapter, aware families are also screened to see whether they can help or even take over certain decision-making responsibilities. They are asked about alternative treatments, operation strategies, different forms of hospitalization, disclosure to the patient and—the most crucial issue—whether the patient's life should be prolonged, given the specific contingencies of the case. These grave responsibilities can be delegated to the aware family only if it is prepared for the patient's demise.

Under some conditions, nurses treat a family member as if he were another *patient*. The mother of a dying premature infant is formally a patient. But family members who are not formally patients may break down or become paralyzed with the news of their kinsman's impending death and, for the moment anyway, they become patients, given sedation, comfort, and consolation and put to rest in the hospital or at home. Nurses with a psychotherapeutic orientation turn family members into patients in helping them prepare for the death of their kinsman. And a nurse sometimes relieves the strain of a status-forcing scene, as we have noted, by shifting the focus of her involvement from the patient, whose case is hopeless anyway, to the family member who is pressing for more care. In essence, she turns from a patient who is lost to a patient who will live and can gain substantially from her efforts, thus sparing herself the frustrating helplessness of being able to do nothing for the moribund patient. In "object switching" she directs her efforts to where rewards can be anticipated.

In sum, the relaxation of visiting rules alters the relations between nurses and family members. When the rules are enforced, family members are allotted a specified time alone with the patient, and the nurse schedules her work accordingly. Her interaction with the family consists mostly of greeting relatives and ushering them in and out. But when the visiting rules are relaxed or waived, the nurse may be in more or less constant contact with the family, and she must find a way to integrate these exchanges with her work routine. She can do this most advantageously by assigning the visitor a role— preferably as a worker, but also as a patient who fits into the hospital routine. This tactic also helps resolve the privacy-versus-work dilemma. The family helper has a useful period of privacy with the patient, and the family patient can legitimately be separated from the dying patient for rest and quiet preparation.

PREPARATION FOR DEATH

Degrees of Preparation. Staff and family members both benefit from disclosure to the family, for disclosure makes it possible for the family members to compose themselves with preparations for their relative's impending death. Depending on the way the staff handles the disclosure, and the type of expectation the family is given at the time, disclosure may result in various degrees of preparation. Perhaps the most important condition is the type of death expectation given the family when it is brought into awareness. On the basis of this expectation the family establishes the delicate balance between accepting and not accepting the patient's fate. This balance results in a degree of preparation which, in turn, determines the family's relative ability to remain composed during dying and at death.

Maximum forewarning occurs when the family is told that the patient is certain to die at a specific time. In this situation, the family members can time the settling of affairs and manage their feelings of grief so as to be most fully prepared; and at death staff members will probably say, "They are taking it very well," "She was wonderful," or "She was trembling, but weren't we all."

Family members who are told that the patient will die, but at an unknown time, will be relatively well prepared at the end, but less so than if they had known when death would occur. Not having had a time limit, they will still have some arrangements to make. The death may still come unexpectedly, and therefore be more disturbing than it might otherwise have been. Families usually give the patient more time than he has, if the doctor does not specify time of death; and since doctors tend to prefer a gentle disclosure in which time is often not specified, most families find themselves in this situation.

When the family is told that death is uncertain, they are in effect alerted to begin preparation without giving up hope. If the time that they can expect a resolution of the uncertainty is also unknown, their preparation is likely to be very slight. Some families simply refuse to begin preparing, and just continue to hope. Staff members find that families in this situation are hardest to handle, since death comes to them as a surprise, and they have made virtually no preparations to help maintain their composure. A family with this degree of awareness may therefore act similarly to an unaware family.

Staff members (employing the transition strategies mentioned in the last chapter) therefore try to help the relatives change their expectations as the patient's condition worsens, so that they will begin to settle the patient's affairs and consider what life will be like after his death. The general process of revising the family's expectations to fit the patient's true condition is contingent on other factors that both help and hinder the revision. Altering the family expectation only with cues is apt to leave it on a suspicion level of awareness, still in doubt. The family that still has doubts is likely to continue hoping, which in turn reduces preparation. On the other hand, staff members are reluctant to announce a definite time; although

they are sure of the time they do not like to be held accountable
for it. A nurse put it so: "I do not like to play God." In one
case, a mother spent her days at her son's bedside, expecting
him to die but, since time was unknown, not expecting death
for a while. Suddenly she noticed that the boy's breathing
had become more difficult, and thinking he might soon die, she
asked the nurse about it. The nurse avoided the issue, leaving
her suspicious but uncertain, so that when the boy did die
the blow was harder than it would have been had the nurse
verified her suspicions.

We reiterate, families tend to give patients more time than
they have—it is a way of sustaining hope. Without a roughly
specific idea of the time of death, family members may tend
to delay their preparations on the basis of a short-run expectation that the patient will continue to live for a while. They
expect him to be alive the following day, even when they are
certain he will die sometime. They expect, therefore, a daily
or even a weekly living relationship with him, forgetting the
end must come. But doctors and nurses can encourage family
preparation, and thereby enhance composure, by keeping family
members up to date with realistic expectations. To this end, it
is advisable for staff to give accurate responses to family members who are testing suspicions, even though this may require
them to make the statement of probable time of death that
they are generally reluctant to give.

The disclosing of time of expected death is also paced
according to the period of illness, both of which in turn affect
the amount of time the family has to complete preparations.
The patient who is certain to die, but at an unknown time, and
whose illness is a long, lingering one, provides the best opportunity for family preparation. Cases like this afford both
stimulus and time for grieving and for arranging affairs. The
problem here is to see that family members are told the expected time of death early enough to allow them to complete
their preparations. Of course, if the doctor gives no certain
expectation that death will occur in the foreseeable future, as is

most often the case, then the long illness may be of little benefit in allowing the family to prepare itself. When a transition
in expectations finally does occur, the family may have no
more time for preparation than the family that learns of the
impending death. only a few weeks in advance. Adequate
preparations take time—even when the family members are
told that the patient is certain to die in a few weeks so that
they are stimulated to make full preparations, these few weeks
may not be enough. Short-term illness, or a fatal accident,
often leaves the family only a few days or hours, but even
then an adequate expectation (certainty, known time) is necessary to stimulate even the minimal preparation that is possible.
Often, however, even on emergency wards where the patient
may be on the verge of dying, the family is only given an
uncertainty expectation. Thus even deaths expected by the
staff can be very surprising to a family that has not had adequate death expectations to stimulate its preparations.

   Illnesses associated with reprieve patterns—that is, the
patient is on the verge of death many times but recovers somewhat—hinder full preparation. Reprieves spark hope, so that
the family is never completely prepared for the death: They
think the next reprieve may be complete, not temporary. Thus,
even when the doctor announces a time of death, usually a few
days ahead of time, the family members may feel that the
"miraculous" return to life they have watched before might
happen again. As one uncle said, "It was hard to fully reconcile
ourselves since we've seen her revive before and she could
do it again." When a pattern like this is established, the family
may refuse to give up all hope even if the doctor tells them
they must, which may put the family through many "tortuous"
episodes—after each, wishing the patient had died. Further,
the short notice he is able to give them is usually not enough
to allow the family members time to reconcile themselves and
begin preparations.

   Linked with lingering and reprieve-pattern illnesses is the
ever constant hope that medical researchers will find a cure

in time: "They are working on it constantly." Some families travel from medical center to medical center and even make telephone calls to research centers all over the world to see how close "they" are to "the cure," adjusting their preparations accordingly.

Helpers of the Family. Family preparations are considerably affected by the people who step in to help them arrange affairs, listen to their grieving and reinforce their belief that death is certain. These helpers may form a well organized team, as in a Catholic hospital where a nurse reported: "If I'm with the patient and their relatives break down, I flash the signal light, and a head nurse comes to take them to sister or the priest." In this hospital there were three "floating" sisters whose only job was to help families and patients through critical periods. Whenever a patient's condition became dangerous, the nun was called right away to help family members prepare themselves. She would give them a rationale for their current death expectation: "It's a blessing that he goes now rather than linger on for months." She may take them to the hospital chapel to pray and show them religious pictures. Grieving family members characteristically want to talk to someone about their impending loss: for the most part this talk is not focused, and it requires only a good listener. The sister's job is to listen patiently and sympathetically.

In other hospitals, chaplains, social workers and ward clerks help the family, thus relieving the nurses of a burden that might otherwise interfere with their normal obligations to other patients. When the hospital has no facilities for aiding families, and does not require the nurses to help the family (that is, their patient loads are not allocated with this consideration in mind), then family members are likely to be treated as "non-persons." In one such hospital for lower class people only the nurses whose hearts were touched—"these people are so neglected"—would bother to stop and talk with the relatives, sometimes offering them coffee from their own urns.

To be sure, the pattern typical of most hospitals is that both nurse and doctor spend a little time with the family. They listen for a few minutes and reinforce the family's death expectations with a supporting rationale. Other hospitals try to find social workers and chaplains who will help the family while the patient is dying, not just at death.

Helpers of the family can furnish support even when they are not aware that an individual is grieving. They need only be sensitive to the fact that the person is "going through something" and treat her with "great care so as not to make her spill over." One woman, sitting with a dying patient, became restless; tears trickled down her face, she tried to read, she went in the bathroom to freshen up, she went to the waiting room to be alone. The nurses did not think of her as grieving, but they realized that she was upset and did not "push" her by asking questions. They left her alone, ready to help her if she approached them.

This kind of support from nurses who are not precisely aware that someone is grieving helps to keep the relative from breaking down under the strain of waiting for the patient to die. If the nurse does not treat the relation as a grieving person, he is less likely to collapse just from receiving sympathy, and this in turn causes her to respect him for his emotional stamina.[12] Not only does her respect furnish additional support, but his apparent emotional control during waiting makes her more tolerant of minor breakdowns as the patient's end approaches. Had she been aware that the relative was grieving all along, she might have expected increasing restraint, and have been annoyed by even a minor breakdown at the end because by now he *should* have been well prepared. Thus paradoxically, giving explicit training in helping people prepare themselves for a death in the family is perhaps less important than using sensitivity as a criterion in selecting staff members to help the family.

[12] In another context it has been noted that undue sympathy breaks down the composure with which a person may be coping with a disagreeable physical condition: Fred Davis, "Deviance Disavowal," *Social Problems*, 9 (Fall 1961), pp. 122-125.

Stages of Grieving. Within a single family, individuals may be at different stages of grieving because each member may form a different kind of death expectation, or may be brought into awareness at a different time, or may require more or less time for grieving. Some relatives may spend more time with the patient, which stimulates more grieving. Usually a very close relative is "ahead" of the others; he has known for a longer period that death is certain, and he has probably spent more time with the patient. Having had more opportunity to complete his preparations for the patient's death, he is more likely to have finished grieving as well. But when a distant relative who arrives late on the scene is overcome with grief, he forces the more intimate one to act very sad, if not equally overcome, so as not to appear unduly callous about the loss of someone so close. (This "status forcing"—as in being forced to play the "wailing wife"—often occurs also at funerals.)

When lingering is very prolonged, family members may finish grieving before the patient is dead, which may be a source of strain to the family members. They may begin almost to resent the constant visiting. Men want to get back to work, women to their households. Money is being drained away. Beginning to wish the patient was dead, famliy members may feel intensely ambivalent or guilty. In situations of this kind, nurses and other helpers of the family can be most helpful if they have been aware of grieving and can sense the point at which it is ended. Then, as in cases we observed, nurses can assure the relatives that their feelings are normal and nothing to feel guilty about. They offer to spell the family at the patient's bedside—"Go home and wash up, I'll keep watch for you," "Go get your rest," or "Go get some coffee." Thus the family member relinquishes his position on the medical team little by little, as the nurse resumes the tasks she allocated to the family when the increased visiting began. Even if the patient is still alive, the family members gradually cease to help the staff, and their visiting diminishes, sometimes to the point where they do not visit at all. If money becomes short or the family does not want to pay hospital bills indefinitely, the lingering (often aged) patient may be sent to the geriatric ward (referred to by some personnel as the "vegetable patch") of a state hospital. There he is fed and given routine care, but he receives only infrequent visits from his family. One patient became comatose but lived on for years with scarcely a visit. In contrast, nurses who are less sensitive, or are unaware that family members can finish grieving before a patient dies, may feel disgusted with "rejecting" relatives, and of course this will affect their relations with the patient's family.

Nurses also grieve for their patients, though they may reserve emotional outbursts for later, private occasions. A pediatric nurse told us that she did not break down until a week later, and then when she was at home—only then did she realize that she too had to grieve for her patients. Because a nurse is usually less involved than family members, and because she is apt to be better informed about the patient's condition, she is normally at a more advanced stage of grieving at any given time. This gives her the stability and sympathy necessary if she is to help grieving relatives. Being at roughly the same stage of grieving can cause the nurse to avoid family members for fear she and they both will break down! If a nurse falls "behind" family members, perhaps because of denial or too brief a period of awareness or too short a time on the case, she risks treating an intimate relative in terms of her own grief, assuming that he too is still "very sad." This may revive the more painful stages of the relative's feelings of impending loss, which he has already gone through once. She also, like the family member who is "behind" the close relative in grieving, may force the relative to act "overcome."

INFORMATION

When a dying patient's family is brought into awareness, the members' need to keep abreast of the patient's condition is intensified; hence their demands for information increase. Staff members necessarily develop many interaction tactics to control both family questioning and the information they will give. Since we have already presented a good many of these tactics and their consequences, we shall devote this section to some special problems in managing the aware family's constant search for information.

Staff members in wards with closed doors can control their accessibility to visitors with various "door norms"—norms for behavior which are associated with the side of the door each party is on—and thus limit demands for information. Once a family member has been allowed to pass through the door, he has the "right" to request information on the patient as he walks to the bedside, and the nurse must answer the query as best she can. At the same time, however, she can also give rules as to how long he may visit and how often, again limiting the family's access to her for more information. Nurses may find questions especially bothersome because the family member is sometimes in a mild panic and does not listen to the answer anyway: as one said, "You try and explain to them, but they can't hear." Thus nurses learn to answer with as little information as possible to avoid a sense of futility and wasted effort.

If family members are *not* allowed through the door, then of course, the staff is inaccessible to queries. If the door is left ajar, visitors may be able to glean information from voices or from glimpses of the activity within. Sometimes a relative is told he cannot enter, but must return to the waiting room and wait for the nurse to bring news to him. The nurse may, however, intend to keep this promise only when she is going somewhere else and the waiting room is en route, or when a drastic change occurs in the patient's condition. Partly because it is so hard for them to get information, family members tend to regard the first nurse who steps out the door as fair game for questions. As they do with nurses in an open nurses' station facing outward, they ask about "their" patient regardless of her familiarity with the case.

Bringing the family into awareness sometimes stimulates constant phone calls to the ward for information about the

patient. To avoid tying up the lines, staff members may repeat
a routine report over and over—"No change," "Rested and
ate well," and so on—or they simply tell the switchboard
operator not to put such calls through or to repeat the routine
report. A family member who does reach the ward nurse is
likely to "crowd" the call, asking as many questions as possible
in rapid succession before the brief span of an appropriate call
is ended and the nurse cuts off the conversation. Of course,
this makes it hard for either party to get or keep anything
straight.

Family awareness eases communication for both staff and
family, as we have indicated. Staff members do not have to
avoid certain sensitive topics, and the relatives can ask more
intelligent questions. But even in this open awareness situation,
dimensions of the patient's condition—such as mode of dying
—may still be closed; or staff and family may have different
expectations as to certainty or time of death, so that ambiguities
of communication exist (as discussed in Chapter 6).

Another kind of communication difficulty is associated with
staff *announcements* to the family. In this section we have
focused on the family's problems in obtaining information, but
as we have suggested previously, staff members must announce
information at various stages in the patient's dying, and then
they encounter additional obstacles. Family members may be
difficult to locate in time for a quick bulletin on the patient's
changed condition, for example, and there are always questions
about how the news is to be broken—abruptly or gently—
and whether the staff member should display emotion. Not the
least important are techniques for getting away from the kinsmen after making the announcement.

11
"Nothing More to Do":
The Problem of
No Recovery

Perhaps the most crucial phase in dying begins when there is "nothing more to do" for the patient. "Nothing more to do"—the designation used by the staff in every hospital we studied means that the patient no longer has a chance for recovery, either through natural processes or through medical help. As long as there is still a question as to whether the patient will recover, then all parties concerned are uncertain in their death expectations. The "nothing more to do" phase begins with the certainty that death will occur, at either a known or an unknown time. Certainty may occur at any time during the patient's dying. It may begin with the original diagnosis, though the patient may linger for years. In cases of this nature, however, periods of uncertainty about death are bound to occur because of partial reprieves or new drugs or surgical techniques. Or, the "nothing more to do phase" may occur only moments before death, when the staff, working intensively to save the patient, realizes just before death that the case is hopeless. In sudden death, of course, this phase is missing.

The "nothing more to do" phase of dying is crucial because at its inception *the fundamental goal for the patient changes from recovery to comfort,* and as a consequence, the activities of the staff change radically. Before this phase begins the staff focuses its efforts on saving the patient with all available means. After this phase begins, any effort to save the patient becomes

superfluous, and staff activities are focused on ways to make
the patient comfortable until death. With this change of goals
and activities occurs a change in the rewards the staff derives
from patient care. For the personnel, the highest professional
reward is in the patient's recovery and return to his normal
personal and social life.[1] Making the patient comfortable is
less rewarding, partly because it requires less medical and
nursing skill, and especially because merely providing comfort
to a patient who is dead-in-anticipation is still a kind of medical
failure: there is no longer any chance to achieve the primary
success, recovery.

Since the staff member's strongest motivation to become
involved in patient care is the chance to cure the patient,
"nothing more to do" patients are excluded from some wards,
particularly the intensive care units which are geared to intensive, split-second heroics. On these wards all patients should
have the possibility of recovery to avoid any dilution of high
staff morale and motivational involvement. To this end, screen-
ing measures are used to insure that any "nothing more to do"
cases sent to the ward are refused entrance. Without such
measures, the ward might become a "dumping ground" for
the dying, and this might damage staff motivation to continue
all-out intense efforts to save other patients.[2] On most wards

---

[1] This paragraph delineates the two principal goal-reward patterns
of medical personnel and the institutionalized priority between them,
and how the motivated involvement in patient care of personnel varies
accordingly. The goal-reward patterns of positions provide a useful
basis for analyzing work behavior. See for clear example: Howard S.
Becker, Blanche Geer, Everett C. Hughes and Anselm L. Strauss, *Boys
In White* (Chicago: University of Chicago Press, 1961); James Coleman,
The Adolescent Society (New York: Free Press of Glencoe, 1961);
Barney G. Glaser, *Organizational Scientists: Their Professional Careers*
(Indianapolis: Bobbs-Merrill, 1964); and Warren O. Hagstrom, "Anomy
in Scientific Communities," *Social Problems*, 12 (Fall, 1964), pp.
186-195.

[2] Ruth Laub Coser found in one ward that was a dumping ground
for nothing-more-to-do elderly patients that the staff developed a
"vicious circle of rejection" of these patients. We might suggest that
this rejection process was in the service of maintaining the staff's motivation to achieve recoveries. See *Life on the Ward* (East Lansing:
Michigan State University Press, 1962), p. 123.

that contain dying patients there is some typical stable ratio of both certain and uncertain death. In most ward situations, then, the lesser rewards of providing only comfort are usually balanced by a sufficiently large number of terminal patients who do provide the challenge of potential recovery.

Linked closely with the change in goals of patient care, from recovery to comfort, is the moral dilemma of whether to prolong life, and if so, for how long. We shall present later in this chapter some of the standard resolutions to this complex and continually debated issue. Suffice it to say here that before the patient reaches the "nothing more to do" phase, the recovery goal requires prolonging his life at all costs, since the patient still has a chance. But after the "nothing more to do" phase begins, after those responsible for his care are certain that the patient will die, prolonging life can become useless. It may require meaningless effort from the staff; and if it means excessive pain for the patient, it conflicts with the goal of providing comfort, which is also disturbing to staff. Excessive prolonging may induce intense emotional pain in the family, another problem for staff. All this pain is senseless and unnecessary, from the perspective of many staff members. Thus, the problem is to bring the "nothing more to do" phase to a close in an appropriate manner.

Since this major change of goals has such a profound impact on patient care, the particular awareness context relative to the "nothing more to do" phase is an important consideration. Much of the interaction among staff, family and dying patient hinges on whether each party is aware that the patient is certain to die and whether the time of death can be predicted. In this situation, there is much room for differential expectation among all parties. Legitimately, doctors are the first to decide that there is nothing more to do for the patient; as we have seen, it is the doctor's prerogative to decide whether or not to tell nurses, family and patient, who may already be suspicious, if not aware. Typically, the doctor is aware before the nurse is. She, in turn, is typically ahead of the family, and all are usually aware before the patient is told. Even when disclosure proceeds directly toward an open awareness context, there will be moments when individual death expectations are different or when the awareness context is closed or suspicious, which will create problems of interaction and patient care. To take an unusual example, suppose that a doctor on an emergency ward suddenly stops trying to save a patient. Other doctors and nurses are dumbfounded, and family members promise themselves to bring a malpractice suit. The burden is clearly on the doctor to disclose, as quickly as possible, that there was really "nothing more to do," giving the reasons for his own sudden transition in awareness. This clear-cut situation seldom occurs, because it is complicated by numerous contingencies, as we shall indicate presently. A far more likely outcome is that the doctor is so intensely involved in striving to save the patient that other doctors and nurses become aware first and must tell him that "it is hopeless" and time to give up. Or family members, suspicious of the truth, may beg him to stop and let the patient die gracefully and in comfort. In short, the problem is more often undue prolonging and how to stop it.

In the "nothing more to do" phase, doctors' activities in response to the change of goals can be placed on a continuum, ranging from ceasing all recovery efforts to still trying valiantly to save the patient. We shall consider these activities as they bear on the interaction between the doctor and nurses, family members and dying patient, in different types of awareness contexts.[3]

PRIORITIES IN PATIENT CARE

Once the doctor is convinced that there is nothing more to do for the patient, his problem becomes one of spending his time legitimately, according to professional values. Because

[3] Confining our discussion of interaction within awareness contexts limits for this chapter an otherwise very extensive topic. In another book, *Passage Toward Death*, we shall consider staff activities in terms of timing the patient's passage through the "nothing more to do" phase. See also, "Temporal Aspects of Dying as a Non-scheduled Status Passage," *American Journal of Sociology* (June 1965).

his scarce skills must also be applied to a large number of patients who *can* recover, his "nothing more to do" patient has less valid a claim on his time; the simple priority assigned to patients who can be helped tends to take him elsewhere.[4] As one doctor put it, "If you know it is necessarily ultimately fatal, then you may not work too hard."[5] The increasing absence of a doctor who has previously been more attentive can make an unaware patient suspect that he has been given up for lost, since he obviously isn't getting better. Thus, this basic structural feature of medical practice—the high priority assigned to patients who can recover—linked with the "nothing more to do phase" may endanger a closed awareness context, for most people know that doctors disappear only when either recovery or death is certain. The patient's suspicion can easily change to open awareness, if the doctor cannot adequately counter the accusations of neglect and incompetence (one patient yelled: "You're no longer a doctor") leveled by a suspicious patient when the doctor makes one of his brief, infrequent visits.

SENDING THE PATIENT HOME

The standard mechanism for handling this problem of priority in care is to send the patient home, if this is feasible. The doctor who tries to "get rid" of the patient justifies this action by referring to another fundamental value in medical

[4] The private doctor, compared to the hospital doctor, is likely to withdraw less time from the patient because of his location in the lay referral system compared to the hospital doctor's location in the professional referral system. See Eliot Freidson, *Patient's View of Medical Practice* (New York: Russell Sage Foundation, 1961), Part 2, for the contingencies of both the lay and professional referral systems that control the doctor's behavior.

[5] "All of us have seen the patient who is slowly dying of a chronic, debilitating illness and has been placed in the room farthest from the center of the ward. The doctors drop in briefly during rounds, glance at his chart and leave almost immediately. The general attitude of the wards is: 'There is really *nothing more* we can *do* for him—after all, he's dying anyway.'" [*underlining* is ours] *Time*, November 20, 1964, p. 42. We see and hear this kind of statement quite often, which continually validates our point.

practice—hospital space is reserved for the people who can benefit from hospital care. In some cases, a terminal patient must remain in the hospital because he needs its facilities for sedation or its special equipment. In other cases the doctor may send the patient home, though he expects him to return for his last few days, when he will require the attention of a larger, well-equipped staff. Sometimes the doctor can send equipment home with the patient. In some of these cases, the family simply sends the patient back to the hospital when it can no longer tolerate his mode of dying. If his pain and condition can be handled at home, however, and if his family can take the ordeal, the doctor is often willing to send a patient home to die. Implicit in this action, he knows, is a decision not to prolong the patient's life, since the home will normally not have the equipment or supplies to sustain a dying patient's life for very long if he is close to death. Also at home there are fewer people to observe or hear the patient die, and the family will usually agree to no prolonging after having lived with this last stressful stage of dying.

To a sentient patient, the implications of being sent home are ambiguous. Especially if the doctor does not visit the home very often, the patient may infer that he has been given up for lost. But most patients are eager to go home, if they have a home; and if they have no cause for suspicions they may even be pleased, since going home may also indicate progress toward recovery, or at least the end of the crisis. Thus, the doctor's decision to send a dying patient home will not necessarily jeopardize a closed awareness context.

The family's awareness is another matter. If the family has been unaware that he is dying, the patient's return can cause a shocking transition into awareness, for now it is quite obvious that he may not be going to recover.[6] Otherwise, the

[6] In contrast to the pessimistic outlook for the dying patient when he returns home, the outlook is optimistic for the recovery patient: "For the child and family the homecoming was a great event. Regardless of the child's condition or handicap, the recovery outlook of family members took a more optimistic turn when he returned home." Fred Davis, *Passage Through Crisis* (Indianapolis: Bobbs-Merrill, 1964), p. 83.

probable result is a suspicion awareness context, muffled by mutual pretense, during further interaction with doctors and nurses. Before a patient is sent home, someone, often a social worker, or a private doctor, usually tries to find out whether the family can care for the dying patient, either unaided or by hiring a practical nurse. Sometimes, in such a situation, the social worker joins forces with aware family members to ascertain what is best for both patient and family, regardless of the doctor's orders. One patient had a sister who felt that she couldn't "take" it and said so directly: "No, I don't want [the patient] home." The social worker recommended "no" to the physician. In other cases, a family member and a social worker, both aware that the patient's death is very near, may try to persuade the doctor to let the patient stay in the hospital during his few remaining days. A relative in one of these cases said he felt that it was "useless" to send the patient home because he had such a short time to live.

The expected time of death after there is "nothing more to do" is important in determining whether the patient will be sent home, thus saving hospital space and medical skills. If he is slated to linger, the family, aware or not, is under very strong pressure to accept him at home. If they cannot or will not do so, the patient can be sent to a nursing home or to a terminal ward in a state hospital. These latter alternatives permit the doctor to exert pressure on the family to accept the patient, for the idea of the state hospital is ofen repugnant to relatives, and most nursing homes may be too expensive. Some families, however, may welcome these alternatives. But when the family knows that the patient has but a few days to live, they can use this expectation to force the doctor, and the hospital, to keep the patient at the hospital.

Sending the patient home is sometimes of course the most satisfactory solution for patient, staff, and family.[7] The patient dies in a familiar environment, surrounded by his kinsmen,

---

[7] Preference for dying at home has been shown by two other studies; see Robert Fulton, "Death and the Self," *Journal of Religion and Health,* 3 (July 1964), p. 364.

and the staff is spared a period of strain, if not an ordeal. The ideal conditions for dying at home are difficult to achieve, though when all or most of them are present the family is usually relatively eager to have the patient at home. The patient should be fairly free of pain and not physically deteriorating too rapidly, so that he is neither comatose nor completely blurred by sedation and he is presentable. Family members should have already had sufficient time to grieve, so that they do not break down. Ideally, too, the awareness context should be open enough for the family to openly take leave of the patient.

EXTRAORDINARY PRIVILEGES

As an alternative to discharging the "nothing more to do" patient from the hospital, doctors may balance their reduced attention by allowing or ordering extraordinary privileges for him.[8] These privileges are never included in routine treatment of a curable physical condition, and they are strongly taboo for patients who will recover, but they are both compensation for lack of medical attention and a source of comfort during a patient's last phase of dying. For example, the patient may be given a pass to leave the hospital for a day or a weekend to go home or to town, though a patient in comparable physical condition, who was recovering, presumably would be bedridden and watched constantly. Another privilege is arranging for the patient to go out for a ride. The patient may also be allowed to eat what he wants—his "last meals"—whereas if he were recovering he would be on a stringent diet. Other special excep-

[8] See the related discussion by Renée Fox on the "red carpet treatment" of patients in which the special privileges are used to induce patients into an experiment and to keep them happy while in it. Some of the privileges accorded the nothing-more-to-do patient for his comfort and to compensate loss of attention would preclude being a research patient (e.g., steak dinner or a pass). Thus, the content of the privileges and their purpose vary, but the common factor between our two studies (and for that matter in all studies of total institutions) is that the people in charge have the power to select from a broad range of privileges, some to give to their inmates to achieve their purposes. Renée Fox, *Experiment Perilous* (New York: Free Press of Glencoe, 1959), pp. 88-89.

tions have to do with ward routines—dying patients may be allowed to remain in bed, for instance, when others must walk a bit (or vice versa), or to skip taking baths, or take extra ones.

For the previously unaware patient, the relief that comes with deviance from stressful routine may fail to compensate for the growing realization that he has these privileges only because the doctors can no longer help him. Thus, these privileges may become transition conditions that are very likely to transform the closed awareness context into a suspicion, pretense, or open context. But to compensate somewhat for disclosure, the doctor's reduced attentions are no longer misunderstood, and if the patient accepts his fate, he can appreciate the increased comfort afforded by the privileges.

Staff and family members who are not yet aware of the patient's certain death may become aware rather quickly if they see the patient eating an unusually choice or large meal, for example. Implicit in these privileges, in fact, is a decision not to prolong the patient's life unduly and sometimes even to shorten it somewhat for comfort's sake. Thus, a student nurse was shocked when she saw a patient with a serious liver ailment eating a steak dinner. Not realizing the patient's true status, she remarked, "It will kill him!" In actuality, it probably did shorten his life by a few days, compared with what routine treatment might have accomplished at the price of more pain. Staff and family often feel relieved that the dying patient is spared the stress of a rigorous medical regime during his final hours.

THE "INTERESTING" CASE

Although it contradicts the usual priorities in patient care, a patient dying in a medically "interesting" way, or suffering from an "interesting" condition, may receive special attention as an object of study and as a teaching "case." [9] This increased attention does not necessarily make the unaware patient sus-

[9] See related discussion on "medical stardom," in Renée Fox, *op. cit.,* pp. 148-153.

picious. He may feel that his chances of recovery are improved by the attention of so many doctors. The unaware family, too, may become very hopeful when they find numerous experts concerned with the patient's condition.

Hope for the patient wanes, however, and even turns to high suspicion if his case is so "interesting" that the doctors decide to keep him alive "for the rest of the semester" and start applying various kinds of equipment to prolong life. Medical equipment can be one of the surest indicators to patients and families that death is certain, but is being delayed. Once aware of dying, the patient may then have to ask for his own death, to put a stop to undue prolonging. A nurse told of a patient who was "kept alive for over three weeks on a pacemaker for teaching purposes." This was so hard on both the patient and her family that the patient, knowing she would die, told the doctor to stop the pacemaker. She was dead within thirty-six hours.

"DO SOMETHING" CARE

Doctors who are fearful that reduced attention will bring an unaware family or patient into awareness—possibly with unpleasant scenes, "hopeless" depression, withdrawal, suicide, or retreat to marginal doctors or quacks—often "do something" in order to preserve the closed awareness context for the patient or his family.[10] That is, they *act* as though they were still trying to save the patient's life. The easiest tactic is to "pass off" an effort to make the patient comfortable—by sedation, for example—as a way to cure him. The extreme example is surgery, actually intended to make the patient comfortable, but presented to the family as a means of helping him recover. Or the doctor can make meaningless trips (that is, for no medical reason) to the patient's bedside, to maintain the illusion that he is still trying to save his life. The doctor makes these actions as visible as possible, examining the patient briefly and then

[10] See related "do something" activities on Fox, *op. cit.*, throughout Chapter 3.

spending his time comforting the patient and his family. In this way the doctor gets credit for doing something, and even if the family still insists on seeing a professionally marginal doctor, with his highly promising treatment, the original doctor retains a measure of control over the patient's dying. In his periodic examinations, he can make sure the marginal treatment is doing no harm while it keeps the patient occupied and hopeful.

The doctor usually buttresses "do something" care by advising patience ("Give the new treatment time to work") and by referring to research promise ("They are working on it at the Mayo Clinic"). Sometimes the doctor who uses these rationales must eventually admit that his hospital cannot provide the equipment or the unique specialized care and knowledge to handle the case. He may then recommend sending the patient to a university medical center where it can be handled more adequately. Often this decision is quite realistic: a case that is classified as "nothing more to do" in one hospital is not necessarily so classified in another. In an urban university medical center, for instance, superior resources and facilities may improve a dying patient's changes for survival immeasurably, compared with what they would be in less advantageous an environment.

The extent of "do something" care varies among hospitals and types of medical practice. Private doctors, pressured by the client referral system, practice "do something" care constantly, sometimes making several trips to the hospital each week.[11] State, county, and veterans' hospitals, where many patients are a non-paying, captive clientele, induce less involvement of physicians with the patients, and "do something" care is applied less often. When dying patients have several doctors, it is likely that no one doctor will feel greatly responsible for inattention to them in the final stages, and so these patients will receive less "do something" care. Lingering patients who remain in the "nothing more to do" phase for months or years

[11] See Freidson, *op. cit.*

are likely to receive a good deal of this kind of attention, especially from private doctors. It keeps them from becoming aware, if they are not already aware, and it helps the doctor convince the family that "we did everything possible," since it keeps him visibly busy with the patient until the end. "Do something" care for lingering patients may constitute a test for a new treatment, and it may even save the patient, for the longer a patient in this condition hangs on, the more probable it is that research will find a way to save him.

"CLINICAL RESEARCH"

The goal of recovery, with its high priority for the doctor's attention, can be reinstated, at least provisionally, by enrolling the dying patient in a clinical research project. In general, the basic legitimate condition for this proposal is the doctor's absolute certainty that, given present knowledge, there is "nothing more to do" for the patient in any available hospital. (For patients with sufficient personal financial resources, "available" hospitals may include those in Britain, France and Germany.) At this time, the family and patient must be presented with the facts of "nothing more to do," even if they were hitherto unaware. Then they are given the alternative: to risk the research with its promise of recovery, however slight. The negative side effects of the treatment or drug are not always presented. If the patient is adult and sentient, he must consent in writing; otherwise a family member must consent. Sometimes, however, "captive" patients are put on a study drug unawares. Parents who "donate" their child often do so without letting the child know that he is dying, so that the closed awareness context is maintained, at least in the beginning.

Recruitment into research is timed according to the current type of death expectation and the availability of a testable treatment. Among patients in the "nothing more to do" phase there are more potential research *cases* than research experiments. A cancer patient, for instance, certain to die, may have been lingering for months when a new chemical drug to be tested is sent from the National Institutes of Health to the hospital; the patient is then asked to be a research case, with, if necessary, an attendant change in his awareness. Unaware patients and families may be converted to awareness for naught, if they do not agree to the experiment. The longer a patient lives in the "nothing more to do" phase, the more likely it is that an effort to recruit him for research purposes will occur which may alter his own and his family's awareness.

On the other hand, sometimes an experiment requires waiting until a particular dying patient has reached the "nothing more to do" phase. Having watched the patient closely, until they are virtually certain of his impending death, doctors negotiate with patient or family immediately to try a new drug or a transplant, for example. In one instance:

> The death watch went on while the surgeons did everything possible to pull Callahan through; they even dropped the temperature of his entire body to decrease his brain's need for oxygen. But he showed no sign of regaining consciousness. On Monday, when all hope had faded, Dr. Russell tackled his most difficult task. He told the woman who was about to be widowed what his colleagues wanted. [The wife] replied without hesitation: "Go ahead if it will help someone else." [12]

Once the "nothing more to do" phase had started, the doctor in this case could legitimately ask the wife for the patient's liver, which was to be transplanted to another patient in the "nothing more to do" phase who had volunteered for the test. Again, negotiating for a research project requires an open awareness context, which sometimes must be instituted quickly —say within an hour—and sometimes must be readied weeks or months in advance.

For patients who are *not* to be recruited for research, however, especially when experiments with a high probability of

[12] *Time*, October 4, 1963, p. 87.

saving the patient are going on at the hospital, doctors have
a stake in maintaining a closed awareness context for both
patient and family. For, if the family became aware that the
patient was certain to die, they might demand that the patient
be given the experimental drug or that the new machine be
tried. Since for most experiments, resources are limited, there
are not enough chances to go around. This situation becomes
even more difficult for the doctors when the news media make
known that a new machine or drug with great promise is being
tested. In a university medical center, of course, both the
facilities for research and the pressure to give a patient a chance
to participate are much greater than they are elsewhere.

A patient can also volunteer for basic rather than clinical
research. In basic research the objective is to find possible cures,
not to test potential ones, so there is no implicit change back
to the goal of recovery. Yet for a lingering patient the hope
is always present that "his" project will succeed in finding a
cure, and he will be the first subject to recover.[13] Thus, some
people volunteer to continue their dying at the National Institutes of Health, for example, where basic research is done
along with clinical research.

In clinical research, the chief drawback for all concerned
is that it takes time, and this means that for some patients life
will be unduly prolonged. Once committed to the research, the
patient and his family are expected to see it through to the
end. Certainly most research doctors are highly committed;
generally, their attitude was, "If it is a study, we go all out."
One doctor did say, "If a patient is in the study and *near
death,* we provide ordinary treatment. Don't use extra measures
just because they are in the study. If he is in agony, I wouldn't
keep a man alive just because of a study."

Nurses, on the other hand, tend to go along with research
in the beginning, but their collective mood in response to undue
prolonging is "Why not let him die?" When the doctors
continue to prolong the patient's life, the nurses often feel

[13] Fox, *op. cit.,* p. 150.

frustrated by their helplessness in being unable to let him die. Occasionally they refuse to acknowledge the legitimacy of the research effort—the well-being of future patients—suspecting that the research patient is really being exploited for personal career purposes, and making statements like: "They keep them alive until the research report is written." Yet, the nurses remain helpless since, as one put it, "Usually you hate to say anything like, 'Why not let him die?' "

Resolution of this problem of unduly extending research patients' lives often depends on the awareness context. If the patient is unaware, as in the case of a child committed by his parents, or a comatose adult, then family members must decide. This is not an easy decision to make, because often they can see the possible benefit to future patients and so feel morally obligated to allow an indefinite prolonging. As one nurse said, "The mother felt obligated, if it teaches them something."

Aware patients react to prospective prolonging according to their death expectation—whether they think of themselves as lingering (time of death unknown) or believe that without excessive staff effort they would die quickly. A patient who thinks he will linger anyway may expect the research to make a possibly uncomfortable fate less so; hence he will probably stay with the study. But if he feels that the research is increasing his discomfort, he may ask to be released from it so that he can live out his last weeks in comfort. A patient who is aware that without research medication or equipment he will die quickly, must weigh this against the pain of having his life prolonged, and decide accordingly. Again, this is a difficult decision to make, and a patient's intention to remain in the study is always subject to reversal.

Because the equipment necessary to prolong life may be so elaborate, many research patients readily become aware that death would come within a few hours or days if they were not in the project. Thus, when prolonging becomes very painful, the patient is apt to lose any moral commitment to the research he might have had, abandon any prospect of recovery, and want simply to be left alone to die. A basic principle in clinical research is that a subject should be allowed to withdraw when he feels that continuation is mentally and physically impossible.[14] But this principle is most appropriately applied to clinical research patients who are either not certain to die, or who are expected to linger on fairly comfortably for weeks or months. They have a moral right to save themselves discomfort; imminent death is not the issue.

A patient expected to die quickly if released from the experiment, on the other hand, may find it difficult to get out of the research if he is not in undue pain. The doctors' point of view may be that his comfort, to be attained through his imminent death, is less important than the success of the experiment if it can be achieved in a few more days or a week. A patient in this situation can withdraw most easily by having his family request it, but family members are not always willing to do this. Much as they might like to help the patient, they may be influenced by the potential benefits to medicine in prolonging his life, or they may still harbor the hope that recovery is a real possibility. If the patient negotiates for dismissal, doctors, who tend to be highly committed to the research, usually try to persuade him to go on with the research, using the idea that it is better than immediate death.

A patient who succumbs to a doctor's argument, however, may have second thoughts after the doctor leaves and try to take measures into his own hands, in spite of his personal obligation to the doctor and the potential benefits to mankind. One research patient, having recovered from the side effects of chemotherapy, was sent back for more. He asked the nurse to remove his restraints, and she agreed, saying they would be

---

[14] Fox, *ibid.*, p. 47. It will be shown, however, in following pages that this rule is often not the operating criteria for deciding on a withdrawal. It is easy enough to say that the patient in his distraught condition is not mentally capable of deciding whether he is mentally and physically capable of continuing. It must, therefore, be decided for him(!) by family or the doctor, and thus the patient loses this apparent control.

ordered back on in the morning. The patient nodded that he understood. After the nurse left the room, he wrote on a slate that he didn't want to go back for more treatment and pulled his catheter out. When the nurse returned, she found him in a pool of blood. She did, however, keep him from killing himself.

Nurses who adhere to the "let him go" belief, based on the comfort goal, try to help the research patient. They may ask the doctor indirectly why he does not let the patient die, by asking why he is prescribing a treatment—for example, tracheotomy or more blood—that will prolong life. The doctor's reply is likely to be on the order of "because he needs it!" So the nurse either must ask directly, "Why not let him die?" or must carry out her tasks of helping to prolong the patient's life, with no satisfactory answer. Other nurses—only a few—simply walk out, indicating they will not give the treatment or prepare the patient. In reply one doctor said to a departing nurse: "I think we ought to give him the blood right now!" One nurse felt morally obligated to help a patient in his struggle if he said he wanted out. She said, "When he tells me that I want to die, it is at this point that I would go right up to the doctors and say, 'Let him die.' "

As we have noted, the research proposal itself may disclose to the patient that he will die, and the change of awareness sometimes induces depression (see Chapter 8). In part, however, the proposal reinstitutes the recovery goal, and this carries a "lift" for patients whose awareness has just been transformed, as well as for those who are already aware. Indeed, an apparent reprieve often does occur in the first days or weeks of the experiment: tumors go down, transplants work, the progress of the cancer is halted, and so on. But often the new treatment eventually fails, the patient's awareness is transformed back to the "nothing more to do" phase, and his depression is all the worse because he has lost a renewed hope. Again, he must go through the process of responding to the disclosure of fatal illness outlined in Chapter 8.

PROLONGING LIFE

Apart from the needs of teaching and research, several conditions encourage unduly extending the life of patients in the "nothing more to do" phase. Some of these conditions preclude changing the goal from recovery to comfort, so that the doctor continues to strive for recovery even though he knows that death is very certain. Other conditions permit a change in goal from recovery to comfort, but still generate efforts to prolong the patient's life.

Change of goal and time of death. Knowing when the patient will die, after he has reached the "nothing more to do" phase, is crucial for the doctor's decision as to whether he should begin a treatment that may prolong life indefinitely and therefore excessively. If he is sure when the patient will die, he is less likely to prescribe a treatment that will prolong life even for a short time, preferring to let the patient die in the "natural" course of the illness. One doctor told us that if a condition, symptom, or disease is secondary to the major problem, then it will not be treated if the effect might be "to prolong death," which is "certain and close by." Thus in a case of metastic cancer, a patient developed pneumonia in the two days preceding her death. The doctor did not treat the pneumonia, suspecting that to do so might prolong her life and assuming that the new illness might make her go "a little quicker."

If the doctor is not sure when the patient will die, however, he is likely to order treatments—blood transfusions, antibiotics, an operation—that may extend the patient's life. Without a firm expectation as to time of death, he is usually not willing simply to wait and let the patient die, since unless something is done, the patient may live on indefinitely in much greater discomfort. "Comfort" surgery may be performed to allow the patient to eat, or to breathe more easily; antibiotics or blood transfusions may be given to improve the patient's over-all physical condition; and equipment may be used to help keep him alive. Striving for comfort may thus prolong the patient's life, sometimes with much more comfort, but sometimes, too, with increased suffering near the end. The difficult problem is to decide whether, in giving the patient more time, the likely outcome is more comfort or more suffering. In practice, the criterion is clearly that "buying time is worth it if you can make them comfortable." A surgeon in one hospital became famous for performing the "comfort miracle." He operated, however, mainly on patients who were expected to linger on painfully, *not* those who were expected to die shortly.

A major social source of uncertainty about time of death, which in turn encourages prolonging, is dissension among the doctors involved in the case. All may be certain that the patient will die, but the attending, private and resident physicians may differ on the anticipated time. Aware of these differential expectations, the doctor on the spot when bleeding starts, for example, may feel obligated to prolong the patient's life even though he believes that "she could go anytime." If his colleagues expect the patient to live for some rather considerable length of time, he may doubt his own expectation or fear an accusation of negligence. Disagreement with experienced nurses can also create this doubt. The immediate social influence of relevant "experts" can force adherence to the ideal medical goal of sustaining life, though this goal is conventionally ignored in most such cases.

Change of goal and closed awareness. In a closed awareness context, relaxing efforts to sustain the life of a "nothing more to do" patient very nearly constitutes an abrupt disclosure that death is imminent. As we suggested in our discussion of "do something" care, the doctor may prefer to keep the patient of family members unaware for the time being, to avoid the problems that such a sharp blow a few hours or days before death might create. Although he has altered his goal from recovery to comfort, if the patient takes a turn for the worse the doctor will continue to act as if he could still save him, and thus prolong his life. The doctor will treat the pneumonia, give blood, perform the tracheotomy, and so on. This gives him time to bring about a more orderly transition to awareness, after which he can let the patient die according to the normal course of his condition.

In gaining this time, a doctor not only avoids unpleasant scenes associated with a sharp break into awareness, but he also protects himself from accusations of negligence by demonstrating that he "did all he could." This demonstration is, as we have said, one of the principal functions of "do something" care, which is often necessary to soothe unaware family members who might otherwise contemplate a malpractice suit after an abrupt change in their awareness followed by the patient's fairly quick death. To them it may have seemed that the doctor "just let the patient die." And as we have emphasized, all parties are better off if both family and patient are made aware of the impending death early enough to give them time to prepare for it. Therefore, prolonging the patient's life extends somewhat the time they have to prepare and softens the blow when the doctor breaks the news to them. And the doctor is also allowing himself time, perhaps to reappraise the patient's condition, before he drastically revises the awareness context by announcing that death is imminent.

An orderly transformation of family awareness involves more than one stage of interaction, taking all the extra time that the doctor gains by prolonging the patient's life. Before approaching a family member, he may talk with the nurse to see whether she agrees that they should let the patient die. She usually assents implicitly, without making an explicit statement: she suggests that the doctor speak to the family about it. This is a way of saying that she will cooperate by helping the family handle the disclosure of imminent death. It also indicates to the doctor whether the family is, in the nurse's judgment, ready to receive the news, and even whether a family member can be approached with a request to permit the patient to die—an action which may further reduce the doctor's burden of responsibility. From his discussion with the nurse, the doctor appraises the support he can count on from nurses and family, and what he must do on his own with some risk of having people turn against him. This information enables him to manage a more orderly transition to awareness than would have occurred had he simply let the patient die, with a consequent shocking transition to awareness for the family.

Change of goal and open awareness. When everyone is aware that there is "nothing more to do," the goal of recovery has, in effect, been changed to a goal of comfort. This is the ideal situation for ceasing to prolong a dying patient's life, but several conditions still tend to prevent letting him die. The doctor must decide on the means by which a patient is to be eased out of life, and whether it should be done covertly or with the explicit collaboration of others.

The means by which a patient is allowed to die depends on whether his life is being prolonged naturally or by equipment. If the patient is lingering on simply as a result of his natural condition, then the basic method for letting him die is *not* to resort to "heroics," such as giving blood or using equipment if he should take a turn for the worse. The patient is simply eased out of life comfortably with pain-killing drugs. Withholding heroic treatment is by and large the only control the doctor has over this form of prolongation. The patient must be given basic sustenance—"You can't let him starve to death"—but not emergency treatment.

The medical ideal, of course, is to prolong at all costs, but according to one doctor, "The family will never say 'Keep him alive as long as possible.' " In cases of extreme pain or deterioration, this condition may influence the doctor to help the patient die sooner than he would have "naturally." Under very loose orders from the attending doctor, the resident doctor or the nurse performs an "invisible act." The standard one is to manipulate the patient's narcotics, giving either an overdose or a premature dose. By this time, negotiations with both nurse and family have been carried out, to insure that letting or helping the patient die will have no adverse consequences for staff members. Normally, these people feel relieved that the patient is out of his misery; often all parties, even including the patient, are involved in the decision—one reason that the invisible act is seldom jeopardized by publicity.

In a few cases family members may insist that the patient be kept alive by any means available. This insistence usually arises from two conditions: painless dying and a reasonable expectation of a cure from research. Provided the physical deterioration is not excessive, painless dying allows the patient and his family to await a cure with hope not trampled by misery. But if the research hope becomes illusory, the doctor or a nurse may still perform the "invisible act," concealing it with attempted heroics or a belated acknowledgment that the patient's condition had deteriorated.

Allowing a patient to die who is being kept alive by equipment poses different problems. In one sense, equipment gives the doctor much greater control over the patient's life than he has with natural prolonging; he also has more time to plan, to calculate risks and negotiate with the family and nurses. At this stage nurses invariably favor letting the patient die, realizing, of course, that they do not actually have to "pull the cord." Only the doctor has this power, preferably with the family's permission. If the family is unwilling, and can afford the cost, the patient's life can be prolonged for some time; but when the money runs out, there is great pressure on the family to allow the equipment to be stopped. At this point even the hospital administration may become involved. In one case a daughter had paid everything she had; when she was out of money, the hospital wanted to send her father to another hospital where the equipment was available free of charge, although it was obvious that the patient would die if moved.

In the face of financial ruin, if for no other reason, a family member usually consents to stopping the equipment. Otherwise the staff may carry out the "invisible act." According to a nurse in one denominational hospital, this is bolstered by the rationale: "The church says we are under no moral obligation to use extraordinary means to keep the patient alive." (Equipment is considered extraordinary.) The invisible act is also rationalized by the staff member's desire to avoid letting an aware family member, unable to make a judgment under stress, use up all his money for "nothing," that is, for no good medical purpose.

Family members in this stressful situation often cannot decide whether the patient should be allowed to die at any given time, even when they are aware that death must occur in the near future. But when a relative *is* aware he usually must be consulted. The doctor may have to wait until the relative has reached an advanced stage of grieving and is prepared sufficiently to discuss the matter. This may take so long that again the doctor is forced either to prolong the patient's life unduly or simply let the patient die on his own responsibility. This is still another situation in which it is important to the staff to have available a strong family member who can make decisions on a rational basis during a time of emotional crisis.

Another condition that tends to encourage extending the dying patient's life is the rule that next-of-kin must be notified when the doctors are sure that the patient will die soon and there is no hope. If relatives live many hundreds of miles away, the doctor is under pressure to prolong the patient's life until they arrive. In this instance, adherence to the standard rule of notification, thus creating open awareness for the family member, may have adverse consequences for the patient and the staff members who must watch him. If the doctor knows of this possibility beforehand, he may evade these consequences by delaying notification and leave the closed context intact until after the patient is dead.

No change of goal and discounting awareness. Under certain conditions the doctor does not change his goal from recovery to comfort even when he realizes that there is "nothing more to do" for the patient. Instead, he discounts his own awareness in favor of other purposes or regards it as an illegitimate basis for action.

The inertia of intense heroics sometimes leads a doctor to continue an all-out effort to save a lost patient even though he is dimly aware that there is no hope. This kind of discounting can easily be reversed by a nearby colleague or nurse who is not too intently involved to observe that the only possible outcome is death. In one emergency case a patient who was not very sick, and certainly was not expected to die, suddenly had a seizure and stopped breathing. The doctor in charge made a heroic effort to revive him with chest massage, but finally another doctor asked gently, "Do you want to continue that if his pupils are fixed and dilated?" This query brought the intense doctor to his senses; he said, "No, I guess not," and stopped the chest massage. In this case the inertia was particularly strong because death was unexpected. Although the doctor stopped, he still could hardly believe what he was quite aware of now—"He didn't seem that sick; he wasn't that sick; what was wrong?" He went on to ask the family for a post mortem, and in addition engaged in a lengthy verbal post mortem with his colleagues to figure out why he had not been able to *recover* the patient.

Only half believing that the patient is lost, a doctor may feel that, having stopped attempting recovery, he must wait at the patient's bedside until either he dies or there are indications that he will recover after all. One doctor turned off a respiratory machine because the patient was no longer breathing. He realized there was "nothing more to do" and stopped recovery efforts—but he was not yet ready to give up all hope of saving the patient. So he waited, alone, by her bedside for two hours to validate his awareness by seeing her die. More typically, however, the doctor trusts his judgment that a case is hopeless and returns to the patients who can recover, leaving word with the nurses to notify him should the unlikely reversal occur.

Although the medical ideal of prolonging life—at all costs and with all possible facilities—conflicts with the awareness that prolonging is useless and unduly painful, the ideal often wins out. As one doctor said, "There are too many instances, in my opinion, in which patients in such a situation are kept alive indefinitely by means of tubes inserted into their stomachs, or into their veins, or into their bladders, or into their rectums—and the whole sad scene thus created is encompassed within a cocoon of oxygen which is the next thing to a shroud."

Prolonging based on this medical ideal most often occurs in particular hospital contexts and with particular doctors. The atmosphere in research medical centers, whether foundation, university or institute, is liable to stimulate more than the usual zeal to prolong life. Jewish community hospitals also seem to have an intensely "saving" atmosphere that often produces undue prolonging. One doctor said of such hospitals, "Intense hospitals make for intense doctors and *intensive* care." Intensive care units in any hospital, with their atmosphere of heroic recovery, are geared to prolonging at almost all costs. Equipment is clustered near every bed, so that prolonging may be just a matter of leaning over and hooking the patient up. The atmosphere in these wards counters staff attempts merely to make the patient comfortable and let him die. In contrast, other hospitals (*e.g.,* Catholic) de-emphasize the ideal of prolonging at all costs by discouraging extraordinary efforts unless they are deemed clearly worthwhile.

Well aware that circumstances like these may force discounting the verdict of "nothing more to do," a group of doctors in one research hospital "have solemnly shaken hands and agreed that under no circumstances will we keep treatment going indefinitely if one of us has an overwhelming stroke and is being kept alive by tubes." The doctor reporting this added,

"This is not only true of us; it holds true for many groups of doctors." These doctors are trying to ensure that awareness of "nothing more to do" will prevail over the strongly emphasized and organizationally supported medical ideal that life must be sustained at any cost. They have established an "invisible system" to assure that the "invisible act" will be performed.

Doctors, particularly the younger ones, often cannot bear the thought of losing a patient, which comes with recognizing that there is nothing more to do. Fired with the ideal of saving, they put patients on life-prolonging equipment, in the vain hope that they can achieve recovery after all. They search the literature for clues to new treatments. (A young doctor in a hospital in San Francisco found such a treatment, saved his patient and became famous for it.) For the most part, however, the effort is of no avail, and eventually the doctor realizes he is responding to a deeply internalized ideal that can no longer be fulfilled. Accordingly, he changes his goal and ceases prolonging. One doctor rescued a patient who suddenly hemorrhaged but later recognized his lost opportunity to let the patient die: "If I had given it a second thought, I wouldn't have saved him." This also occurred to a nurse who had automatically inserted a falling tube but wondered, immediately afterwards, why she had done it.

Several other conditions, linked with the medical ideal of prolonging, result in discounting awareness of nothing more to do. It is often very hard just to watch a patient die. The sense of helplessness—also a consequence of the medical ideal —may cause a doctor to reinvoke the recovery goal and try to prolong the patient's life, hoping to save him later. For the moment, at least, this reduces his frustration and helplessness at being unable to do anything effective. Some doctors feel that a patient's death puts their professional competence in question, rather than the state of medical knowledge generally; and as a consequence they will not relinquish the recovery goal until they feel assured (often after reminders from colleagues and nurses) that their own skill is not at issue. A favorite rationale of the doctor who persists in the ideal of indefinite prolonging is an assertion that he is simply an instrument of society. He feels that society has vested in him the duty of sustaining life and that he is therefore obliged to abdicate personal responsibility for judging the advisability of whether a particular life should or should not be prolonged.

12
"Nothing More to Do": The Problem of Comfort

In the previous chapter we spoke of nurses primarily in relation to doctors' efforts and activities. Now we shall focus on what the nurse does on her own when she becomes aware that there is "nothing more to do" for the patient, and changes her primary goal from recovery to comfort.

When the patient is expected to recover, his primary source of care is the doctor who specifies and supervises treatments. But when the patient is in the "nothing more to do" phase and comfort is the only goal, the nurse takes over as the main custodian of care. It is her responsibility to insure patient comfort within the limits of the doctor's orders for sedation, meals, privileges, treatments and such. Of the many problems this responsibility poses for the nurse, we shall consider only those linked with the awareness of the parties involved in the dying situation. We shall discuss the nurse's transitions into awareness of "nothing more to do"; how she then insures comfort; and when painless comfort is no longer possible, what she does about the collective mood that develops among nurses to "let him die."

THE NURSE'S TRANSITION TO AWARENESS

The doctor may tell the nurses that a patient is dying, but usually not that he is in the "nothing more to do" phase of dying. The doctor withholds this information for several reasons. To the nurse involved in the case, the change in the patient's condition may be so obvious, as when he suddenly

loses consciousness, that the doctor does not need to say anything. Even if the nurse can see no change, she can tell from
the doctor's slackening of effort that there is nothing more to
do. This meaning is clear when, for example, the doctor suddenly stops blood transfusions. Or, the doctor may post the
patient's name on a critical or terminal list, so that this information is routinely distributed to the nurses involved. And the
nurse spends so much more time with the patient that she
is very likely to witness this strategic change in his condition
before the doctor does, and rush to tell him.

As the nurse comes to realize that there is "nothing more
to do," she adjusts her goal from recovery to comfort care.
One nurse expressed the goal change this way, "You can still
make the patient comfortable and you can still entertain him
and you can still distract him." Thus, in relinquishing the
prospect of recovery she was planning comfort activities. As we
noted in the previous chapter, however, losing the chance to
achieve the primary medical goal of recovery, and with it the
highest nursing reward, often results in less involvement and
effort in patient care.

Because this reduced effort is such a common reaction
among nurses, a doctor may again be reluctant to tell a nurse
that there is nothing more to do, if she is not already aware.
His purpose is to keep the nurse alert to recovery as long as
possible, until she becomes aware on her own and starts
thinking in terms of routine comfort. If the nurse's awareness
is on the level of suspicion because the doctor has not validated
her suspicions, she is likely to remain doubtful and alert for
counter-cues, still hoping for recovery. Her tendency is to wait
and see; as one nurse put it, "If he comes out of it, we'll work
on him. He only has to give us the slightest cue." Should the
doctor stop working himself, a nurse who still thinks there is
a chance may be horrified and blurt out, "Do something,
doctor!" A nurse who is sure the patient is in the "nothing
more to do" phase might hesitate to continue working, for
her efforts might result in painful prolonging. For nurses who

are committed to and responsible for painless comfort, pain is legitimate only in the service of recovery.

Nurses are judged by both superiors and doctors according to the effect the change in goals has on their work. Those nurses who tend to work as hard or almost as hard after the news is out may be assigned to patients who need comfort care. As one doctor said, "I always try to get her for patients who can't be saved. She still works so hard to make them comfortable. She's wonderful." So far as this appraisal of the nursing staff is the basis for a clear-cut division of labor, it tends to balance the drawbacks of reduced challenge, involvement, and effort. Some nurses volunteer for comfort care, while others avowedly find they cannot do it because they give up.

In many instances, as mentioned, the nurse becomes aware there is nothing more to do before the doctor does, which, as we shall see presently, creates a number of additional problems. It may be a nurse who must get the doctor to post the patient on a seriously ill list, to notify the family, to order more sedation, or to stop prolonging the patient's life; and it is her job to reach him outside the hospital to find out what to do when a patient suddenly "turns worse." In sum, the differential death expectations between doctor and nurse guide the transition into awareness of "nothing more to do," and the subsequent interaction and purposes of each party.

"GOOD WILL" COMFORT

In the previous chapter we reviewed some of the "extraordinary" privileges granted to the "nothing more to do" patient to make him more comfortable. To the privileges ordered by the doctor, the nurse can add others within her power to bestow. She, too, may excuse the patient from having baths, being turned in bed, or taking walks; she may release his constraints or give him passes and better meals. Comfort can also be achieved through exceptional attentions, or "good will" care. The nurse puts herself out to chat with the patient, helps female patients with hair combing and makeup—so necessary for feeling good and for family visits—keeps the room cheerful, spends time with the patient for companionship, and lets the patient set the pace for much of their interaction, whether routine or not.[1] For non-routine interaction she is ready to comply with the patient's requests. For routine care, giving the patient a measure of control over the activities linked with hospital and medical routine is in itself an act of good will. Of course, in situations such as those in wards for aged in state hospitals, the small number of nurses and aides in attendance over many patients makes it virtually impossible to give the patient much control of this kind.

In closed awareness contexts, the unsuspecting patient enjoys this apparently beneficent attention and the leeway in his hospital life, but "good will" care, like "extraordinary privileges," can also be a reliable cue to an unmending patient that something is awry. Thus, a suspicious patient is likely to respond by badgering the nurse with questions about the implications of "good will" attention, and she must control his assessment of these implications (as discussed in Chapter 3).

In the open awareness context, responses to "good will" care depend on the way the patient is taking his dying. The patient who is preparing himself for death may feel that good will care is his due, since his status is exceptional. He may simply enjoy the attention, or he may interpret it as a hypocritical compensation for not really being able to help him.

[1] Letting the patient set the pace of interaction is a gift of control over his situation to the patient. If it is true, as Fox says, that "the sick person is expected to cooperate with his physician, and in this way do everything he can to facilitate his recovery," then the pace of interaction is, to begin with, mostly under the control of the staff, and the patient must cooperate with the pace offered him in treatments, comforts, baths and so forth. Thus, to offer the patient some control over this pace of interaction is indeed a gift from the nurse, for it is a relinquishment of a power the nurse has to begin with and need not give up, but may, since she no longer expects the "nothing more to do" patient to "facilitate his recovery." Pace of interaction is an important category for the study of how interaction is controlled, a problem of traditional concern in social interaction theories.

A patient who denies his own dying may refuse any attentions that segregate him from typical or recovering patients, while a withdrawn patient ignores them just as he ignores all efforts to pull him out of his withdrawal. Nurses who go out of their way to engage in "good will" care are distressed by refusal or disregard, for the loss of contact reduces them to helplessness. They can then give only rudimentary forms of comfort (perking up a pillow). There is almost nothing to do until the patient allows himself to be reached again. Withdrawal is the patient's most extreme control over the pace of interaction with nurses.

PAINLESS COMFORT

Most of the nurse's energy is concentrated on maintaining *painless* comfort for the patient. While painlessness is a goal that is desirable for all patients, it takes on added importance for a patient who has nothing left to hope for but painlessness. For such a patient, lethal risks to insure painlessness through narcotics are legitimate, though they would never be taken for patients who can be expected to bear pain in the service of recovery.(The possibility of addiction is now irrelevant because the dying patient can *never* be taken off the narcotics.)

Painless comfort is a goal strongly emphasized by doctors, family, nurses and other patients (as well as the patient himself), for few people can stand another's pain. If a patient is in too much pain, everyone is upset by the "scream at the end of the hall," which threatens to disrupt the routine work as well as the staff's collective moods and feelings—the sentimental order of the ward. Thus, the nurse is under considerable social pressure to control the patient's pain successfully.

Differential Death Expectations. To accomplish this task, a nurse must have adequate sedation orders from the doctor. How adequate the doctor's instructions appear to the nurse depends on their differential appraisal of the patient's stage of dying. If both doctor and nurse are aware that the patient is in the "nothing more to do" phase, then the doctor's instructions are very likely to allow the nurse to use her own discretion in the dosage necessary to keep the patient free of pain. She may even risk lethal dosages. "None of the (nurses) believe in euthanasia, but it's just that as you give these heavy doses of narcotics you think that this may be the last one he can take." One nurse reported that her instructions gave her a leeway that would allow the patient to die in the line of *her* duty. The implicit instruction was: "Give [this degree of medication] to the patient every —— hours until dead."

If the doctor is aware that there is nothing more to do for the patient, and gives very loose instructions to a nurse who is unaware of the patient's condition, she may be frightened by so much discretionary power. She will "cover" herself by phoning the doctor to check dosages or to request lower dosage orders, checking with the head nurse, sticking as close to the order as its looseness permits, and so on. She fears that if anything happens to the patient she could be accused of negligence in her interpreting of the loose orders. She also fears loss of self-control when faced with pain that she knows she can within the limits of her orders blot out with a heavy, but potentially lethal dose.

A nurse who realizes somewhat before the doctor does that the patient is either in, or soon will be in, the "nothing more to do" phase, faces other interaction problems. If the doctor, in preparing to leave the ward, has not given her sufficiently loose instructions to ensure painless comfort, she must act fast. She will have to corner the doctor and either remind him that he has left no instructions or suggest to him possible changes in old or current instructions. Saying she might need them, and asking what she should do, she prods the doctor into giving leeway. If this tactic fails, or if she is too shy to try it, two alternatives remain. One is to engage in "invisible acts" of increased dosage: some nurses, particularly private nurses, do take matters into their own hands. The other alternative is to try to reach the doctor by phone when the patient's pain becomes uncontrollable under present orders. This is one condition under which the nurse and her supervisor will make every effort to reach the doctor, no matter where he is, what he is doing, or what time it is. Having reached him, she tries to bring the doctor's awareness into line with hers by pointing out changes in physical condition, indicating that there is nothing left to do but insure painlessness. Then she requests a change in sedation orders.

Patient's Awareness. The patient's part in the means the nurse uses to insure his comfort depends on the awareness context. A nurse may ease the transition to an open awareness context by promising painless comfort until death. A typical sequence of interaction is the following: The doctor tells the dying patient that there is basically not much more to do for him medically *except to control his pain.* This announcement immediately leads the patient to develop tactics for securing sedation. Normally, a patient in this stage does not worry about becoming an addict,[2] or about becoming immune to any one painkiller. He is concerned only with minimizing his pain, and he starts by trying, by various interaction tactics, to control the nurse's management of it. The pressure of this attempt often makes a nurse wish she were maintaining comfort under the cover of a closed awareness context; for then the patient, still motivated to recover, will put up with some pain—and leave it up to her to manage it.

Furthermore, the announcement by the doctor usually leaves the patient very depressed. To cope with this initial response, the nurses stand by with medication to relieve emotional as well as physical pain. As one nurse put it, "If no one had helped him that day I think he might have committed suicide; he was in an awful state. We gave him medication." And thus he was immediately introduced to the looser regulations

[2] Unaware cancer patients do worry about addiction, but patients who are aware they are in the nothing more to do phase tend to ignore it since the pain will not cease, death is inevitable, and therefore narcotics must be taken to the end.

surrounding sedation. He would no longer have to put up with as much pain; he could depend fairly well on the nurses to insure comfort.

Most often, the patient wants the nurse to increase dosage; and a common tactic for this is using verbal indicators of pain— moans, complaints, and so on. The nurse must judge whether the patient is in physical pain and, if so, to what degree. This task is difficult since the indicators of pain are often poor or unreliable: a patient who says he is in pain may be expressing, to one degree or another, only emotional pain. Although a disturbed patient may have to be tranquilized, a narcotic should not be wasted on emotional pain, for its effectiveness, which declines with tolerance, must be reserved for physical pain often over a long period of time. Thus, when a patient uses "moaning and groaning" tactics to obtain more sedation than ordered, the nurse must use countertactics to test him if she has reason to doubt the physical origin of his pain. She may give him a placebo or tranquilizer; she may walk past his room a few times to see whether the "moaning and groaning" occurs only when her footsteps are audible, and so on.

Maneuvering of this kind tends to result in irregular dosages and fluctuating levels of pain for the patient, which in turn may make him wish to control the scheduling of injections and dosages. Some patients dispense with manipulation of verbal indicators and proceed directly to try to establish control over schedules. The patient on a periodic (rather than demand) schedule may concentrate on trying to shorten the time between injections. He may act confused in his time perspective, ringing for the nurse at the three-and-a-half hour point and asking for another shot on the grounds that his four-hour interval is up. Or he rings for the nurse after two hours to say: "You'll be sure to be on time for my next injection, won't you?" thus trying to control the schedule by enforcing it. He may also get family members to keep close watch for transgressions. Patients also try to negotiate for a different schedule on the grounds that the regular one is not adequate.

Patients on demand schedules depend primarily on their

handling of indicators of pain, since "demand" means when the nurse judges the patient needs it. Such a patient may also stick his hand out for medication every time a nurse passes. If these tactics do not work, he may threaten suicide or try to negotiate for a regular schedule, or he may go through other staff members to put pressure on the nurse. He can ask the doctor to order the nurse to give him regular or more frequent sedation, or he can enlist the aid of family members. A family member can create a status-forcing scene, saying it is the nurse's job to relieve the patient's pain, but she is, it appears, negligent in this duty. (Needless to say, anxious family members often do this without prompting.) Lastly, a chaplain may be asked, as a neutral, to institute a conference of patient, nurse, doctor and family to arrange a sedation schedule that is satisfactory to all.

The demand schedule can be very demoralizing to the aware patient, since it necessarily means more pain for him. Because the nurse is watching for symptoms, the patient must withstand some pain before it is reduced by her action. This pain may make the patient think "I am surely going this time." On the other hand, a patient who finds himself supporting longer and longer periods without sedation may think he is improving and feel hopeful, though he is experiencing only a temporary reprieve. His pressuring the nurse to increase or reduce sedation will be guided by these conditions linked with the demand schedule.

We have described the typical situation but not the infrequent patient who is aware that death is certain but refuses narcotics, perhaps to keep clear-headed enough to arrange his affairs before the family takes over, or perhaps merely to demonstrate his prowess. (These patients too, however, are often given narcotics in spite of their wishes, if their pain disturbs others, for the nurses' job is to protect the sentimental order of the ward as well as to preserve the hospital routine. This is one instance in which patients are not allowed to manage their own dying when it interferes with the social organization of the hospital.)

To reduce dosage, patients may use a "no complaining" tactic. Then the nurse must watch for other indicators of pain since, in the interests of others on the ward, she cannot let the patient support so much pain that he breaks down or sets a "bad" example of nursing care for other more fearful patients. The goal of painless comfort must be pursued, but under these conditions it is very difficult to achieve, for when a patient says very little it is hard to ascertain how much a given dosage reduces his pain.

"Can't Talk." A patient on a demand schedule increases the pressure on the nurse if his physical condition deteriorates to the point where he can no longer ask for sedation because he is "snowed" by sedation. This problem applies particularly to research patients who are kept on a demand schedule for painkillers, to minimize narcotics interference with the study drug. As one nurse said, "They are kept under sedation, but there is this carelessness. They don't give medication unless it's asked for and these patients often aren't in a condition to ask, yet I am sure they are in pain." Nurses use several methods to establish degree of pain: turning the patient to watch his response or asking him to blink or move his hand if he is in pain. Sometimes the nurse talks with the patient about this stage of dying before it arrives, either on her own initiative or because the patient negotiates with her. In one nurse's words, the response is: "We always reassure them that we will give them whatever they need to keep the pain under control." This promise, however, ignores the fact that when verbal contact with the patient is lost, indicators of pain are harder to read and verify. Thus, "We sedate heavily in the end," a nurse told us; this is one way of playing it safe.

Under this "can't talk" condition, before death, the nurse is relieved of several pressures emanating from the patient. She no longer needs to "explain," or parry the patient's request for an explanation, every time she changes a periodic schedule or after each demand-schedule injection. As he approaches death, a patient on a periodic schedule puts less and less pressure on the nurse, when a regular increase in dosage is built into the periodic schedule. This causes the patient at this stage to be either too "snowed" by narcotics to talk effectively, or not to be able to talk at all. Thus, the nurse no longer has to worry about avoiding talk of death, nor does she have to listen to "Why don't you let me die?" or "For God's sake, let me die," or "Don't let me die," nor must she handle his negotiation for more narcotics. In the last phase of dying, nurses are particularly vulnerable to the patient who begs for help, especially for painkillers. They want to provide more sedation as a way of "doing something" within their power in order to relieve their own feelings of medical helplessness. It is also very difficult for them to take a patient's indeterminate state of pain; and one way to control the amount of pain is to "sedate heavily."

Some of the benefits otherwise inherent in the open awarenes context are lost when the patient can no longer talk. From the patient's point of view, he loses whatever control he had established over insuring painless comfort, and over management of his dying, when he loses the ability to negotiate for more narcotics. One advantage of open awareness is that the patient can take leave of his family, but when he is heavily sedated this advantage is lost too. (In the words of one nurse: "They're snowed and can't talk to their relatives.") Even if the patient can communicate, heavy sedation makes him mentally vague, which tends to disturb relatives who wish to make final farewells. Patients in this condition are also unable to sustain useful relations with a chaplain or social worker. In short, the aware patient who cannot talk cannot interact very well even on the basis of open awareness.

"LET THE PATIENT DIE"

When painless comfort is no longer possible for the dying patient, nurses are reduced to a state of helplessness, which one nurse expressed as follows: "You can't do anything, even to relieve the pain in the end, sometimes, and the patients keep wanting things done for them." [3] They can no longer achieve the only goal of patient care that remained to work for. As they watch a patient lingering or having his life painfully prolonged, a collective mood develops among the nurses, an urgent wish to "let him die." This is their most frequent response to their inability to provide comfort. (A less preferred alternative is to put the patient into living sleep with drugs—a social death.) One nurse stated this "let die" alternative to painless comfort explicitly: "We can't relieve her pain, everybody wants her to die for her sake, meaning her suffering, we can't even help her. Once we can't help her, let her die for God's sake, for our sakes as well as theirs."

Other nurses are less articulate but as direct: "The quicker she dies, the better without suffering." "Why should he be saved to go on living like a vegetable?" "Why should he be saved for a life of continual suffering?" "Maybe it is for the best, maybe it is a blessing if he goes." And in reference to research patients, "I think a man should be left to die in peace with plenty of narcotics." When the patient does die, the collective mood of the nurses changes to one of great relief. No longer must they be frustrated by their inability to provide comfort and by the "waste and senselessness" of undue lingering or prolonging.

To be sure, this collective mood runs counter to the medical ideal of prolonging life. A student nurse displayed clear recognition of this ambivalence: "We had a patient, a cancer patient, who wanted to come to the hospital. Everything was done for him, even if he didn't want it. They gave him everything

[3] Sheldon Messinger, in a private communication (September 13, 1963), gave us a comparative view of helplessness. ". . . you mention 'medical helplessness' in passing. A most impressive phenomenon. Death isn't the only place where it is found, although it may be among the most salient. I remember an MD at Napa telling me that she used EST (electric shock therapy) in a particular case not because she thought it likely to do any good in the long run, but because 'the patient was in pain and I'm trained to help. I had to do something. What else was there to do?' "

to prolong, to save this person, if that is what you want to call it. This isn't actually saving, but once you come to the hospital everyone is concerned to preserve your life, the person has no choice; well, it is just a question of ethics." She realized that in the "nothing more to do" phase, prolonging is *not* saving and can only be justified in terms of an "ethic," which is weak support indeed in these cases. Thus, most nurses feel that "let him die" is the best alternative to painful prolonging, though some remain ambivalent. One nurse, evidently wanting to support the ideal, questioned her judgment that the patient was really in the "nothing more to do" phase: "How do I really know he is going to die; how do I really know; therefore, how can I possibly let him die?" Another nurse resolved her ambivalence by means of unquestioning compliance with the ideal.[4] She registered annoyance, indignation and irritation at the thought of *not* prolonging at all costs as well as at the thought of actually helping the patient die. Other nurses regard the ideal as a public shield over the invisible acts, or system of acts, by which they let the patient die.[5]

Patients and Open Awareness. In the closed awareness context the collective mood of "let him die" develops spontaneously among the nurses, regardless of the patient's overt demands. In the open awareness context, however, this mood may be supported and even initiated by the patient's requests to be allowed to die. A patient's longing to die—"Please God let me go"—is reciprocated by the nurses' "It's a blessing if he goes." Just as a patient's struggle to live encourages nurses to help him, his struggle to die may arouse their sympathy and

[4] The resolution of problems of work by using formal rules—termed "rule tropism" by Alvin W. Gouldner—is an important aspect of nursing care that is worthy of future research. See Alvin W. Gouldner, "Comopolitans and Locals: Toward an Analysis of Latent Social Roles —I," *Administrative Science Quarterly* 2 (December 1957), p. 299.

[5] See Anselm L. Strauss, Barney G. Glaser and Jeanne C. Quint, "The Nonaccountability of Terminal Care—An Aspect of Hospital Organization," *Hospitals,* 36 (January 1964), pp. 73-87.

prompt them to help him attain his objective. One nurse, mentioned in the last chapter, stood by for a patient's request to die, so that she could step in and ask the doctor to "let him die."

"Request" is too mild a way to describe this behavior: many patients actually beg and plead to be allowed to die. A doctor has lucidly described this pattern, covering the two essential conditions of "nothing more to do" and too much pain: "A cancer patient for which every conceivable avenue of treatment has been explored with total failure, and this patient moreover is suffering from excruciating pain and is pleading for release." [6] Patients who say, "Please leave me alone, I want to die, I don't want any tests like this," or "Why don't you let me die?" confirm the nurses' conviction that the best way out is death. Statements like "I'm dying right now, get me out of my misery," may express a transition from a closed awareness context to an open one; the patient registers a "let me die" mood as he registers realization of his change of status. Such a quick change in awareness context can bring into the open the nurses' collective hidden desire to let him die, and prompt their active assistance in achieving the mutual goal. Too quick a transition, however, may cause an unaware nurse to doubt the patient's reading of his own condition and consider him "morbid."

Family and Open Awareness. The nurses' collective mood may also be shared by aware relatives of the pain-ridden, "nothing more to do" patient. They are often permitted to make the final decision, but sometimes they may be forced to plead (*"Please* turn that drip off") if the doctor still considers prolonging the best course. Of course, unaware family members would be horrified by the nurses' collective mood, and sometimes even aware family members who encounter it create a status-forcing scene to remotivate the nurses.

The ordeal suffered by family members at this time also

[6] *San Francisco Chronicle*, June, 1963.

supports the nurses' collective desire to let the patient die. "It was torture, we felt more sorry for her [mother] than for him [patient] at times." Nurses may shift the object of their involvement at this time (as we have suggested in Chapter 10): the patient cannot be comforted now, but the family member can. As the new object of the comfort goal, the "very much alive" family member takes on the patient status, and the nurses, as a result of this "object switching," now have a goal to work for and a reward to expect. This shift of involvement may, at the same time, paradoxically reverse the nurses' intentions to let the patient die, when the only way to keep the family member comfortable seems to be to comply with his desire to postpone the patient's death.

LETTING THE PATIENT DIE

In the last chapter we indicated how a doctor, with the help of the nurse, may let a patient die; here we shall discuss some means available to a nurse acting on her own for letting the patient die. The use of these means depends on differential death expectations between nurses and the doctor and on awareness contexts.

"Non-rescue" Tactics. The tactics available to the nurse depend on whether she agrees with the doctor's evaluation of the patient's status. If she and the doctor *agree* that there is nothing more to do, she can exercise "non-rescue" tactics to let the patient die, without fear of reprisal from the doctor and with confidence that he will protect her from family accusations of negligence. Since she spends more time with the patient, the nurse is more likely than the doctor to be in a position to save—or not save—the patient from immediate death with split-second operations should he turn "worse." She can replace a fallen tube, ring for help, give an injection, massage his chest; or she can, if she chooses, let the patient die. Lack of action is in itself consistent with the reduced effort characteristic of this phase of dying, but it is hard to resist

rescuing the patient during the critical moments when action must be taken instantaneously if it is to be effective, and there is little time to ponder more alternatives. Consequently, a nurse who performs a split-second rescue maneuver may wonder later why she went to the trouble to preserve or prolong a patient in vain.

Several conditions lead a nurse to rescue even when she would prefer to let the patient die. First, the medical ideal of prolonging, however senseless it may seem to her, is too deeply internalized to be overcome readily in the final act, especially where there is no time to think. Another condition depends on the physical setup of the ward. In an intensive care unit, for example, it is easy to follow the natural response and simply to hook the patient up to the necessary equipment, which is right next to his bed. On a medical ward, though, some difficulty in requisitioning supplies or equipment quickly enough might encourage a nurse to use "non-rescue" tactics. A third reason is admiration for a doctor who has made heroic efforts to save the patient against low odds for his survival. In this situation the doctor is more important to the nurse than the patient; again her involvement shifts from a dying patient to a "very much alive" person. In the words of a nurse who experienced such "object switching": "I was so concerned in trying to suction in everything. I guess why I did this is because he was Dr. X's patient and he had worked so hard to save him, it really upset me." Another contributing factor here was the high degree of social loss; the patient was a young man with a good future.[7]

Another condition pressuring the nurse to rescue, when she can count on even the doctor's support for non-rescue, is the probable *visibility* of her failure to act.[8] Non-rescue tactics

[7] See Glaser and Strauss, "The Social Loss of Dying Patients," *American Journal of Nursing*, 64 (June 1964), pp. 119-121.

[8] An aspect of nursing care needing future research is how the hospital structures the visibility of a nurse's work from specific parties to it. On "visibility" see Robert K. Merton, *Social Theory and Social Structure* (New York: Free Press of Glencoe, 1957), referenced on page 645; and Erving Goffman, *The Presentation of Self in Everyday Life* (New York: Doubleday Anchor Books, 1959), Chapter III.

are easiest on night shifts, in single rooms, in restricted areas such as premie wards (except during baby viewing times), or on private duty. When her behavior is likely to be witnessed by staff members not connected with the case (whose death expectations presumably are more optimistic), or by family members, then the nurse will rescue. When family members are present much of the time, as they so often are during the final stages of dying, opportunities for applying non-rescue tactics are particularly scarce. Even if the relative is aware that there is nothing more to do and wants to end the painful prolonging, a nurse may be reluctant to let the patient die in his presence as a result of her inaction. Linked with visibility of her inaction is the *time* it takes the patient to die. If the patient takes too long to die in front of a relative or unaware staff member, the nurse is forced to rescue. She can do nothing for only a few minutes, unless her behavior is unusually well shielded from observation. If the doctor disagrees with the nurse, maintaining that the patient is *not* in the "nothing more to do" stage, she can risk a "non-rescue" tactic only if she can avoid being seen for a long enough time, since as a nurse she is expected to save any patient whose death is not considered inevitable.[9]

In addition, several structural conditions facilitate the nurse's use of "non-rescue" tactics, apart from her agreement with the doctor and the visibility of her actions. Hospital policy may specify that extraordinary efforts—especially the use of equipment—are not to be taken for patients clearly in the "nothing more to do" phase of dying. General, legal and medical rules as well as hospital rules bar nurses from using such rescue devices as certain kinds of equipment, certain

[9] Under what general conditions of work are professionals forced, allowed, and helped to act unprofessionally in order to get a professional job done is a problem in the study of professions worthy of future research. Present study tends to focus on how professionals are trained to act professionally, not how they are forced, allowed, or helped to act unprofessionally for professional goals. This is an important problem in nursing care. See Merton, *op. cit.,* pp. 343-345, for his notions on institutional evasions, which may help such research.

types of injection, or certain procedures such as open heart massage. Thus, in some cases a nurse can withhold her own actions with impunity, though she still must try to reach a doctor.

Reaching a doctor can itself be used as a "non-rescue" tactic. The doctor may have left no instructions to follow in case of emergency; no resident may be in attendance to take over (this depends on the hospital or the daily work shift). Or, a resident on duty may be unwilling to go too far with a private doctor's patient, as may other doctors who happen to be on the ward. Reaching the doctor responsible for the case may be difficult or take too long for quick action, so that inaction for a time is unavoidable. These conditions, of course, might lead a nurse to use rescue procedures forbidden by the rules, but she is forestalled since illegal efforts to rescue a patient from death could jeopardize her position as a nurse and even result in a manslaughter charge if she fails. A nurse may risk an illegal rescue effort when she *disagrees* with the doctor, and is less certain than he is about the inevitability of the patient's death. But when doctor and nurse agree that there is nothing more to do, a nurse who cannot reach the doctor in charge of the case has a perfect opportunity to ease the patient gently to his death.

Sedation Tactics. When doctor and nurse *agree* that the best course is to let the patient die, the doctor may order cessation of most or all equipment in use and give the nurse loose sedation orders to insure painless comfort until the end. These sedation orders allow the nurse much discretion and therefore encourage her to use active tactics to help the patient die (as opposed to the more passive non-rescue tactics). Under these conditions she can manipulate sedation with little or no fear that she will be accused of negligence. By manipulating sedation, or its counteractants, she can ease the patient to death when adverse conditions multiply and become too much for all concerned: the patient is begging for death, he is deteriorating physically, pain cannot be controlled, the family are going through an ordeal that is pushing them to the breaking point, and so on.

Loose sedation orders give the nurse enough latitude to administer potentially lethal doses in the hope of achieving painless comfort. In this way she can help the patient die. One nurse said, "It may kill her, but why not let her go free of pain?" Another said, "None of the (nurses) believe in euthanasia, but it's just that as you give these heavy doses of narcotics you think that this may be the last one she can take." If the dose does turn out to be fatal, then the nurse can withhold the counteracting stimulant. If it is not fatal, then she can increase the dosage next time. And since she is following—or stretching —the orders of a doctor who agrees with her assessment of the patient's fate, she need not fear accusations of negligence from him, and she can be confident that he will protect her should others raise questions about her "interpretation of orders." Another factor encouraging this strategy is the patient's attempt to control or increase sedation. The nurse can purposively yield to a patient's "moaning and groaning" or distorted time perspectives so that she eventually is giving sedation oftener.

Non-rescue tactics depend on whether the nurse's inactivity during a crisis can be observed by others, but sedation tactics are not nearly so contingent on visibility. A nurse can apply the needle or give the pill in the presence of others, since it is part of her job, and the patient need not be in an obviously critical condition. Any adverse effects are too subtle for most observers to distinguish from those of routine medication. When charting what has happened, however, the nurse generally must be backed up by a doctor's orders. Thus, a nurse who *disagrees* with a doctor about the patient's fate takes quite a risk in manipulating sedation. She must falsify or avoid recording her "invisible act," and this is too drastic a deviation from professional standards for her to contemplate usually. Normally, as we have indicated, a nurse in this situation will first try to convince the doctor that the patient's case is hopeless and that letting him die is the sensible thing to do. They may also talk with a relative to obtain the family's consent and support.

When a nurse *disagrees* with a doctor who is certain there is nothing more to do and accordingly gives flexible sedation orders, she may be alarmed, as we noted before, by the responsibility implicitly given her for the patient's survival. Her tendency then is to seek more control in her orders, to prevent her from going too far in striving for the patient's comfort. Of course, this is a problem only for a nurse who still believes that the patient *can* survive.

Several structural conditions inhibit use of sedation tactics to let the patient die. If the patient is a research subject, even a doctor who agrees that he is in the "nothing more to do" stage may not give sufficiently flexible orders to allow the nurse much latitude. She is supposed to minimize sedation, so that it does not interfere with a clinical experiment, and if she gives overdoses on her own, the doctor is not likely to back her up. She is expected to keep the patient going until the end of the study.

In a closed awareness context, the patient may beg not for death but for a reduction in narcotics, because he is afraid of addiction. Sometimes unaware family members have the same concern. If social and family affairs are still unsettled, use of sedation tactics is often precluded by patient or family request. And if a family member is traveling from afar for a last visit with the patient, sedation can be manipulated only to prolong life while keeping the patient conscious.

Open Awareness and Auto-euthanasia. Another tactic for letting the patient die, which is possible in the open awareness context, is to permit auto-euthanasia. The prelude is a distressing scene in which a pain-ridden patient begs to die, while the nurse has no way to help or cannot bring herself to help him. But she may tacitly agree to let the patient take his own life. She may even provide him with a "setup" for his suicide by leaving pills at his bedside, removing his constraints, or leaving him alone in his room or in a bathroom. The next thing she knows is that the patient has pulled out all his tubes, or is sitting in the bathtub with his throat slit, or is lying in the street below. Such attempts, though, usually take so much time that another nurse will often discover—and be forced to rescue—the dying patient.

Auto-euthanasia is, of course, also attempted by patients without a nurse's surreptitious assistance. In one case a patient refused to give the doctors or nurses any information on what she had done to herself. Since her condition could not be counteracted, she thereby insured her own death. Sometimes the ward arrangements are such that patients are put in a separate "dying" room (which is a more convenient place for the patient to attempt auto-euthanasia), and left unwatched for comparatively long periods of time. Even when auto-euthanasia is anticipated, the ward may have no room available with barred windows, for example, or staff shortages may preclude adequate surveillance.

Nurses understand and even sympathize with patients in great pain who attempt auto-euthanasia, since it is consistent with their own collective desire to "let him die." Their collective reaction is usually relief, not moral indignation or feelings of professional incompetence. Just as letting the patient die seems a realistic alternative for them, auto-euthanasia seems a realistic alternative for the patient, as far as they are concerned. The patient's awareness of this alternative is a basic "turning-point" in his passage toward death,[10] for at this point he grasps the most important implication of his condition—that there is nothing more to do—and realizes that the medical staff is merely managing this last phase of his dying as best they can. When he also realizes that his physical condition will soon prevent him from trying to manage his own dying, as well as

[10] On "turning points" see Anselm Strauss, *Mirrors and Masks* (New York: Free Press of Glencoe, 1959), Chapter IV. The essential idea behind "turning points" is the awareness that "I am not the same as I was, as I used to be."

the staff's managing of it, he recognizes auto-euthanasia as the only alternative to giving the staff complete control over his fate.

Nurses are trained to motivate patients to recover, and patients soon learn, if they do not know already, that they are supposed to be willing to get well. But this goal, like many other medical ideals, is inappropriate for a patient in the "nothing more to do" phase. It makes more sense to motivate him to die; that is, to get him to accept his impending death and prepare for it. A nurse who is able to help motivate the patient to die (most nurses we met are not, however) can teach him how to die "gracefully." And this tactic may abet the tacit permission for auto-euthanasia, for he may also learn that it may be best, in the end, for him to manage his own death, to arrange a painless, easy departure and forestall an indefinite prolonging—which, toward the end, he may be powerless to prevent. In this way he can insure a shorter ordeal for his family and a more presentable, undeteriorated physical condition for the last farewells. Indeed, we have known active people in the prime of life, many years before this stressful turning point, to contemplate just such a plan when they ask themselves, "What would I do?"

13

Awareness and
The Nurse's Composure

Despite many adverse circumstances in the dying situation, a nurse must make every effort to maintain her professional composure, for both her own work and the assistance she gives other staff members depend on it.[1] The combined requirements of dying patients, their families, and the staff for appropriate levels of involvement in and attitudes toward patients, and also their kinds of collective moods and degrees of composure, create and define an overall "sentimental" order in the ward— and each nurse's composure is vital to maintaining that order. Nevertheless, nurses can become very upset, and a nurse's great fear in the dying situation is that she might lose control over herself.

While many structural conditions help a nurse maintain her composure, other conditions tend to break it down. To cope with situations that threaten to destroy her composure, a nurse must develop strategies to maintain it. Some strategies are general—avoiding dying patients, for example—and therefore appropriate under many different circumstances; other strategies are more specialized. Some strategies involve interaction; others consist of collective moods or patterns of behavior. Some are standard and acceptable to all nurses, so that anyone may use them; others are developed privately and may or may not be condoned by other staff members.

Maintaining professional composure is a complex problem, in view of the multitude of disturbing conditions that nurses

[1] The study of professional composure is, as yet, an unresearched area in the sociology of professions.

226

encounter. To delimit the following discussion and integrate it with the theme of the book, we shall focus on the conditions and strategies related to the nurse's awareness. We shall show how the means by which a nurse maintains her composure are largely determined by her expectations about the certainty and timing of the patient's death.

The *general defense strategy* by which a nurse tries to maintain her composure, during the entire time it takes a patient to die, is to manage her emotional involvement with him according to her expectations regarding his death. This general defense strategy is a *developmental process,* comprising a progressive accumulation of strategies (pertaining to work, to talk with the patient, and to collective moods that develop among the nurses), which serve to reduce involvement in the patient as he approaches death. By reducing involvement as the ordeal increases, the nurses are less likely to become upset and possibly lose composure; if they do lose composure, it is easier to regain. Our purpose in this chapter is to describe this process.

DYING IS UNCERTAIN

In this early stage, when nurses are not yet certain that the patient will die, and do not know when this uncertainty will be resolved, they perceive little need to protect their composure. They therefore do not avoid conditions of working and talking that induce or encourage involvement with the patient, though, during the later stages of dying, they will use counteracting tactics in the same conditions.

Nurses have a general conception of the death ratio—*i.e.,* the proportion of patients who die—on their ward. When the chances are slim that any patient will die unexpectedly ("We don't have very many patients who die"), nurses permit themselves to become involved quite freely, to the limit imposed by the sentimental order of the ward. They do not need to think in terms of possible death. On wards with a relatively high death ratio, such as cancer wards or intensive care units, the prevailing sentimental order limits involvement more, as a general defense against the higher probability that death will occur. In short, the death ratio typical of the ward is articulated in its sentimental order, determining the degree to which a nurse's involvement in a patient's fate is considered appropriate.

At this stage of dying the goal of recovery is in full force, though some staff members may have begun to doubt that recovery is possible. In working for recovery, nurses are apt to become involved with a patient to the allowable limits of the ward's sentimental order, and sometimes to a greater extent than is warranted by the real probability of his death. High involvement is also more likely when the patient has a high potential social loss value. A youthful patient, or one whose occupation is prestigious or important, or whose family is devoted to him, or who is gifted or beautiful, has a high value—and the slightest possibility that such a patient will die distresses nurses and makes them work harder to save him. For example, the thought that he might be dying caused one nurse to become over-protective of a 15-year-old at this stage of dying. Nurses are usually well aware of the loss a patient's death would entail, because at this stage they listen freely to family members who discuss his value.[2]

Working on the evening shift also tends to induce involvement with patients at this stage of dying. The patients are awake, and since the bulk of the day's work is over, nurses have more time for them. Only a few auxiliary personnel and doctors are present to dilute the nurses' attention. Few nurses are on duty, so that although each nurse has more patients to care for, each patient sees the same nurse more often. And

[2] In listening to family members they "learn" characteristics of the patient's social loss which serve to correct and to balance out "apparent" characteristics of his social loss. See Barney Glaser and Anselm Strauss, "The Social Loss of Dying Patients," *American Journal of Nursing*, 64 (June 1964), pp. 119-121. Occasionally, also, a nurse gets involved with a recoverable and highly valued patient, but then meets him on another floor at a later stage of his illness when she then finds it difficult emotionally to disengage herself from the relationship.

members of the family usually visit during evening hours. All these factors combine to produce cooperative, talkative, involving relations with the patient and his family. Nurses on the night shift, when the patients sleep, are least likely to become involved, but even these nurses have an opportunity to involve themselves with dying patients if the hospital policy is to rotate nurses among shifts.

Since the fear of not being able to avoid the topic of death is minimal, conversations can be frequent and talk not usually closely controlled at this stage of dying, so that nurses may also become involved with patients through conversation. Long-range future plans for work and family, to be carried out when the patient has recovered, can be discussed. The nurses feel free to motivate the patient to get well—which further involves them in his fate—even if they feel slightly dubious about his prospects. These conversations may also increase the patient's social loss potential, in the eyes of nurses, since they learn more about him and his importance to others. Nurses and patient can also discuss the latter's physical condition with little or no anxiety, since even "realistic" interpretations are unlikely to lead to talk of dying. Should a nurse's interpretation of a physical symptom point to the possibility of dying, the nurse can pass it off as inconsequential without losing the patient's confidence. Treating a symptom as unimportant is such a standard tactic in all nursing care that it need create no "terminal" suspicions on the patient's part.

EXPECTED RESOLUTION TO UNCERTAINTY

When the patient's fate is uncertain, and the nurses can expect certainty at no definite time, their collective mood becomes unsettled. The situation is indeterminant: should hope for recovery or concern for comfort be the appropriate stance? But when they know the time when the patient's fate—living or dying—will be determined, this mood of indecision is relieved. Now they can begin to prepare themselves for the outcome by managing involvement so as to maintain their composure while they await more definite news. They begin by applying the standard strategies—avoiding both the patient and topics of dying and death—as well as starting to develop strategies that can be applied if the patient's death becomes certain.

Intense Work. The basic characteristic of this stage of uncertainty is that it gives staff members a specified amount of time for saving the patient's life. Though this stage of dying may occur on all wards, certain wards are organized with reference to it—intensive care units, wards for premature infants, emergency rooms and operating rooms with their adjunct wards. Here the best available in talent and equipment is concentrated. On these wards the nurses have a fairly definite idea of the time it will take a patient to get through a crisis, so that his fate can be predicted accurately. Operations take several hours; a premie's chances can usually be determined in 48 to 72 hours. If a patient does not die within one day in the emergency room he is sent either to a medical ward, if he is expected to live, or to an intensive care unit for further treatment. The fate of an intensive-care patient, however, may not be predictable for as long as several days, or it may take only a few hours.

In contrast, on cancer, medical, and neurological wards patients often pass directly from uncertainty, with no expected time of resolution, to the certainty stage of dying. The period during which the nurses know when uncertainty will be resolved is usually very short, if not imperceptible, because on these wards certainty that the patient is dying usually reflects a sudden, unexpected change in physical condition. Consequently, staff members have little or no time to intensify their efforts to save the patient's life.

Nurses on the wards that are devoted to this stage of dying are usually totally engaged in the fight for life during this waiting period, and the intensity of their effort may involve them very deeply in the patient's fate. As one doctor put it, "Intensive care makes for intense nurses." This situation is one of the most challenging for nurses, because, as we have mentioned, they have been trained to regard saving a patient as one of the highest achievements in nursing, and failure to save may seriously threaten their composure. In the words of one intensive care unit nurse: "Staff feels different about the seriously ill [uncertainty] and the terminal [certainty] patients. They might have saved the seriously ill so they feel worse, perhaps, that they didn't." At the same time, however, the intensity of the work tends to take a nurse's mind off the patient's fate, reducing her conscious involvement and helping her to maintain composure during the crisis. Even during periods when intense work is not necessary, they keep themselves as busy as possible in order to maintain their composure while awaiting the outcome.

However long the crisis period lasts, the prospect of failure —that is, when it seems likely that the patient will be certain to die—also causes the nurses to work even harder, to forestall any accusation of negligence (a direct threat to composure) from themselves, other staff members, or the patient's family. They want to be sure that "no stone is left unturned," that there is no implication that "they could have done more." To withdraw their involvement from the patient they engage in "object switching" (changing the object of their involvement) by concentrating on helping patients who have a chance to live, or on the "poor" doctor who has tried so hard to bring the patient through. They also turn to each other for mutual support in giving up the patient. To each other, they say that there is "nothing more to do," or they rationalize the patient's social loss. "Even if he had lived he would have had brain damage" may be said of a young father with everything to live for.

The risk of losing composure through excessive involvement is especially high for nurses on the premature infant wards. Nurses tend to become very involved in saving a premature baby who lives through its first days, when they know the mother wants it, especially if the baby has no physical defects, but they can become equally involved in saving a premie that the mother does not want, because it is alone and helpless in the world. They "adopt" the babies, give them names, and watch over them closely to the end. While the nurses may be well insulated from the mother, they cannot avoid being aware of her wishes because she either telephones the ward incessantly or does not phone at all.

Involvement in the baby's fate may even lead a nurse to phone when she is off duty to keep track of its condition. This radically departs from the standard strategy to reduce involvement in patients—seldom following a case on which they are not immediately working, and seldom following their own cases when not on duty. During the crisis period the very involved nurse may become quite upset should the premie turn "bad," and some loss of composure is readily understood by her coworkers. If the premie dies they fall back on the standard strategies of object switching, absolving themselves of negligence, reducing social loss, and referring to God's will.

Handling the family during this crisis period is also strategic for maintaining composure. The intense work on all these wards is somewhat shielded, by doors and "door norms," from the family. This structural arrangement reduces nurses' involvement in the family, and prevents family members from disturbing the nurses' composure by creating a scene or asking many questions. Since the family is unlikely ever to know who the nurses on the case were, they cannot bother the nurses afterwards by asking why the patient could not be saved. This means, however, that any nurse passing through the door may be approached for information (as we mentioned in Chapter 10). Nurses also try to insulate themselves from the family by putting relatives in distant waiting rooms, empty treatment rooms, offices, or main lobbies to wait out the crisis. A glass-walled office is a preferred place to insulate family members waiting out a crisis because they can be watched without actual contact and thereby be prevented from drifting back to the ward or nursing station. In isolating relatives, a nurse often finds it helpful to tell them that she will bring news of any change in the patient's condition, but as likely as not she then either forgets that they are waiting or simply avoids them when she passes the waiting room. Forgetting, like avoiding, is a standard strategy for maintaining composure.

Talk. During this stage the nurses start to control their conversations with the dying patient. They may discuss his future plans with him, but they tend to restrict the scope of their talk to the short range. They talk about getting back to his work and family when all this is over, not about the patient's future occupational career. They interpret physical symptoms less freely, making sure that what they say points to recovery to keep up the unaware patient's motivation to get well. During the crisis they refrain from asking the patient, "How do you feel?" to avoid prompting him to ask about his chances. They also avoid the subject of dying if the patient starts testing his suspicions. Even when the awareness context is open, as before surgery to explore for cancer, they try to deny that death is a possible outcome, saying, for example, "No one knows yet for sure," "We all die sometime," or "Don't be so morbid." Or, the nurse keeps very busy in the patient's presence, and she responds to invitations to talk with a "professional brush-off"—a silent, pleasant smile, a "We're doing all we can" or "We'll pull you through."

All these strategies enable nurses to maintain composure by keeping both *themselves* and the patient away from the subject of dying, for a patient's loss of composure is sometimes as upsetting to nurses as the fact of possible dying itself.

During a crisis the patient is often under anesthesia or sedation, or is comatose, so the nurses need not employ conversational strategy. Once they have determined whether the patient can still hear even though apparently comatose they accordingly can or cannot discuss, in his presence, his condition and his chances for recovery, in order to mutually support each other's composure.

The premie ward, however, does offer a unique conversational strategy for maintaining composure that is not available on other wards where patients can listen and respond. The nurses tell their "adopted" infant patients anything; they can talk of love, act possessive, reprove them for not being more cooperative, get angry, joke, and so on. All of this adds up to a catharsis that helps maintain composure, since stored feelings may accumulate to break the nurses down, as does happen frequently on other wards.

Collective Moods. At this stage of dying the nurses' collective mood amounts to hope that the outcome for the patient will be recovery. Hope keeps them working hard to save the patient and to motivate him to get well, and hope keeps up their own morale. If the patient's condition is vacillating between certainty and uncertainty, so that the outcome cannot be predicted, the nurses are not sure whether to accept that the patient is dying or continue to hope—any outcome would be a relief. As one nurse put it, "You know, she is looking much better the last couple of days. I came back after the weekend expecting to find her looking bad but she's looking better, she really is. She goes back and forth. We would like her to die and get it over with, yet if there is something going on that she is getting better, maybe. . . ." When cues fail them and "maybe" perplexes them, they seek certainty from the doctors: "If the doctor knows that a patient is going to die, I prefer to know it." They need to know what to expect so that they can control their composure. Some doctors will tell the nurses if they know, but others, as we have seen, will say nothing, wishing to keep the nurses working hard to save the patient even when there is "nothing more to do" for him.

DYING IS CERTAIN BUT TIME OF DEATH
IS UNKNOWN

When the nurses are finally certain that the patient will die, but at an unknown time, the conditions of work and talk that threaten their composure multiply rapidly. The progressive building up of strategies begins to snowball. Previous strategies to manage involvement and maintain composure, are refined and used more often, and new strategies must be developed.

Work. Since there is "nothing more to do" for the patient in this stage of dying, nurses begin now to design their work to make the last days, weeks, or months of the patient's life comfortable and painless. Nurses work especially hard to make the patient comfortable at this stage, to overcome their feelings of negligence by achieving the only goal of patient care remaining. The need to feel justified was clearly expressed by the nurse who said, "I feel especially that I want to know I did everything I could to make the patient's last days comfortable. So if anything I see it as more necessary rather than less." Self-accusations of negligence are common during this stage of dying. For example, one nurse said, "Sometimes a death will linger in my mind. I feel I could have done more to make her comfortable." In this case, self-accusations of negligence made it impossible to carry out the major composure strategy of forgetting the patient and thus reducing involvement in his death.

Family members may also accuse nurses of neglecting to keep the patient comfortable; they may start a status-forcing scene to get the nurses to do what they feel will insure comfort —"the nurses' job." To avoid such scenes the nurses isolate the family in waiting rooms or avoid them and call in other helpers—a social worker, chaplain, orderly, policeman, or ward clerk. Although the strategy of "role switching" (referred to in Chapter 9)—turning family members over to others—to avoid disturbing scenes and to reduce involvement in their sorry plight is begun at this stage, the strategy becomes more important at the last stage of dying. At the present stage composure is also maintained by turning the relative into either a helper or patient, for this gives him a position on the ward with which a nurse can deal in a composed manner, in her capacity as the relative's supervisor or nurse. To avoid being exposed to scenes or bombarded with questions by a free-floating family member with unlimited visiting privileges, nurses try to structure the situation so as to maximize their control of family members, and reduce threats to their own professional composure.

Providing comfort, which reduces the feelings of negligence that threaten composure, is not always easy. Flexible sedation orders from the doctor make it fairly easy—as we have seen, nurses give potentially lethal dosages to insure painless comfort. Sometimes, however, they must overdose without the sanction of flexible orders, using this invisible, uncondoned strategy to cope with their own emotional reaction to a patient's pain. Thus, a nurse can maintain her own composure by ensuring complete painlessness for the patient. Overdosing may be against the expressed wishes of the patient, who wants to be alert to settle his affairs, and/or the doctor, who wants sedation used sparingly to prevent too early tolerance of it. Most often, however, no one knows this very occasional strategy has been used.

The location of the pain, or the limited scope of the doctor's orders, sometimes makes it impossible to keep the patient comfortable. At this point the nurses collectively experience an overwhelming mood of helplessness, and to maintain their composure, they try to avoid the patient and reduce involvement with him. They wish for his death: "We can't relieve her pain. Everybody wants her to die for her sake, meaning her suffering. Once we can't help them, let them die for God's sake and our sake as well as theirs." If the patient is a research subject, the insuperable obstacles, both to letting him die and to relieving his pain, combine to distress the nurses. To help regain their composure, some nurses develop a "miracle rationale," hoping that something miraculous will arise from the research to save the patient after all. At best, slender hope offers weak consolation.

Another way of making dying patients comfortable is to give some routine care in a somewhat expressive and considerate manner. When nurses employ the composure strategy of avoiding the patient, dying patients sharply feel the nurses "pulling away." But when it comes to the duties of medical care, nurses cannot literally avoid the patient. They can, however, employ "expressive avoidance"; that is, they avoid him as a person while they are fulfilling their medical duties. They ignore him, treat him as a body (that is, socially dead), wear bland professional facial expressions, exude dignity and efficiency, and refuse or evade conversation, or else do their chores quickly and "get out" before the patient can say anything.

One nurse expressed her failure to make the patient comfortable in this regard as negligence: "I felt guilty after she died because I could have made her life a little bit more comfortable." Another nurse engaging in "expressive avoidance," while accomplishing routine duties with a 13-year-old patient, was asked by the patient to play cards with him. This request for continuous, relatively intimate contact forced her literally to avoid him; she mumbled something about being very busy and ran. But even her feeling of negligence later on was less threatening to her composure than was the prospect of close contact with a patient whose capacity to involve her emotionally was, because of his high social loss value, virtually irrestistible.

In another case a nurse involved with a young patient who was dying began to avoid him expressively, but he countered her strategy:

He began to make demands that she would come back into the room and that she would spend more time with him. Then he began to accuse her, saying that she wasn't as much fun as she used to be or you hate me, and she said that was really very rough, not only that but he would say this to the doctors and then urge them to ask her to spend more time with him. She handled it by just spending more time with him.

To keep from being judged negligent by the doctors, this nurse was forced to abandon her strategy and spend more time with the patient.

Expressive avoidance tactics contradict the impulse to provide "good will comfort" that we described earlier. While comfort of this kind does make a nurse vulnerable to excessive involvement, it may also help some nurses keep their composure in the face of helplessness to save the patient. It gives them something, however ineffective, to do for the patient.

In general, a nurse confronted with a patient known to be dying, for whom there is nothing more to do, finds it easiest to maintain her composure when the patient can be made comfortable with sedation and a minimum of expressive care. Under these conditions, nurses can forget and avoid the patient except for routine duties, thus minimizing both their feelings of helplessness and negligence and the risk of emotional involvement.

These ideal conditions for maintaining composure are not always easy to achieve, however, for many circumstances tend to induce involvement with a dying patient. Some nurses cannot help feeling upset about a patient who is left alone to die, for example, when no family member is in attendance. It is also hard for any nurse to remain detached when the patient's social loss value is very high.

Occasionally some aspect of a case—the patient's age, sex, marital status or occupation, for example, or the similarity of his illness to one the nurse herself or someone close to her has had—leads a nurse to over-identify with the patient. As an extreme form of involvement, this is disturbing to composure. "I found it so hard to talk to him, and he, of course, knew

enough about medicine to realize what his condition was." The
interviewer asked: "He was close to your age?" The nurse answered, "Yes, he was, I think this was part of what made me
feel so badly." And the dying patient whose illness is similar to
one the nurse or a member of her family actually has, or is sus-
ceptible to, provides a distressing rehearsal of a potential fate.

A dying patient who lingers on can present special problems: he cannot be avoided or forgotten all the time, and nurses
tend to become involved simply as a consequence of long-term
contact with him and his family. "We get so attached to our
patients because they are long-term." They expect to see the
patient each day as a part of coming to work. They may become
good friends with him, expecting regular exchanges with him
and enjoying the daily job of making him comfortable. If
he is alternately going home and returning to the ward as his
condition varies, he is welcomed as an old friend each time
he returns. After a time, some nurses may develop a "never
will die" expectation for the patient, which weakens their
emotional defenses so that when he finally dies, loss of composure is more likely.

Nurses are also likely to become upset at the long arduous
struggle of some lingering patients, a struggle which in the
end only makes the dying harder on everyone. They may become particularly concerned about the family members who
must go through an emotional ordeal while their financial
resources are being drained away for naught. Patients' deaths
may leave their family destitute financially as well as socially
This attachment to lingering patients and their families makes
it as difficult to avoid or forget patients as it would be if they
were friends known prior to hospitalization. When one such
patient died, the nurses "were all with her," mutually supporting
each other's composure. Such a collective form of involvement
reduces the strain on composure that each nurse would otherwise suffer alone. In the end, as one nurse put it, "The longer
you know the patient, the harder it is to forget." Another nurse,
talking about death in general, said, "We talk over death here,

get our feelings out, then forget it and go home." But she also said, referring to a lingering patient. "These are the kinds of deaths that stay with you."

Talk. Outright avoidance and expressive avoidance are both strategies for precluding conversation as well as controlling work. However, once a conversation has begun, other strategies can be used to protect a nurse from involvement or distress. With patients approaching death, nurses avoid the subject of death in general. This subject may easily come up in discussions about another patient further along with the same disease, thus allowing the first patient to use another dying—or deceased—patient as a reference for gauging his own chances.[3] When the awareness context is closed, or one of suspicion, a nurse cannot discuss another patient's impending death without virtually giving the first patient's fate away. When the context is one of mutual pretense, she might thereby destroy the comfortable illusion that others, including the patient, have carefully established. In an open awareness context, she must still decide how much the patient should be told, or wants to know, about *how* he or another patient is going to die. Since at this stage neither the nurse nor patient knows *when* he is going to die, telling the aware patient when another patient might die or did die may lead him to false and distressing assumptions. Thus, giving him too many details may cause him to break down or withdraw from all communication; either outcome threatens her composure.

Selective listening is another conversational tactic. Nurses listen only to information from the patient and his family that will help them with their work, without increasing their involvement. They turn a deaf ear, if possible, to details about the indicators of social loss—children, spouse, job, talent—that make the impending death so distressing.

[3] The use by patients of other patients as references for ascertaining facts about their own condition has been thoroughly studied for the tubercular patient. See Julius Roth, *Timetables* (Indianapolis: Bobbs-Merrill, 1963).

Other strategies for controlling talk are designed to reduce feedback in questions from the patient which may further involve the nurse with him, thus threatening her composure. Temporal references are sharply restricted, the nurse now limiting herself to perfunctory descriptions of what will happen to the patient in the following days or weeks, and eliminating references to what he will do when he gets out of the hospital, since these may occasion responses. "Tomorrow you are going to x-ray," or "See you next week" (when the nurse takes her weekend off). Nurses depend more on cues they can gather from the patient's condition and less on asking him verbally how he feels—since the patient is likely to ask, in return, for an interpretation of the way he feels. Interpretations of this kind must be managed so as to mislead a patient in a closed, suspicion or pretense awareness context, and to avoid mentioning death in an open context; in either case they take an extra effort to maintain composure. A standard strategy is not to speak until spoken to and then to say as little as possible. This strategy carries anticipatory rebuff of questions not yet asked, and so discourages questioning.

Another strategy to cut down feedback is to select from a patient's talk the least compromising subject and respond only to it. A patient said: "Yes, I'm afraid, I'm afraid, I'm afraid—I can't breathe and I do a lot of coughing." The nurse, to spare herself a discussion of the drastic consequences of inability to breathe, or of fear of death, tried to focus on the coughing. Another nurse was asked directly, "Am I going to die?" to which she responded with the "over-generalizing" strategy: "Well, we all go sometime." Another tactic is to sidestep the "Am I going to die" question by saying "no," then talking a blue streak about nothing in particular, steering clear of his fate and covering her own feelings. Another effective strategy to cut off feedback is to parry this fateful question with the standard "role switching" strategy: "Talk to your doctor." She told the interviewer that when asked this question by a nine-year-old girl, "You feel just like you swallowed your tonsils and you really don't know what to say. It is terribly hard to handle." Her response was intended to stop further discussion. Actually many nurses simply flee the room when asked this question directly, sometimes seeking a private place to cry and regain composure.[4] On one pediatric ward the head nurse prohibited crying on the ward; it had to be done in the coffee room away from the children. Nurses in this stressful situation often feel a need for self-examination, and they must use tactics to maintain composure with the patient until they can find privacy and perhaps a friend to talk it out with.

Death Talk and Awareness Context. We have already indicated that the current awareness context largely determines the strategy a nurse uses to maintain her composure. Many of the strategies just mentioned are also used in maintaining a closed or pretense awareness context—indeed, maintaining such a context often depends on the nurse's remaining composed. But whether a closed awareness context helps or hinders the nurse depends on her personal tolerance for talk about death.

A nurse who cannot tolerate talk about dying or death feels less threat to her composure in a closed or pretense awareness context because the patient cannot force her to discuss the subject. She can use the strategies we have described to evade death talk without feeling that she is evading a conversation that would be legitimate in an open awareness context. In an open or even in a suspicion context, evasion of this type may risk damaging the patient's confidence in the staff, but in a closed awareness context, disclosure is the doctor's responsibility.

When a nurse, who wishes not to, feels that an open awareness context requires her to talk about death, she may be able to turn the patient over to a nurse who is noted for her ability to discuss death—a "death talker." Thus, sometimes a division

---

[4] "Back regions" are structures provided by the hospital, one use of which is for regaining composure; see Erving Goffman, *Presentation of Self in Everyday Life* (New York: Doubleday Anchor Books, 1959), Chapter II.

of labor may develop among nurses to protect those who are unable to handle this aspect of an open context. One nurse reported, "I can talk to patients about death. In fact, nurses call me in to talk to patients because I am able to do this." In a Catholic hospital, three of the older nuns, retired as nurses, were on call for talking with patients about death and dying. Chaplains, social workers, and psychiatrists are sometimes able to take over this task. In these instances the nurse employs the "role switching" strategy to maintain composure.

The nurse who is able and even wants to talk with the patient about the implications of his dying may feel quite uncomfortable in a closed awareness context. To keep the patient unaware, she is forced to put up a false front, which is a burden on her composure because it affords protection she neither needs nor wants. Unless she receives instructions to the contrary, she must not indulge in talk or behavior that would indicate to the patient that he is dying. Yet, to display some involvement, to talk about the death and to act natural would enhance her composure. For this reason some nurses often feel frustrated and distraught in the closed context, and in order to stay composed, avoid the patient, although they would rather give him companionship.[5]

This threat to composure that a closed context gives to nurses who wish to talk is increased if the patient lingers, starts to suspect his fate, or signals that he wants to talk about dying. The nurses begin to debate among themselves whether the patient really knows, and, if so, how awful it is that they cannot help him by talking about it. Further, they do not like having to risk losing his trust by acting as if he will recover when, possibly, he knows he will not. They are also upset by family problems—relatives moving in on the patient's estate, or a child who will not be able to say goodbye—that could

[5] Nurses in this situation were highly likely to go to a sociologist interviewing on the subject to vent their frustration. We later used this as a tactic to obtain information, for most often we were the only people available to nurses for listening to the stresses and strains of such a sensitive situation.

be resolved if they could discuss the patient's death with him. Under this sort of pressure, nurses occasionally break the rules and tell a patient his true fate in time for him to settle his affairs. These nurses appear rather composed after this transgression.

Collective Moods. When the nurses are certain that the patient is dying, they begin developing several collective moods (italicized below) which serve to reduce their involvement in the patient and maintain their composure. The moods continue with refinements and reinforcements through the last stage of dying (when time of death is known) until death. The nurses derive continual mutual support and self-control from these collective moods.

First, nurses begin, collectively, to prepare themselves for the ordeal ahead by viewing the patient's death as *inevitable* and even *desirable*. At the same time, they develop collective rationales to explain and condone their *acceptance* of his death ("It is best for him and his family"). Respites in these moods may occur when the patient rallies for a time before proceeding downhill again ("So you feel better, even though you know she couldn't live"). A lingering patient who can be made comfortable and never seems to die also provides a respite— as he becomes familiar to the nurses they begin to forget that he is dying, thereby altering their moods for a time. A patient whose social loss value is high ("He was a young boy who had everything to live for"), however, may reduce the composure drawn from acceptance by lingering on interminably. The ordeal becomes too much to bear and a mood of *sadness* overcomes the nurses. Their collective impulse is to *"let him die,"* if he is being kept alive with drugs or equipment (see Chapter 12.)

The collective mood of acceptance is accompanied by one of *relief*—a mood with many aspects. Nurses are relieved to know the patient's fate; it at least makes the situation definite. Since there is nothing more to do they no longer need to hope for recovery or be unduly disturbed about failing to save the patient. They can anticipate additional relief after they know when to expect his death and still more after he dies. These anticipations counteract potential distress during the ordeal of these last two stages of dying. They are also relieved when a patient is sent home or to a nursing home, another hospital or another ward. This mood of relief compensates for any guilt generated by the wish somehow to be rid of the dying patient. At death, relief results in a collective mood of *gladness* that the ordeal is over for themselves, the patient and the family. If they have had trouble making him comfortable and free of pain the ordeal is increased, and the relief is greater when he finally leaves the ward or dies.

At this stage of dying—when time of death is not yet known —the nurses' *morale* now becomes a critically important collective aspect of the sentimental order of the ward, and therefore an important underpinning of their composure. Their morale is intimately linked to the patient's. If he is withdrawn or depressed, the nurses must sustain their morale on their own through mutual support with no support from the patient. (This becomes a strong reason for avoiding the patient.) If the patient's morale is good, however, he becomes the pacesetter for the morale of the ward, for it would not do for a nurse to be less cheerful than a patient. Nurses are literally forced to "one-up" the patient by having higher morale. This is one very good reason why nurses are so grateful and appreciative when a patient dies gracefully and cheerfully. Such patients make it comparatively easy to maintain composure, especially when they could, because they are known to be dying, legitimately exert an emotional drag on staff morale.

A patient wavering between cheer and depression may be controlled by the strategy of professional calm and mild sympathy. Too much sympathy might dissolve the patient's tenuous control over himself, thus straining the nurses' morale.[6] Too much hope might make the patient still more depressed,

[6] On the inundation of expressive boundaries, see Fred Davis, "Deviance Disavowal," *Social Problems*, 9 (Winter 1961), p. 124, *et passim.*

should he later suspect or discover his true fate. By remaining calm, nurses hope to settle the patient into a middle-range morale, which in turn will help them maintain their own composure with a minimum of strain.

EXPECTED TIME OF DEATH

In this, the last stage of dying, the strategies used in the previous stage are still very useful, but to cope with the unsettling effects of the death watch, presence at death, the death itself, and handling the family, the nurses develop additional composure strategies. For patients who pass directly from either stage of uncertainty to this last stage, the strategies reviewed directly above must be developed now in the remaining time before death. In many cases, the specific time when death is expected is known for only a few hours or days at the end of the unknown-time stage, though it may be expected for a longer period.

The doctor's participation in this last stage may help or hinder the nurses in maintaining their composure. Nurses can more easily ascertain that a patient will die than they can tell *when* he will die, but knowing when death can be expected will affect their management of the patient, his family, and their own behavior. By telling the nurses when to expect death, and thus initiating this stage for them, the doctor helps them prepare themselves to face the last days or hours with maximum composure. They reassure each other not to feel badly when death comes, reinforcing their collective moods of acceptance and relief and reducing their feelings of helplessness and failure due.to inability to save the patient's life. They also start planning strategies to avoid imposing on a single nurse the strain of the death watch and presence at death.

The Death Watch. Nurses may implement the standard strategy of creating an informal team for the death watch. All members participate in the death watch, no matter which nurse was assigned the patient. Each of the nurses on the team will look into the room as she goes by and all will take turns answering the patient's calls. In some cases, however, one nurse may have to sit with the patient for eight hours, being relieved only for meals and coffee. This "trap" can be quite distressing, especially if the patient has a high social loss value which exacerbates the feeling of helplessness. One nurse watching a 14-year-old girl during her last hours said: "I felt badly about it, you know, here was a young girl and just to see her lying there, and there really wasn't too much you could do for her, you know, only to keep her comfortable and then she wasn't even aware of that. I think more than anything, it's just a help-less feeling, sort of a loss feeling, you just don't know what to do and you couldn't do too much in this particular case."

One strategy to reduce the strain on composure imposed by the death watch is to ask the doctor for flexible sedation orders. Once the doctor has told the nurses when the patient is likely to die, they may legitimately request flexible orders, to insure a comfortable ending for the patient. For the nurse who must participate in the death watch, this gives her an opportunity to alleviate her own distress as well as the patient's sometimes final agony.

Nurses can also find ways to delegate the death watch, usually to someone who is not quite aware of the task he is being asked to perform (another use of "role switching"). If the dying patient is in a room with an alert patient, the nurse may leave the room with a "pressing work" excuse, asking the alert patient to call her immediately if he notices a change in the other patient. Nurses will also ask an ever-present family member, or perhaps a chaplain, to sit with the patient. If no one is available, a patient may be left to die alone, between periodic checks, though nurses find this outcome most disturbing unless he is already comatose.

When the patient approaches death, a number of pre-announcements have to be made; keeping a death watch is a necessary preliminary to these announcements. A doctor must be called, and calling him either too soon or too late is em-barrassing, and hence threatening to composure. (Doctors can relieve nurses of this source of strain by making recurrent visits to the patient.) If the patient is a Catholic, the Catholic chaplain must also be called. Family members must be notified if they exist, but nurses may also have to interrupt or prevent a routine family visit to the bedside, in order either to avoid announcing the imminent death to those unable to bear the shock or to keep relatives from witnessing the death. Timing and handling these announcements with composure is possible only if the doctor has given the nurses a fairly precise indication of when death is likely to occur. Otherwise a sudden change for the worse may disrupt the ward and upset the nurses. Some nurses, therefore, will ask the doctor when to expect death when they are not told (if they can find him).

Presence at Death. The nurses' composure is crucial during the entire final stage of dying, but, especially at the moment of death, when the likelihood of breaking down is greatest. For this reason nurses usually prefer to avoid the death scene. During the first stage of certainty, a collective mood of wishing not to be present at the patient's death tends to develop among them. Since they do not know, at that stage, when to expect death, they can do little but sustain themselves hopefully on the fiction that "patients die at night."

Once they know when to expect death, however, they can make active efforts to be absent. They can take vacations, or request ward changes or different patient assignments, or they can simply disappear when the time comes. And sometimes staff nurses are saved by a routine rotation off the ward. If the doctor or chaplain is present, the nurse can sometimes excuse herself for other work. On some wards special nurses take care of the moribund during the death watch and death, relieving the staff nurses of responsibility for the dying situation altogether. One staff nurse in this situation, however, did say that she was bothered by not being able to take care of her patient at the end.

For the many nurses who cannot avoid being present at death, several conditions affect composure. On wards that seldom experience death, such as obstetric and some pediatric or medical wards, nurses lack experience and may be terribly upset by watching a patient die. These nurses are also likely to become upset because death represents a failure among many successes, and because the ward's sentimental order has let them become deeply involved with the patient and his family. As mentioned earlier, these wards allow much involvement with patients, not only because of the low death ratio but because when a patient starts to die he will often be sent to another ward, such as an intensive care unit, for saving. On wards with a high death ratio, where involvement is not condoned and experience is greater, nurses make less effort to avoid being present at death. In general, just as they do after failing to save a patient in the second stage of dying, nurses who must participate in a death watch and be present at death try to transfer their involvement (object switching) to family members, doctors, or other patients, maintaining composure by helping the living.

At the time of death, it is the doctor's duty to announce it to family members, but in some cases they appear on the scene unexpectedly, unprepared for the death, and demand to know what is happening. The nurse may have no time to remove the relatives or to get a doctor to pronounce death. If she lies about the patient and removes the family she risks a scene in which all parties might lose composure. She is, therefore, forced to announce the death herself, while the family actually watches it take place, hoping her own composure, if she can maintain it, will help the family members keep theirs. One nurse, horrified to find an unsuspecting aunt coming to inquire about her nephew after his brain tumor operation, told the aunt directly that he had died. Having regained her own composure, she was then able to help the stunned aunt control herself.

Forgetting. At death, another collective mood develops to help the nurses maintain composure—"forget the patient." A patient is easiest to forget if his dying follows the pattern expected for his condition. (Ease in forgetting a dying patient is one of the more useful consequences of death expectations.) But if the patient dies in great pain, or after prolonged lingering; if the death involves some negligence or failure on their part; if he had unusual habits—such as drinking shaving lotion; or if his social loss value was high, he may be very hard to forget. In interviewing nurses about their past experiences with dying patients, they invariably mention first those patients who were hard to forget.

In many cases the collective effort to forget will preclude further discussion of the patient, and each nurse is therefore left to find her own individual means for "giving up" the patient and regaining composure. In extreme cases of failure—an unanticipated suicide or negligence—the collective mood may be curiosity instead of forgetfulness. The nurses discuss the case among themselves and with doctors to figure out what went wrong, why the patient died, or died as he did. To forget the patient once and for all, they must rid themselves of feelings of guilt or negligence. It is not uncommon for nurses to be reminded with a sense of distress of a patient who is hard to forget, when passing the room where only a few days before he was alive. Requesting transfers to another ward alleviates these reminders, and it is done occasionally.

UNEXPECTED DEATH

We have described the progressive accumulation of strategies by which a nurse tries to maintain her composure as guided by her changing death expectations for the patient as he approaches death. This developmental building up of strategies does not occur for nurses who have (1) no death expectation; and it is compromised to a degree for nurses with either (2) radically changing expectations or (3) an inaccurate expectation. Thus, these are three principal sources of the unexpected or surprise death of a patient, which in turn become sources of reduced control over both involvement with the patient and professional composure. The underlying point is that any death expectation but the accurate one leaves the nurse open to the shock of an unexpected death, though the threat to her composure varies with the degree of inaccuracy.

When death is really unexpected, and the nurses have no death expectation at all, they have no cause to develop strategies to maintain composure. Sudden death therefore catches them in a most vulnerable state. Lack of awareness among nurses is due, as we have indicated, to an absence of appropriate cues, or from the doctor's failure to reveal his own awareness, or both. Insufficient experience is also a factor, of course: students must learn, first, to recognize an impending death and, then, to manage involvement in terms of death expectations, so as to maintain their composure. From her shock at an unanticipated suicide, one student nurse realized that she had started to cope with dying and death according to her death expectations: "Yes, boom [a suicide], therefore I am frustrated because it happened so quickly. Last time I wasn't frustrated because I knew it would come sooner or later. I wasn't much prepared for it the other time either, but emotionally I was more prepared for it."

Inaccurate expectations may cause a nurse to be too careful, or not careful enough, in managing her involvement with the patient. If she is careless, she is liable to be very upset by a death that could have been anticipated correctly. If she is too careful, her strategies for managing involvement may do unnecessary damage to her relations with the patient and his family. For example, she may avoid a patient or limit talk with him to such an extent that he does not trust her, and this in turn may make her less effective in patient care and unnecessarily hard on the patient and his family. Again, failure to form an accurate death expectation may be due to inexperience, inadequate information from the doctor, or misreading cues.

Radically changing expectations also make it difficult for a nurse to manage her involvement. She may never quite know whether involvement will ultimately destroy her composure: at one moment the patient is going to die, at the next, he will linger some time, the next he may recover, and so forth. In these cases, the patient's physical condition changes constantly, making it difficult for either doctor or nurse to establish a reliable death expectation. Similarly, a vacillating doctor can leave the nurses at a loss as to how much they should guard their composure. In such an unstable situation a nurse's relations with the patient and his family suffer because her talk and avoidance patterns fluctuate in accordance with her changing expectations. And the death may catch her off guard, devastating her composure.

Negligence in Work. The surprise death is particularly upsetting to nurses' composure because it implies that they might have been negligent in nursing care. This implication varies with the three sources of the surprise and with the nearness of the patient to death. If the patient was only seriously—not fatally—ill, or if his death was still not certain, his unexpected death immediately raises a question in the nurses' minds as to whether they could have saved him by watching him more closely. Having had no expectation of death or having been, inaccurately, so certain of death that they concentrated on comfort rather than recovery, nurses may in fact have been negligent. As one nurse put it, "The initial shock of a sudden death bothers you. What could I have done? Could I have noticed something that would have been a warning?" She will be very upset if she remembers something that should have alerted her to the possibility of saving the patient.

After an unexpected death, the nurses may go over the patient's last days in great detail, to see if any of them were negligent in any way. In one case—a woman who committed suicide but who otherwise would have lived—this discussion went on for weeks and was linked to a coroner's inquest and an autopsy. Usually, however, the post-mortem discussion is finished in a few days and any negligence accounted for.

When the patient's death was in fact inevitable, his comfort may have been neglected somewhat by a nurse who did not expect death or who believed that death was not certain. She might have focused on recovery to the detriment of comfort care. When such a patient dies, she regrets not having done more to make the patient comfortable, instead of insisting on a treatment, perhaps a rigorous one, designed to cure him. Of course, a nurse in this situation is still less upset than she would be if she had neglected recovery care in favor of comfort.

Whether their feelings of negligence refer to recovery or to comfort, a surprise death may very well lead distressed nurses to blame the doctor for not telling them what was going on. To some extent, they can thus attribute any apparent negligence on their part to his negligence or incompetence in keeping them informed. To forestall such accusations, the doctor can try doubly hard to obtain an autopsy in cases for which he cannot give an adequate explanation. Another tactic is to accuse himself first. In one very dramatic case a mother hemorrhaged on the delivery table and both she and her baby died. The husband was shattered and "absolutely lost his mind." The nurses were terribly upset, and the doctor broke down and cried. While his crying was genuine, its effect was to forestall accusations of negligence or incompetence based on his failure to foresee trouble beforehand. That is, he was not hiding his "awareness" from them. Having to support the doctor also helped the nurses regain composure.

Forgetting. Collective forgetting after death is inhibited and delayed when the patient dies unexpectedly. The nurses must discuss what happened and whether any negligence was involved. In this way they help each other cope with their distress, and regain some composure, but the restorative process of forgetting the patient is delayed. Once the question of negligence is settled, however, they can begin to forget the death, which, as we have seen, forces the discussion to end. Telling nurses on other wards about the surprise death also enhances forgetting and restores composure. The other nurses may find the circumstances of the death interesting, or they may have known the patient themselves. Telling another nurse, especially one who was not involved in the case, allows the nurse to organize the tragedy and account for it to herself; this helps her forget it and regain her normal composure.

This method of regaining composure may, however, have unpleasant consequences. Sometimes the news is shocking enough to reverberate through the hospital and even to the newspapers. Others in the hospital may be disturbed because they are in some way implicated, as the head of nursing services, for example, would be implicated as the overseer of negligent nurses in a preventable suicide.

In the process of forgetting, the nurses' composure is least threatened when they can remember only the general circumstances, not the individual or the agonizing details of his few last days and his death. In a surprise death, the details of the last days are constantly mulled over afterward, making it difficult to forget them. These details may remain in the nurses' memories to disturb them much later, sometimes to the point that they cannot face other dying patients with composure and have to arrange for transfer to wards where they are unlikely to have to deal with them.

Overdue Death. Another surprise inherent in the dying situation occurs when a patient does not die at the expected time. He may linger on interminably, beyond all reasonable expectations for his condition. For example, a child with a congenital defect was supposed to die at five or six years of age and lived on to thirteen. One nurse found this so disturbing that she avoided the patient, especially his continual requests to play cards. After he died, his seven years of lingering were very hard for her to forget. (Unfortunately this particular patient had been taken care of for six years by nurses who had well-developed guards against involvement. His life as a patient would have been much easier if the nurses had known that his death would be so delayed, for then they could have permitted a more appropriate degree of involvement during the years of lingering.)

One strategy to handle an overdue death is simply to avoid and forget the patient. This is sometimes aided by the collective mood: "It's senseless." When the patient lingers on indefinitely in a comatose state—physically alive, socially dead, nurses may just stop thinking about him. One nurse said in such a case, "It makes no sense for her to live beyond the point where she went on living and that was by some months."

The patient who is expected to die on the operating table, but instead lives on for three or four days, is another example of overdue death. In one such case, during this short but intensive overdue period, nurses who had participated in the operation became quite upset. They felt that perhaps more could have been done for the patient if the doctors had approached him with the expectation that he was going to recover, and that everyone had been negligent. Each day, as they came to work, they asked whether the patient had died yet. Only after he died could the nurses who were involved convincingly regain their normal composure. Thus some overdue patients are forgotten before death, and others never forgotten.

PESSIMISM AND COMPOSURE

Built into the development of strategies to manage involvement and maintain composure while the patient is dying, is an element of pessimism. The nurses base their defenses on a conservative estimate of the patient's chances, preferring excessive caution to the risk of breaking down at the wrong moment. As we have indicated, this too-careful guarding of composure may be hard on a patient who is really not as close to dying as the nurses believe. The nurses' pessimism, therefore, is a source of slightly inaccurate death expectations.

If the patient recovers—"comes alive"—a nurse with a well-developed strategy against losing composure may be distressed by the realization that she failed him. She was negligent. If she had not been so careful to guard her composure, she could have treated the patient as if he were merely seriously ill, talking with him about almost anything and motivating him to get well. Not only could she have applied her training more effectively, but the patient would have had more companionship.

In general, this implicit pessimism causes nurses, too often, to "pull away" from patients sooner than necessary—and, indeed, why should it be necessary at all? If the patient has been unaware that he is expected to die, this pulling away may risk a premature, abrupt disclosure of his impending death which can be very distressing to the patient and unnecessary if he is still in the uncertain stages of dying. One uncertain-to-die patient who later recovered told us, "When I felt the nurses pulling away from me, I knew I was dying and I became terribly depressed."

Part Four

Conclusions

14

The Practical
Use of Awareness Theory

In this chapter we shall discuss how our substantive sociological theory has been developed in order to facilitate applying it in daily situations of terminal care by sociologists, by doctors and nurses, and by family members and dying patients. The application of substantive sociological theory to practice requires developing a theory with (at least) four highly interrelated properties. (As we have demonstrated in this book and will discuss explicitly in the next chapter, a theory with these properties is also very likely to contribute to formal—*i.e.*, general—sociological theory.) The first requisite property is that the theory must closely *fit* the substantive area in which it will be used. Second, it must be readily *understandable* by laymen concerned with this area. Third, it must be sufficiently *general* to be applicable to a multitude of diverse, daily situations within the substantive area, not just to a specific type of situation. Fourth, it must allow the user partial *control* over the structure and process of the substantive area as it changes through time. We shall discuss each of these closely related properties and briefly illustrate them from our book to show how our theory incorporates them, and therefore why and how our theory can be applied in terminal care situations.[1]

---

[1] Applied theory can be powerful for exactly the reasons set forth by John Dewey, some years ago: "What is sometimes termed 'applied' science . . . is directly concerned with . . . instrumentalities at work in effecting modifications of existence in behalf of conclusions that are reflectively preferred. . . . 'Application' is a hard word for many to accept. It suggests some extraneous tool ready-made and complete which

FITNESS

That the theory must fit the substantive area to which it will be applied is the underlying basis of the theory's four requisite properties. It may seem obvious to require that substantive theory must correspond closely to the data, but actually in the current ways of developing sociological theory there are many pitfalls that may preclude good fitness.[2] Sociologists often develop a substantive theory—theory for substantive areas such as patient care, delinquency, graduate education—that embodies, without his realization, the sociologist's ideals, the values of his occupation and social class, as well as popular views and myths, along with his deliberate efforts at making logical deductions from some formal theory to which he became committed as a graduate student (for example, a theory of organizations, stratification, communication, authority, learning, or deviant behavior). These witting and unwitting strategies typically result in theories too divorced from the everyday realities of the substantive area, so that one does not quite

---

is then put to uses that are external to its nature. But . . . application of 'science' means application *in,* not application *to.* Application *in* something signifies a more extensive interaction of natural events with one another, an elimination of distance and obstacles; provision of opportunities for interactions that reveal potentialities previously hidden and that bring into existence new histories with new initiations and endings. Engineering, medicine, social arts realize relationships that were unrealized in actual existence. Surely in their new context the latter are understood or known as they are not in isolation." *Experience and Nature* (Chicago: Open Court Publishing Company, 1925), pp. 161-162.

[2] For many years, Herbert Blumer has remarked in his classes that sociologists perennially import theories from other disciplines that do not fit the data of sociology and inappropriately apply sociological theories developed from the study of data different than that under consideration. *Cf.* "The Problem of the Concept in Social Psychology," *American Journal of Sociology* (March, 1940), pp. 707-719. For an analysis of how current sociological methods by their very nature often result in data and theory that does not fit the realities of the situation see Aaron V. Cicourel, *Method and Measurement in Sociology* (New York: Free Press of Glencoe, 1964).

know how to apply them, or in what part of the social structure to begin applying them, or where they fit the data of the substantive area, or what the propositions mean in relation to the diverse problems of the area. The use of logical deduction rests on the assumption that the formal theory supplies all the necessary concepts and hypotheses; the consequences are a typical forcing and distorting of data to fit the categories of the deduced substantive theory, and the neglecting of relevant data which seem not to fit or cannot be forced into the pre-existing sociological categories.[3] In light of the paucity of sociological theories that explicitly deal with change,[4] logical deduction usually is carried out upon static theories which tends to ensure neglect, distortion, and forcing when the deduced theory is applied to an ever-changing, everyday reality.

Clearly, a substantive theory that is faithful to the everyday realities of the substantive area is one that is carefully *induced* from diverse data gathered over a considerable period of time. This research, usually based primarily on qualitative data gathered through observations, interviews and documents and perhaps later supplemented by surveys, is directed in two ways —toward discovering new concepts and hypotheses, and then continually testing these emerging hypotheses under as many diverse conditions as possible. Only in this way will the theory be closely related to the daily realities (what is actually "going on") of the substantive area, and so be highly applicable to dealing with them. After the substantive theory is sufficiently formulated, formal theories can be scrutinized for such models, concepts and hypotheses as might lead to further formulation

[3] Our position may be contrasted with that of Hans L. Zetterberg who, after some exploratory research to determine problems, bypasses development of substantive theory and goes directly to formal theories for help. He says, "We must know the day-by-day issues facing the practitioner and then search the storehouse of academic knowledge to see whether it might aid him." *Social Theory and Social Practice* (New York: Bedminster Press, 1962), p. 41.

[4] This is noted by Wilbert Moore in "Predicting Discontinuities in Social Change," *American Sociological Review* (June, 1964), p. 332, and in *Social Change* (Englewood Cliffs, N. J.: Prentice-Hall, 1963), preface and Chapter I.

of the substantive theory.[5] We have described in the appendix on method how we have proceeded in developing our theory to fit the realities of terminal care in hospitals. Readers who are familiar with this area will readily be able to judge our degree of success in that enterprise.

UNDERSTANDING

A substantive theory that corresponds closely to the realities of an area will be understood and "make sense" to the people working in the substantive area. This understanding is very important since it is these people who will wish either to apply the theory themselves or employ a sociologist to apply it.[6] Their understanding the theory tends to engender readiness

[5] Thus, in contrast to Zetterberg who renders his data directly with a formal theory, we first develop a substantive theory from the data which then becomes a bridge to the use of what formal theories may be helpful. By bridging the relation of data to formal theory with a carefully thought out substantive theory the forcing, distorting and neglecting of data by rendering it with a formal, usually "thought-up," theory is prevented in large measure. See Zetterberg, *op. cit.*, Chapter 4, particularly pp. 166-178.

[6] In contrast, both Zetterberg and Gouldner imply by their direct use of formal theory that the practical use of sociological theory is the *monopoly* of the sociologist as consultant, since, of course, these formal theories are difficult enough to understand by sociologists. Zetterberg, *op cit.* and Alvin W. Gouldner, "Theoretical Requirements of the Applied Social Sciences," *American Sociological Review*, Vol. 22 (February, 1959). Applying substantive theory, which is easier to understand, means also that more sociologists can be applied social theorists than those few who have clearly mastered difficult formal theories to be "competent practitioners of them." Zetterberg, *op. cit.*, p. 18.

Another substantive theory dealing with juvenile delinquency, in David Matza, *Delinquency and Drift* (New York: Wiley, 1964), provides a good example of our point. This is a theory that deals with "what is going on" in the situations of delinquency. It is *not* another rendition of the standard, formally derived, substantive theories on delinquency which deal intensively with classic ideas on relations between culture and subculture, conformity, opportunity structures, and social stratification problems, such as provided in the formal theories of Merton and Parsons and as put out by Albert Cohen and Richard Cloward and Lloyd Ohlin. As a result two probation officers of Alameda County, California, have told us that at last they have read a sociological theory that deals with "what is going on" and "makes sense" and that will help them in their work. Thus, they can apply Matza's theory *in* their work!

to use it, for it sharpens their sensitivity to the problems that they face and gives them an image of how they can potentially make matters better, either through their own efforts or those of a sociologist.[7] If they wish to apply the theory themselves, they must perceive how it can be readily mastered and used.

In developing a substantive theory that fits the data, then, we have carefully developed concepts and hypotheses to facilitate the understanding of the theory by medical and nursing personnel. This, in turn, has ensured that our theory corresponds closely to the realities of terminal care. Our concepts have two essential features: they are both analytic and sensitizing. By *analytic* we mean that they are sufficiently generalized to designate the properties of concrete entities—not the entities themselves—and by *sensitizing* we mean that they yield a meaningful picture with apt illustrations that enable medical and nursing personnel to grasp the reference in terms of their own experiences. For example, our categories of "death expectations," "nothing more to do," "lingering," and "social loss" designate general properties of dying patients which unquestionably are vividly sensitizing or meaningful to hospital personnel.[8]

To develop concepts of this nature, which tap the best of two possible worlds—abstraction and reality—takes considerable study of one's data.[9] Seldom can they be deduced from formal theory. Furthermore, these concepts provide a necessary bridge between the theoretical thinking of sociologists and the practical thinking of people concerned with the substantive area, so that both parties may understand and apply the theory. The sociologist finds that he has "a feeling for" the everyday realities of the situation, while the person in the situation finds

[7] See Rensis Likert and Ronald Lippitt, "The Utilization of Social Science," in Leon Festinger and Daniel Katz (eds.), *Research Methods in the Behavioral Sciences* (New York: Dryden Press, 1953), p. 583.

[8] On sensitizing concepts see Herbert Blumer, "What is Wrong with Social Theory," *American Sociological Review,* 19 (February, 1954), pp. 3-10, quote on p. 9.

[9] Zetterberg has made this effort in choosing concepts with much success, *op. cit.,* p. 49 and *passim.*

he can master and manage the theory. In particular, these concepts allow this person to pose and test his "favored hypotheses" in his initial applications of the theory.[10]

Whether the hypotheses prove somewhat right or wrong, the answers still are related to the substantive theory; use of the theory helps both in the interpretation of hypotheses and in the development of new applications of the theory. For example, as physicans (and social scientists) test out whether or not disclosure of terminality is advisable under specified conditions, the answers will be interpretable in terms of awareness contexts (Chapters 3 and 6) and the general response process (Chapter 8). This, in turn, will direct these people to further useful questions as well as lead to suggestions for changing many situations of terminal care.

In utilizing these types of concepts in our book, we have anticipated that readers would almost literally be able to see and hear the people involved in terminal situations—but see and hear in relation to our theoretical framework. It is only a short step from this kind of understanding to applying our theory to the problems that both staff and patients encounter in the dying situation. For instance, a general understanding of what is entailed in the mutual pretense context, including consequences which may be judged negative to nursing and medical care, may lead the staff to abandon its otherwise unwitting imposition of mutual pretense upon a patient. Similarly, the understanding yielded by a close reading of our chapters on family reactions in closed and open contexts should greatly aid a staff member's future management of—not to say compassion for—those family reactions. A good grasp of our theory, also, will help hospital personnel to understand the characteristic problems faced on particular kinds of hospital services, including their own, as well as the typical kinds of solutions that personnel will try.

[10] Gouldner (*op. cit.*, pp. 94-95) considers in detail the importance of testing the favored hypotheses of men who are in the situation. However, we suggest that the person can test his own hypotheses too, whereas Gouldner wishes to have a sociologist do the testing.

GENERALITY

In deciding upon the analytic level of our concepts, we have been guided by the criteria that they should not be so abstract as to lose their sensitizing aspect, but yet must be abstract enough to make our theory a general guide to the multi-conditional, ever-changing daily situations of terminal care. Through the level of generality of our concepts we have tried to make the theory flexible enough to make a wide variety of changing situations understandable, and also flexible enough to be readily reformulated, virtually on the spot, when necessary, that is, when the theory does not work. The person who applies our theory will, we believe, be able to bend, adjust, or quickly reformulate awareness theory as he applies it in trying to keep up with and manage the situational realities that he wishes to improve. For example, nurses will be able better to cope with family and patients during sudden transitions from closed to pretense or open awareness if they try to apply elements of our theory (see Chapters 3, 8, 9), continually adjusting the theory in application.

We are concerned also with the theory's generality of scope. Because of the changing conditions of everyday terminal situations it is not necessary to use rigorous research to find precise, quantitatively validated, factual, knowledge upon which to base the theory. "Facts" change quickly, and precise quantitative approaches (even large-scale surveys) typically yield *too few* general concepts and relations between concepts to be of broad practical use in coping with the complex interplay of forces characteristic of the substantive area. A person who employs quantitatively derived theory "knows his few variables better than anyone, but these variables are only part of the picture." [11] Theory of this nature will also tend to give the user the idea that since the facts are "correct" so is the theory; this hinders the continual adjustment and reformulation of theory necessi-

[11] Zetterberg, *op. cit.*, p. 187.

tated by the realities of practice. Because he is severely limited when facing the varied conditions and situations typical of the total picture, the person who applies a quantitatively derived theory frequently finds himself either guideless or applying the inapplicable—with (potentially) unfortunate human and organizational consequences. This kind of theory typically does not allow for enough variation in situations to take into account the institution and control of change in them. Also, it usually does not offer sufficient means for predicting the diverse consequences of any action, done with purpose, on those aspects of the substantive area which one does not wish to change but which will surely be affected by the action. Whoever applies this kind of theory is often just "another voice to be listened to before the decision is reached or announced" by those who do comprehend the total picture.[12]

Accordingly, to achieve a theory general enough to be applicable to the total picture, we have found it more important to accumulate a vast number of *diverse* qualitative "facts" on dying situations (some of which may be slightly inaccurate). This diversity has facilitated the development of a theory that includes a sufficient number of general concepts relevant to most dying situations, with plausible relations among these categories that can account for much everyday behavior in dying situations. Though most of our report is based on field observations and interviews, we have used occasional data from any source (newspaper and magazine articles, biographies and novels, surveys and experiments), since the criterion for the credibility and potential use of this data is how they are integrated into the emergent substantive theory.[13]

The relations among categories are continually subject to qualification, and to change in direction and magnitude due to new conditions. The by-product of such changes is a correction of inaccuracies in observation and reintegration of the

[12] *Ibid.*

[13] This theme on integration into a theory as a source of confirming a fact or a proposition is extensively developed in Hans L. Zetterberg, *On Theory and Verification in Sociology* (New Jersey: Bedminster Press, 1963).

correction into the theory as it is applied. The application is thus, in one sense, the theory's further test and validation. Indeed, field workers use application as a prime strategy for testing emerging hypotheses, though they are not acting as practitioners in a substantive area. In the next section, by illustrating how our theory guides one through the multifaceted problem of disclosure of terminality, we indicate how one confronts the total picture with a theory that is general enough in scope to be applicable to it.

This method of discovering and developing a substantive theory based on a multitude of diverse facts tends to resolve two problems confronting the social scientist consultant, who, according to Zetterberg, is "dependent on what is found in the tradition of a science" and, when this fails, is apt to "proceed on guess work" so as not to "lose respect and future assignments." [14] Our method resolves these problems in large measure because it is not limited by the dictum that Zetterberg's consultant must follow: "Only those details were assembled by the consultant and his co-workers that could be fitted into the categories of sociology, *i.e.,* phrased in sociological terminology." [15] As stated earlier in the section on fitness, we do not believe that the categories of sociology can at the outset be directly applied to a substantive area without great neglect, forcing, and distortion of everyday realities. A substantive theory for the area must first be *induced,* with its own general concepts; and these concepts can later become a bridge to more formal sociological categories if the latter can be found. As Wilbert Moore has noted, however, we still lack the necessary formal categories to cope with change adequately.

CONTROL

The substantive theory must enable the person who uses it to have enough control in everyday situations to make its

---

[14] Zetterberg, *Social Theory, op. cit.,* pp. 188-189.
[15] *Ibid.,* p. 139. This dictum is based on the idea: "The crucial act here is to deduce a solution to a problem from a set of theoretical principles." Theoretical principles refer to laws of formal theories.

application worth trying. The control we have in mind has various aspects. The person who applies the theory must be enabled to understand and analyze ongoing situational realities, to produce and predict change in them, and to predict and control consequences both for the object of change and for other parts of the total situation that will be affected. And as changes occur, he must be enabled to be flexible in revising his tactics of application and in revising the theory itself if necessary. To give this kind of control, the theory must provide a sufficient number of general concepts and their plausible interrelations; and these concepts must provide him with understanding, with situational controls, and with access to the situation in order to exert the controls. The crux of controllability is the production and control of change through "controllable" variables and "access" variables.

Controllable variables. Our concepts, their level of generality, their fit to the situation, and their understandability give whoever wishes to apply them, to bring about change, a *controllable theoretical foothold* in the realities of terminal situations. Thus, not only must the conceptual variables be controllable, but their controllability must be enhanced by their integration into a substantive theory which guides their use under most conditions that the user is likely to encounter. The use of our concepts may be contrasted with the unguided, *ad hoc* use of an isolated concept, or with the use of abstract formal categories that are too tenuously related to the actual situation.[16]

[16] At a lower level of generality, in much consulting done by sociologists to industrial firms, hospitals, social agencies, and the like, what is usually offered by the sociologists is "understanding," based upon an amalgam of facts intuitively rendered by references to formal theory and some loosely integrated substantive theory developed through contact with a given substantive area over the years. (Sometimes this is abetted, as in consumer research, by relatively primitive but useful analyses of data gathered for specific purposes of consultation.) Providing that the amalgam makes "sense" to the client and that he can see how to use it, then the consultation is worthwhile. Conversely, no matter how useful the sociologist may think his offering is, if the client cannot "see" it then he will not find the consultation very useful. See also Zetterberg, *op. cit.*, Chapter 2.

For example, the prime controllable variable of our study is the "awareness context." Doctors and nurses have much control over the creation, maintenance, and change of awareness contexts; thus they have much control over the resultant characteristic forms of interaction, and the consequences for all people involved in the dying situation. Also, the interactional modes we have specified are highly controllable variables; doctors and nurses deliberately engage in many interactional tactics and strategies.

If a doctor contemplates disclosure of terminality to a patient, by using our theory he may anticipate a very wide range of plausibly expected changes and consequences for himself, patient, family members and nurses. By using the theory developed in Chapter 8, he may judge how far and in what direction the patient's responses may go and how to control these responses. By using the theory in Chapter 3, he may judge what consequences for himself, nurses and patients will occur when the context is kept closed; and by referring to Chapter 6, he may weigh these against the consequences that occur when the context is opened. Also, he may judge how advisable it is to allow the characteristic modes of interaction that result from each type of awareness context to continue or be changed. From these chapters he also may develop a wider variety of interactional tactics than ordinarily would be in his personal repertoire. If maintaining a closed context will result in too great a management of assessment (an interactional mode) by the nurse—which might decrease the patient's trust in the whole staff when he discovers his terminality—it may be better to change the context to allow the nurse to respond differently.

The doctor may also review Chapters 9 and 10 for judging to what degree opening the context by disclosure will lead to problems in controlling family members, and how the disclosure may affect their preparations for death. Resting this decision upon our theory allows him much flexibility and scope of action —precisely because we have provided many general concepts and their probable interrelations closely linked to the reality of disclosure, in order to guide the doctor in considering the many additional situations that will be affected by disclosure. Simply to disclose in the hope that the patient will be able to prepare himself for death is just as unguided and *ad hoc* as to not to disclose because he may commit suicide. To disclose because the patient must learn, according to formal theory, "to take the role of a terminal patient," is too abstract a notion for coping with the realities of the impact of disclosure for all people concerned.

This example brings out several other properties of controllable variables and, thus, of our substantive theory. First, the theory must provide controllable variables with *much explanatory power:* they must "make a big difference" in what is going on in the situation to be changed. We have discovered one such variable—awareness contexts. As we have reiterated many times, much of what happens in the dying situation is strongly determined by the type of awareness context within which the events are occurring.

Second, doctors and nurses, family and patients are already purposefully controlling many variables delineated in our substantive theory. While the doctor exerts most control over the awareness context, all these people have tactics that they use to change or maintain a particular awareness context. The patient, for example, is often responsible for initiating the pretense context. However, all these people are, in our observation, controlling variables for very limited, *ad hoc* purposes. Our theory, therefore, can give staff, family and patients a broader guide to what they tend to do already and perhaps help them to be more effective.

Controllable variables sometimes entail controlling only one's own behavior and sometimes primarily others' behavior —the more difficult of the two. But, as we have tried to show, control usually involves the efforts of two parties; that is *control of the interaction* between two people by one or both. In the dying situation it is not uncommon to see patient, family, doctor, and nurse trying to control each other for their own purposes. Those who avail themselves of our theory may have a better chance in the tug-of-war over who shall best control the dying situation.

In the hospital, material props and physical spaces are of strategic importance as variables which help to control awareness contexts and people's behavior.[17] We have noted how doctors and nurses use spatial arrangements of rooms, doors, glass walls, rooms and screens to achieve control over awareness contexts. By making such controllable variables part of our theory we have given a broader guide to the staff's purposeful use of them. Thus, to let a family through a door or behind a screen may be more advisable than yielding to the momentary urge of shutting out the family to prevent a scene. Letting in family members may aid their preparations for death, which in turn may result in a more composed family over the long run of the dying situation.

Access variables. The theory must also include access variables: social structural variables which allow, guide and give persons access either to the controllable variables or to the people who are in control of them. To use a controllable variable, one must have a means of access to it. For example, professional rules give principal control over awareness contexts to the doctor; therefore the nurse ordinarily has a great deal of control in dying situations because of her considerable access to the doctor, through or from whom she may try to exert control over the awareness context. Professional rules forbid her to change the context on her own initiative; they require her to maintain the current one. Thus the organizational structure of the hospital, the medical profession, and the ward provide degrees of access to control of awareness contexts by both doctor and nurses—and our theory delineates this matter. Family members have more access to a private physician than

---

[17] Elements of "material culture" should not be neglected in development of substantive theory. Gouldner suggests they are the "forgotten man of social research": *op. cit.*, p. 97.

to a hospital physician; thus they may have more control over the former. Sometimes they can demand that their private physician keep a closed awareness context because of the control they exert over him through the lay referral system (upon which he may depend for much of his practice).[18] The patient has little access in the closed context to a doctor in order to control changes of context. However, like the nurse, he has much access to everyday cues concerning his condition —they exist all around him and he learns to read them better and better. Thus, his access to strategic cues gives him an opportunity to control his situation—and we have discussed at length how he can manage cues to gain controls. Access variables also indicate how best to enter a situation in order to manage a controllable variable while not otherwise unduly disrupting the situation. Thus, we have delineated the various alternatives that a nurse may use to gain control over the "nothing more to do" situation in order to let a patient die.

CONCLUSION

Throughout our monograph we have indicated many strategic places, points and problems in dying that we feel would profit from the application of our theory. By leaving these short discourses on application *in context* we trust they have had more meaning than if gathered into a single chapter.

We have made this effort to establish a "practical" theory also because we feel, as many sociologists do and as Elbridge Sibley has written: "The popular notion that any educated man is capable of being his own sociologist will not be exorcised by proclamation; it can only be gradually dispelled by the visible accomplishments of professionally competent sociologists." [19] By attempting to develop a theory that can also be applied, we hope to contribute to the accomplishments of

[18] On the lay referral system see Eliot Freidson, *Patients' Views of Medical Practice* (New York: Russell Sage Foundation, 1961), Part Two.

[19] *The Education of Sociologists in the United States* (New York: Russell Sage Foundation, 1963), p. 19.

sociology. Social theory, in turn, is thereby enriched and linked closely, as John Dewey remarked thirty years ago, with the pursuit and studied control of practical matters.[20]

Two properties of our type of an applied theory must be clearly understood. First, the theory can only be developed by trained sociologists, *but can be applied by either laymen or sociologists.* Second, it is a type of theory which can be applied in a substantive area which entails *interaction* variables. Whether it would be a useful type of theory for areas where interaction is of no powerful consequence (that is, where large scale parameters are at issue, such as consumer purchase rates, birth control, the voting of a county, desegregation of a school system, and audiences for TV) remains unanswered.

[20] See "Social Science and Social Control" in Joseph Ratner (ed.), *Intelligence in the Modern World, John Dewey's Philosophy* (New York: Modern Library, 1939), pp. 949-954.

15

Awareness and the Study of Social Interaction

We noted in the first chapter that this book would focus upon a set of related questions: What were the recurrent kinds of interaction between dying patient and hospital personnel? What were the kinds of tactics used by personnel in dealing with the patient? What were the conditions of hospital organization under which interaction and tactics occurred? And in what ways did they affect the goals and stakes of patient, family, and personnel in the dying situation? In anticipation of the pages to follow, we remarked that in finding answers to such questions we had discovered that most of their variations could be accounted for by what each party to the dying situation was aware of about the patient's fate. In consequence, we would deal with these questions as they related to the powerful explanatory variable of awareness, which we conceptualized as *awareness context*. ("What *each* interactant knows of the patient's defined status, along with his recognition of the other's awarenesses of his own definition—the total picture as a sociologist might construct it—an 'awareness context.' It is the context within which these people interact while taking cognizance of it.")

In part II of the book, we discussed four types of awareness context of great import for "what goes on around the patient": closed, suspicion, mutual pretense, and open awareness. We assumed, for simplicity's sake, that only two interactants were involved in the given awareness context: the patient and the hospital staff (taken as though all its members shared the same awareness). Each discussion was organized around a paradigm: (1) a description of the given awareness context; (2) the social structural conditions that enter into the context; (3) the consequent interaction, including various tactics and countertactics; (4) the change of interaction from one type of awareness to another; (5) the ways in which various interactants engineer changes of awareness context; and (6) various conseqences of the interaction for the interactants, for the hospital, and for further interaction. The discussion in Part III was organized around various general problems associated with awareness context as they bear upon the patient, his family and the hospital staff. In that latter discussion, the paradigm noted above was left implicit but was the analytic bedrock upon which discussion itself rested.

Many readers, notably the health professionals, have undoubtedly read our chapters as realistic, albeit highly organized, *descriptions* of the multi-faceted "dying situation." But as we have previously emphasized, the chapters can also be read as an *integrated substantive theory* about awareness contexts as those contexts relate to interaction in the dying situation. We did not, in this book, concern ourselves with everything that happens around dying patients, but only with the varied events which occur in relation to awareness of the patient's death. Every page touches on some aspects of awareness as it affects interaction around or toward the dying patient.

This kind of theory is, of course, grounded in research on one particular substantive area (dying), and might therefore be taken to apply only to that specific area. Theory at such a "level," however, may have important general implications. We shall now detail the more general significance of our theory of awareness contexts.

FROM SUBSTANTIVE TO FORMAL THEORY

In the preceding chapter we remarked that substantive theory faithful to the empirical situation cannot be formulated by merely applying a formal theory to the substantive area. A substantive theory must be first formulated in order to see which parts of diverse formal theories (originally developed for such conceptual areas as deviance, status congruency, reference groups, stigma, or hierarchy) can then further the substantive formulation. And in its turn, substantive theory may help in formulating formal theory. It may also contribute to the formulation of new formal theory grounded on careful comparative research.

In developing our substantive theory of awareness contexts, we utilized the strategy of choosing multiple comparison groups to study (see Appendix). Those groups were chosen by virtue of the logic of our emerging analytical framework. The reader will recall that we studied, simultaneously or in succession, a series of hospital services designed to maximize differences and similarities in "the dying situation" according to our emerging substantive theory of awareness contexts. We suggested in our opening chapter, and discussed in a recent article,[1] that awareness contexts are not confined to the dying situation, but are found generally throughout the full range of social interaction. Consequently, if one wishes to develop a systematic formal (or general) theory of awareness contexts, he must analyze data from many substantive areas.

When advancing a substantive theory to a formal one, the comparative analysis of groups is still the most powerful method for formulating credible theory. The logic for discovering substantive theory—which provided an efficient guide to multiple groups in one substantive area—also will provide a guide for obtaining more data from many kinds of substantive areas, in order to generate formal theory and to verify or

[1] Glaser and Strauss, "Awareness Contexts and Social Interaction," *American Sociological Review*, 29 (October, 1964), pp. 669-679.

negate its hypotheses. Again, the constant comparison of many groups quickly draws attention to their many similarities and differences, the analysis of which now generates a formal theory.[2]

How this might be done with the theory of awareness contexts can be briefly illustrated. Situations where awareness contexts exist are, for instance, clowning at circuses, buying and selling cars, hustling in pool halls, the passing of Negroes as whites, spying as practiced by nations, and the mutual suspicion of prisoners in Chinese war camps. Quick scrutiny of these situations, as well as our earlier preliminary analysis of differences between some of them and the dying situation, suggests several properties useful for comparing groups within these situations. The *signs* or indicators of an interactant's status may vary in how visible they are to the other interactants. Different *numbers of interactants* can be involved: two, three, or more. Different *numbers of groups* can be represented by the interactants. The *ratios of insiders and outsiders* present during the interaction may vary: one patient and dozens of staff members; five hustlers and one mark; one Negro, five "wise" people "in the know," and millions of white persons not in the know. The statuses of interactants may also vary in *hierarchical* position (same or different status levels) as well as in *degree* of hierarchy. And of course the *stakes* of the interaction may vary tremendously.

Comparisons of each property for diverse substantive groups, as listed above, quickly leads to the development of general categories and the formulation of associated hypotheses. Suppose that one focuses, for instance, upon the identifying signs of status. Some signs are physical (skin color), some are behavioral (speech or gesture), some are marks of skill (the agility of the card shark), some are insignia (uniforms and clothing), and so on. For any given interactional situation

[2] Barney Glaser and Anselm Strauss, "Discovery of Substantive Theory: A Basic Strategy Underlying Qualitative Research," *American Behavioral Scientist*, 8 (February, 1965), pp. 5-12.

certain signs of status may be thought of as primary and others as secondary: in America, skin color is the primary indicator of "Negro," just as genitalia are of respective sex. The secondary signs—those that strongly suggest status, especially in conjunction with primary signs—would be, for "Negro", "kinky hair" and perhaps southern-style speech, and for sex they would be clothing, hair style, and gesture.

The visibility of such signs depends on learned ability to recognize them; for instance, many people have never learned to recognize homosexuals, and others would not know an American Indian if they saw one. Understandably, some interactants may not even recognize the signs of their own status: for instance, the dying person kept in the closed awareness context. Signs can be manipulated, both crudely and with subtlety. For instance, they may simply be removed from vision, as when stigmata are concealed. They can be disguised, as when kinky hair is straightened or, as John Griffin did when passing for Negro, skin color is changed temporarily with chemicals. Signs can also be suppressed, as when an interactant chooses not to flash signs that he is really an American spy, or a Japanese-American visiting in Japan chooses to talk in the native tongue at a department store so as not to be recognized as a "rich American." These, of course, are all tactics for minimizing potential recognition by other interactants.

Countertactics consist of eliciting important "give-away" signs, for otherwise one may have to wait for and hope to recognize those signs. Some countertactics for recognizing persons who are suppressing identity depend upon "passing" as a member of that group (an FBI man posing as a Communist) or on informers from within the group. Among persons of similar status, conventional signs may be used to further recognition; the deliberate use of these signs will vary depending on whether outsiders are present or absent, and whether if present they are "wise" (sympathetic insiders) or not.[3] There are typical spatial locales where the gathered insiders can forgo

[3] See Erving Goffman, *Stigma* (New York: Prentice-Hall, 1963).

efforts to disguise or suppress identifying signs. But they may need (as with drug addicts) countertactics to avoid betrayal even in such secluded places. It is worth emphasizing that sometimes identifying signs need to be rectified—as when a man mistaken for a thief must prove his innocence to bystanders, or even to police and later to a court of law. Sometimes rectification is made, but it false! And sometimes, as we have seen in mutual pretense, the dying patient in some sense rectifies that notion by acting as very much alive and, given the ambiguity of most signs, other people act up to his rectification—until the signs are either so unambiguous that the game is hard to play, or he drops the pretense and admits who he really is. A subjective, and subtle, accompaniment of such ambiguities is when an interactant's rectification is rejected and he himself begins to doubt who he is, as in Nazi Germany when gentiles with faint Jewish lineage came to doubt their true identities.[4]

Such comparisons of diverse groups on the dimension of "signs" quickly lead to both useful concepts and hypotheses about this facet of a formal theory of awareness context. Just as when one is developing a substantive theory, the hypotheses will be concerned with such matters as tactics and counter-tactics, as well as with the structural conditions for them, their consequences, and so on. But it is important to understand that this kind of inquiry can be furthered immensely by systematic analysis not only of a single property but of *combinations of properties*: signs and stakes, for instance; or signs, stakes, ratios of insiders-outsiders, and numbers of group representatives present at the interaction. (In essence, this is how we proceeded when developing substantive theory in Part III of our book.) This kind of analysis becomes increasingly enriched, because it leads the researcher to ask, "Where can I find another comparison group that differs in one more specified respect?" When he finds that group, its examination leads

[4] Arthur Miller's perceptive novel, *Focus* (New York: Reynal and Hitchcock, 1945), portrays this dilemma for a man who looked Jewish but had no Jewish lineage whatever.

him to further verification or to fruitful qualification. By such means, exceedingly complex—and well-grounded—formal theory can be developed. It is precisely by such means that one could extend our substantive theory of awareness contexts upward (in abstractness) and outward (in generality). In doing so, many more useful types of awareness context would be generated and related to interactants' behavior.

ON TO FORMAL THEORY?

Unquestionably most sociologists tend to avoid the formulation of *grounded* formal theory; they stay principally at the substantive level. Aside from the inherently greater difficulties in working with high level abstractions or in feeling confident about broader generalities, we believe there are several reasons why sociologists prefer to stay with substantive affairs.

First of all, a researcher tends to know one or two substantive areas well, and feels increasingly comfortable as he learns more about them over the years. The internal satisfactions and securities of such specialization are augmented by the further rewards of being considered a mature expert in a specialized field—rewards which emanate from colleagues and the wider public.[5] Furthermore, sociologists learn very early the dictum that there is great difference between a dilettante and a true "pro." The latter knows his data inside out. This conviction tends to keep sociologists from researching more widely, and certainly from working more abstractly, than they might. One perceives this vividly in the writings and remarks of colleagues who feel they have to amass and comprehend great amounts of data before they can safely claim "findings." (The historian's critical reaction to invasion of any well-worked historical field by a social scientist is an extreme instance of the attitude that the outsider does not know the field well enough not to commit errors.)

Insofar as the sociologist concerns himself with formal

[5] *Cf.* Fred Reif and Anselm Strauss, "The Impact of Rapid Discovery Upon the Scientist's Career," *Social Problems*, 1965.

theory, he currently tends to handle it in several alternative ways. He may set out to test, in a given substantive area, some small portion of one or more formal theories, derived often from prominent theorists. Such studies are legion. He may apply several formal theories to a substantive area which he already knows well, seeking to give his materials greater meaning. Sometimes he does this as a *post hoc* enterprise, after the data is collected; but sometimes the theories do direct at least portions of his data collection.

A third aproach is to check out upon comparative materials an important body of theoretical writing, as when Robert Blauner systematically scrutinized a number of industries with respect to their degree of "alienation." [6] This latter type of research is typically confined to careful verification or invalidation of the central guiding theory. But except where the old theory seems to require qualification, this very mandate to check out the existing formal theory under diverse conditions tends to block the chances for developing new theory that are afforded by comparative analysis. In short, such conventional use of comparative analysis shows variations in an established general theory and explains them. In contrast, our use of comparative analysis generates and generalizes a new theory; variations and explanations become part of the process, *not* the product.

Probably the most widespread use of formal theory is, however, that when initiating specific researches a sociologist begins with a loose "framework" of ideas, hunches, notions, concepts, and hypotheses about the substantive area under consideration. This framework is often linked with the researcher's graduate training (Parsonians from Harvard, Mertonians from Columbia) and with his further experiences since graduation.

None of these uses of formal theory is to be decried; they are, however, rather different enterprises than the formulation of grounded formal theory through systematic study of multiple

[6] Robert Blauner, *Alienation and Freedom* (Chicago: University of Chicago Press, 1964).

comparison groups. Perhaps the closest relative to such formulation is the kind of essay writing established many years ago by Georg Simmel, and nurtured by such contemporaries as Erving Goffman and David Riesman, where the essayist—with or without systematic data before him—develops a series of general propositions of relatively high abstraction. Such writing tends to be criticized as, at best, full of insights and, at worst, as pure speculation. (Some "insights" may get "tested" by more rigorously minded social scientists.) From our viewpoint, such writing is exceedingly valuable, but as theory it does lack both integration of well defined concepts and sufficiently credible grounding in careful comparative research.

The more prestigious style of logico-deductive, systematic "grand theorizing," in the hands of its most brilliant practitioners is more than merely aesthetically satisfying; it also gives impetus to considerable useful, precise testing of hypotheses. But it provides no directive—any more than a century ago when Comte and Spencer were its spokesmen—to a closing of that embarrassingly noticeable gap between highly abstract theory and the multitude of miniscule substantive studies so characteristic of sociology. It should be evident that we put greater faith in grounded formal theory, of the kind outlined above, to close that gap, for it is a type of formal theory that readily fits "what's going on" in everyday situations. Possibly the main benefit yielded by grand theories is their use of abstract models (such as the various mathematical, system and equilibrium models). The formulation of formal theory often requires guidance from such explicit models more than does substantive theory, if only because the greater level of abstraction of its concepts requires integration according to such models.

AWARENESS CONTEXTS, INTERACTIONAL THEORY AND RESEARCH

As we noted in the preceding chapter, the theory outlined in this book entails interaction variables, because it was developed to gain a greater understanding of and control over interaction in the dying situation. Much earlier we had remarked that a central sociological problem is how to conceptualize and account for social interaction and that many influential theorists (Weber, Durkheim, Thomas, Mead, Parsons, and Goffman among them) had grappled with the problem.

If now we focus upon the relation of awareness contexts to social interaction, what can be said about the writings of such men? In general, they have tended, when discussing the kinds of phenomenon which we have termed "awareness context," to attend only to one or two of the many possible contexts. For instance, Mead was consistently interested in open awareness and Erving Goffman, though not solely concerned with the closed context, is perhaps at his best when discussing the phenomena which we would associate with closed awareness.[7] Of equal importance, such theorists tend to emphasize only certain portions of the basic paradigm developed in this book for the study of interaction. Sometimes they discuss a given awareness context in relative isolation from, or in only loose connection with, social structure. And the relevant interactional tactics may not be fully explored. Sometimes the consequences are barely noted, or only as they bear on one or the other interactant, not necessarily in relation to the social or organizational structure within which interaction occurs.

Essentially the same strictures hold for sociological research when awareness is central to the situation investigated.[8] Also in many research reports the readers are given passing information which suggests that the paradigm of awareness might have provided a very useful addition, even within the framework of the researcher's own analysis.[9] And some substantive theories, based upon extensive bodies of research, turn upon awareness

[7] See our paper, "Awareness Contexts and Social Interaction," *op. cit.*

[8] *Ibid.;* also see Ned Polsky's description of hustler tactics in pool halls: "The Hustler," *Social Problems,* 12 (1964), pp. 3-15.

[9] See M. Dalton's description of organizational cheating in his *Men Who Manage* (New York: Wiley, 1959); also Albert J. Reiss, Jr., "The Social Integration of Queers and Peers," *Social Problems,* 9 (1961), pp. 102-120.

contexts: in our estimation, these sometimes excellent writings require much more extensive analyses of the specific and central awareness contexts in order to increase plausibility and make verification more operational.[10]

To be sure, not all interactional research and analysis requires a central focus upon awareness. We urge, however, that such studies, irrespective of their specific focus and central variables, include in their analysis a consideration of awareness as a *strategic general variable*. Additional data gathering on awareness is not thereby required, for most interactional studies inevitably collect data bearing on awareness; the data need only be analyzed in terms of awareness. Formal interactional theory, in general, could profit from such specific substantive analyses, just as the latter might benefit from an increasingly sophisticated interactional theory. In interactional studies which do not centrally focus on awareness, the specific paradigm which underlies the analysis in our book need not be used in toto. Presumably different enterprises require somewhat different guiding schemes. However, we wish to emphasize that our paradigm forces one's gaze upon two important features of interaction that are frequently underplayed. One feature is the developmental character of interaction. The second is the social structural context within which interaction occurs. Perhaps a fitting close to this book is a re-emphasis upon that second feature. In so much writing about interaction there has been such neglect or incomplete handling of relationships between social structure and interaction that we have no fear of placing too much emphasis upon those relationships. The careful reader of our book may even have noted that these relationships are not entirely one-sided. On occasion, the course of interaction may partly change the social structure within which interaction occurred, as when the transformation of an awareness context alters the structural conditions operat-

---

[10] *Cf.* David Matza, *Delinquency and Drift* (New York: Wiley, 1964), Chapter 2; Alfred Lindesmith, *Opiate Addiction* (Bloomington, Indiana: Principia Press, 1947).

ing at a given hospital service so as to make it "a different place." This interplay of social structure and social interaction is precisely what makes the study of interactional development so richly rewarding, thus binding together two basic concerns of our book and our theory.[11]

[11] And, as we suggested in an earlier paper ("Awareness Contexts . . ." *op. cit.*, p. 678), this is why our paradigm is so useful in relating development and structure: "how does one type of context lead to one another; what are the structural conditions—including rules—in the relevant institutions that facilitate or impede existence of a context, and changes in it; what are the effects of a changing awareness context on the identity of a participant; why does one party wish to change a context while another wishes to maintain it or reinstate it; what are the various interactional tactics used to maintain or reinstate change; and what are the consequences for each party, as well as for sustaining institutional conditions?"

Methods of Collection and Analysis of Data

In our book, we have attempted to develop an integrated theory about awareness contexts as they pertain to dying in hospitals. After a preliminary stage of eleven months this aim governed further collection and analysis of data. As noted in Chapter 1, fieldwork data were gathered at a number of hospitals in the Bay area of San Francisco over a period of three years. Fieldwork procedures are well known to sociologists, but the health professionals may be less acquainted with them. We shall, therefore, write this appendix with both audiences in mind, emphasizing especially the features of field method which make it extremely appropriate for developing *integrated theory* about a *substantive topic* like "dying." [1] In presenting our views, we shall give information about what we did and how we did it, and at the same time we shall give a more general commentary on the characteristics of a credible and pragmatically useful substantive theory.

First, we should note that our concept of "awareness context" was foreshadowed by personal experiences of both authors. Five years before the study began, Strauss participated in what was at first a closed and then a mutual pretense aware-

---

[1] For extended discussions, from which this Appendix is drawn, of discovering and developing substantive theory through the collection and analysis of qualitative data, see Barney G. Glaser and Anselm L. Strauss, "Discovery of Substantive Theory: A Basic Strategy Underlying Qualitative Analysis," *American Behavioral Scientist*, 8 (1965), pp. 5-12;. and Barney G. Glaser, "The Constant Comparative Method of Qualitative Analysis," *Social Problems*, 12 (1965), pp. 436-45. Extensive citation of related source materials on qualitative analysis may be found in these papers. See also the remarks on method in the Preface.

ness context surrounding the dying of his mother. Two years later, he found himself deeply involved with others in what he perceived as "an elaborate collusive game" designed to keep a dying friend unaware of his impending state (closed awareness). Both personal experiences brought to his attention the problems and consequences of lingering deaths as compared with speedy deaths. Still later, during brief observation on a geriatrics ward at a state mental hospital, he was impressed by the immense importance of the ward structure for the staff's handling of dying patients, most of whom were comatose or senile. Consequently, when he initiated a study of dying in hospitals he started by focusing on expectations about certainty and timing of dying—and awareness of these expectations as they affect how the staff manages and how the hospital organization impinges on the dying of patients. After a half year of preliminary fieldwork the project was funded by the Public Health Service, and five months later Glaser joined the project. Glaser, whose father had recently died, had been especially impressed by the importance of death expectations— and who was aware of them—as they affected how family members discussed his father's illness, how the members were handled by the doctors, and how everyone treated his father. He was also struck by the hopelessness of the "nothing more to do" phase of his father's dying.

Shortly after Strauss and Glaser joined forces, they systematically worked out the concepts (and types) of death expectations and awareness contexts, and the paradigm for the study of awareness contexts. Thus, a concern with death expectations and awareness guided the preliminary data collection; the systematic formulation of these concepts and of the paradigm governed further data collection and the ensuing analysis; and this book completes the formulations on the theory of awareness of dying. These formulations should guide others both in research on dying and in developing other theories which must take into account the awareness of people.

We shall begin our discussion of method by noting that

fieldwork is admirably adapted to the development of systematic substantive theory. Fieldwork allows researchers to plunge into social settings where the important events (about which they will develop theory) are going on "naturally." The researchers watch these events as they occur. They follow them as they unfold through time. They observe the actors in the relevant social dramas. They converse with or formally interview the actors about their observed actions. Our own fieldwork procedures did not differ significantly from those described in the literature.

Numerous fieldworkers have also remarked that the formulation and testing of hypotheses inevitably begins early in the research. The earliest hypotheses quickly tend to become integrated, to form the basis of a central analytic framework such as is developed in our book. The analytic framework gets expressed in field notes in two forms: analytic comments are written directly into the field notes; and they are written into occasional memos addressed specifically to matters of analysis. A process of coding also begins at or near the outset of the research, as the researchers think systematically about the data in accordance with their basic analytic categories. In such qualitative analysis, there tends to be blurring and intertwining of coding, data collection and data analysis, from the beginning of the investigation until near its end. As various segments of the analytic framework get built during chronologically different stages of the fieldwork, more data need not be gathered nor analysis be rethought for the segment, unless further theoretical work makes it necessary.[2] When the researchers are convinced that their analytic framework forms a systematic substantive theory, that it is a reasonably accurate statement of the matters studied, and that it is couched in a form possible for others to use if they were to go into the same field, then they are ready to publish their results. This is a schematic but accurate description of how our own analysis was accomplished.

[2] See Glaser, "Constant Comparative . . . ," *ibid.,* for specific procedures of coding and analysis.

The formulation of substantive theory is both facilitated and made additionally credible by the strategy of systematically studying several comparison groups. This strategy—which in our opinion should be more extensively employed—is guided by the *logic* of the emerging analytic framework. In our study, we began by observing on a premature baby service, intentionally minimizing the patient's awareness of dying and maximizing the expectedness of deaths (most "premie" deaths are expected). We then observed on a cancer service, intentionally maximizing the lingering and "nothing more to do" aspects of dying as well as several varieties of awareness of dying. In this fashion, we gradually studied various wards at different hospitals, some of them simultaneously.[3] Our choice of these sites and the directions of our observation there accorded with our aims of verifying (in diverse settings) our initial and later hypotheses, of suggesting new hypotheses, and providing new data either on categories or combinations of categories.

Using comparison groups maximizes the credibility of theory in two fundamental ways. First, by detailing precisely the many similarities and differences of the various comparison groups, the researcher knows, better than if he had studied only one or a few groups, under what sets of structural conditions his hypotheses are minimized and maximized; and hence to what kinds of social structures his theory is applicable. In increasing the scope and delimiting the generality of his theory, he saves his readers work. Frequently, readers of fieldwork must figure out the limitations of a published study by making comparisons with their own experience and knowledge of similar groups. By comparison, they figure that the reported material jibes just so far and no further—for given structural reasons. By using multiple comparison groups, much of this burden of delimiting relevant boundaries for the theory is

[3] The hospitals were: a teaching hospital, a VA hospital, two county hospitals, a private Catholic hospital, a state hospital. The services, or wards, included: geriatrics, cancer, premie, intensive care, medicine, pediatrics, neurosurgery, urology, emergency, etc. The field workers spent between two and four weeks on each ward. In addition, a third researcher later contributed extensive interview data on nursing students' encounters with death.

lifted from the readers' shoulders. In short, replication is built into the research. A second way that multiple comparison groups maximize credibility is by helping the researcher to calculate where a given order of events or incidents is most likely to occur or not to occur (in our study, on what specific wards). This calculus provides him with an efficient logical guide to groups whose study will yield more data to fill in gaps in theory and to verify hypotheses.

Multiple comparison groups also permit and generate the speedy development of analysis. The constant comparison of many groups rather quickly draws the observer's attention to many similarities and differences among groups: these contribute to the generation of theoretical categories, to their full range of types or continuum, their dimensions, the conditions under which they exist more or less, and their major consequences. In addition, the observed differences and similarities speedily generate generalized relations among the theoretical categories, which in turn bcome the hypotheses soon integrated into the substantive theory.

When the field researcher decides to write for publication, then he faces the problem of conveying the credibility of his discovered theory so that readers can make sensible judgments about it. The problem of conveying credibility is divisible into two sub-problems. The first is that the researcher must get readers to understand his theoretical framework. This is generally done by giving an extensive abstract presentation of the framework and its associated theoretical statements, usually at the beginning and end of the publication but also in segments throughout the publication. We have written theory on almost every page of our book.

The related sub-problem is how to describe so vividly the social world studied that the reader can almost literally see and hear its people—but in relation to the theoretical framework. To do this, the researcher ordinarily utilizes several of a considerable armamentarium of standard' devices and we have done so (using pertinent phrases dropped by informants, briefly describing scenes, occasionally quoting sentences or segments of on-the-spot field notes).

The first and second sub-problems of conveying credibility are reflected in the types of concept chosen for writing substantive theory. With regard to the first problem, the researcher's concepts are analytic—sufficiently generalized to designate the properties of concrete entities, (not the concrete entities themseves). With regard to the second problem, his concepts also are sensitizing—they yield a "meaningful" picture—with apt illustrations which enable one to grasp the reference in terms of one's own experience. Our readers will readily recognize that our concepts are both analytic and sensitizing.

Several aspects of the presentation enter into how the reader, in turn, judges the credibility of the theory that the writer is trying to convey. First of all, if a reader becomes sufficiently caught up in the description to feel that vicariously he has been in the field, then he is likely to be more kindly disposed toward the theory than if the description seems flat or unconvincing. In the case of our theory, many readers will have had similar experiences to the people depicted in our book, and will come to the reading armed with numerous, and usually realistic, images. Second, a judgment of credibility will also rest upon assessments concerning how the researcher came to his conclusions. Readers will note, for instance, what range of events the researcher saw, whom he interviewed, who talked to him and under what conditions, and perhaps what experiences he had and how he might have appeared to various people whom he studied. That is, readers will assess the types of data utilized from what is explicitly stated as well as from what can be read between the lines. It is absolutely incumbent to make such judgments about reports based on fieldwork, partly because the publication could conceivably be a complete fabrication, but more usually because any analysis may require some qualification.

Such qualification, we may term "the discounting process." Readers surely discount aspects of many, if not most, analyses which are published (whether resting upon qualitative or quantitative data). This discounting takes several forms: the theory is *corrected* because of one-sided research designs, *adjusted* to fit the diverse conditions of different social structures, *invalidated* by the conditions for other structures through the reader's experience or knowledge, and deemed *inapplicable* to yet other kinds of structures.

This ongoing discounting process of qualification by the reader allows the researcher to write his theory in general form, because the researcher knows that the reader will make the necessary corrections, adjustments, invalidations, and inapplications when thinking about or using the theory. These are qualifications that the researcher could not begin to cover for even a small percentage of one type of reader and, more important, they are qualifications which the researcher must gloss over or ignore in order to write a substantive theory of some generality. Our own theory, for instance, must be qualified to fit various types of hospitals and wards that we did not study—their number is legion. On the other hand, the theory is of sufficient generality, and sufficiently grounded in careful fieldwork, so that the discounting process can usefully proceed. In sum, we and our readers share a joint responsibility.

Probably we need to say a final word about the question of "rigorous findings" versus "credible theory." The presentation of substantive theory, developed through analysis of qualitative data, is often done at a sufficient level of plausibility to satisfy most readers. The theory can be applied and adjusted to many situations with sufficient exactitude to guide thinking, understanding and research. Given certain structural conditions under which sociologists work (such as designing specific action programs, or working in well-developed substantive areas), then more rigorous testing may be required to increase the plausibility of some hypotheses. Under these conditions, it should be a matter of empirical determination as to how the further testing can best be accomplished—whether through more rigorous or extensive fieldwork, or through other methods.

The two essential points in this decision about method are: first, the testing should be more rigorous than previously (but not necessarily the most rigorous of all methods); and second, the more rigorous aproach should be compatible with the research situation in order to yield the most reliable findings. Many researchers share an ideological commitment to quantitative methods, but an increased, required level of plausibility should be based on the method or methods best suited to the socially structured necessities of the specific research situation.

We wish to emphasize that the type of substantive theory developed in our book is often of great practical use long before the theory is tested with great rigor. Both informed laymen and social scientists often manage to profit quite well by the kind of analysis represented in these pages. In the case of our own theoretical analysis, readers should regard it as only the beginning of the search for fruitful ways of understanding, explaining, and controlling interaction that pertains to dying patients.[4]

---

[4] As we remarked in the first chapter, this book does not represent all that we know about such interaction.

Index